WALKI
CAPE TOWN

WALKING CAPE TOWN

GERALD ROSENTHAL

FOREWORD AND ACKNOWLEDGEMENTS

One of the pleasures of my childhood was walking with my parents and hearing the historical and botanical background to our route. My father, Eric Rosenthal (who was known to many South Africans for his involvement in radio quiz teams), was a mine of information on many topics. Together with my mother, who corrected his manuscripts and provided input on natural history, he wrote about 90 books, including an Encyclopaedia of Southern Africa and over 300 histories of people, towns and commercial enterprises. As we walked they would tell me of the places they remembered from their childhood and of the people who lived there. For me, this was sheer pleasure and in many ways this book is my way of sharing these memories with you.

My research for the background to these walks has involved a great deal of study and discussion with many people who have specialist expertise. Of those who have contributed their time and knowledge I would particularly like to thank Graham Avery, Jaana Ball, Anne Bean, Mac Bissett, Margot Branch, Rae Gordon, John Grindley, Shereen Habib, Rosemary Hickman, David Jack, Richard Jameson, Bill Liltfed, Pat Masterson, Clive McDowell, John Rogers, John Rourke, Ute Seemann, Caroline and Louis Silberbauer, Emilia Smuts, Ernst van Jaarsveld, Bernard Wagener, Mike Walker, Dave Wakelin, Gerald Wright and Trevor Wright. The encouragement and patience of Glynne Newlands and Annlerie van Rooyen of Struik are also very much appreciated.

My family's contribution to this, my first book, has been outstanding and I sincerely thank Heather, Philip and Lindy for their loving patience and interest.

Gerald Rosenthal
July 1999

Struik Publishers (Pty) Ltd
(a member of Struik New Holland Publishing (Pty) Ltd)
80 McKenzie Street, Cape Town 8001

Reg. No. 54/00965/07
ISBN 1 86872 114 0

Managing editor: Annlerie van Rooyen
Editor: Glynne Newlands
Design manager: Janice Evans
Concept design: Sonia Hedenskog de Villiers
Cover and DTP: Lellyn Creamer
Colour section design: Petal Palmer
Cartographer: John Hall (based on original material by Gerald Rosenthal)
Proofreader and indexer: Claudia Dos Santos

Reproduction: Disc Express Cape (Pty) Ltd
Printing: National Book Printers, Drukkery Street, Goodwood, Western Cape

If, despite my endeavours to verify details, errors or urban legend remain, I would appreciate readers bringing this to my attention by writing to The Author, *Walking Cape Town*, c/o Struik Publishers, P O Box 1144, Cape Town 8000.

Quotes from *Jan van Riebeeck's Journal* are from HB Thom's translation, published by AA Balkema, 1952.

Front cover: *Kirstenbosch (H von Hörsten/SIL)*; Spine: *Adderley Street flower sellers (M Skinner)*; Back cover: *Sea Point promenade (S Adey/SIL)*; Half-title page: *The Castle of Good Hope (S Adey/SIL)*; Title page: *Table Mountain (S Adey/SIL)*; chapter openers pp 40, 63, 80, 92, 96 and 111 (K Young).

Contents

Introduction 7

Adderley Street, St George's Mall, Greenmarket Square and Strand Street 16

Government Avenue and the Company's Gardens 22

Grand Parade, Castle, Buitkenkant Street and Parliament 28

Bo-Kaap 34

Lion's Head 40

The Victoria and Alfred Waterfront 46

Three Anchor Bay to the Waterfront 52

Three Anchor Bay to Saunders Rocks 58

Table Mountain Pipe Track 63

Milnerton Beach 68

Rhodes Memorial and the Contour Path 74

Newlands Forest 80

Kirstenbosch National Botanical Garden 86

Skeleton Gorge to Table Mountain Plateau 92

Liesbeek River Walk 96

Arderne Gardens 101

Groot Constantia 106

Constantia Nek to Table Mountain Plateau 111

Hout Bay Beach 116

Noordhoek Beach 121

Zandvlei 126

Muizenberg Beach 147

Muizenberg to St James Coast 153

Boyes Drive 159

Kalk Bay Harbour and Clovelly 164

Fish Hoek Beach and the 'Catwalk' 169

Peers Cave 174

Simon's Town 179

Cape of Good Hope Nature Reserve 185

Index 190

Introduction

HISTORICAL BACKGROUND

The Cape Peninsula has been inhabited by people for probably more than half a million years and possibly for much longer. Although we do not know much about the prehistoric occupants, we have some clues about them from finds in rock shelters and caves. It appears that they lived largely on shellfish and fish, which they caught in natural tidal fish traps at places like St James and Kommetjie, and game, including large wild animals such as hippos and elephants, which was plentiful.

The archeological evidence of ancient occupation in the Peninsula includes:

* ashes of fires, which can be dated reasonably accurately up to about 10 000 years;
* stone tools covering a continuous period of about half a million years;
* skeletons that have been found at many places, including rock shelters such as Peers Cave, near Fish Hoek (see pg 177);
* middens – huge piles of shells and other debris, the kitchen waste of prehistoric times.

Many of the oldest stone implements are very large and relate to a period called the Acheulian. The basic tool from this period is an almond-shaped hand-axe about as big as an open hand, or even bigger. Similar tools are found in Morocco, southern Europe and India. The oldest, which are from Africa, are about 1.4 million years old. Stone Age tools from later periods are much smaller as is evident if you visit the excellent displays in the South African Museum in the Company's Gardens (see pg 22).

PHOENICIANS: Some evidence exists that Phoenician explorers passed the Cape more than two thousand years ago. The Greek historian, Herodotus, wrote that in about 600 BC that the Egyptian Pharaoh Necho sent Phoenician ships from the Red Sea: *'He asked them to sail and come back through the Pillars of Hercules* [Straits of Gibraltar] *to the Northern Sea* [the Mediterranean] *and so to Egypt. The Phoenicians therefore set out from the Erythrean Sea* [the Red Sea] *and sailed through the Southern Sea* [the Indian Ocean]. *In the third year they turned through the Pillars of Hercules and arrived again in Egypt. And they reported a thing which I cannot believe, but another man may, namely, that, in sailing round Libya, they had the sun on their right hand.'*

What Herodotus is reporting is that, on a voyage lasting three years, Phoenician sailors rounded Africa (and the Cape) from east to west.

PORTUGUESE, BRITISH AND DUTCH EXPLORERS: During mediaeval times there was a theory that the 'end of the earth' was at Cape Bojador, about 240 km due south of the Canary Islands. This became a challenge for Infante Dom Henrique (1394–1460) (called 'Henry the Navigator' by English historians), the third son of the Portuguese king who established a headquarters for discovery and initiated exploratory voyages southwards. In 1434, after several unsuccessful attempts, one of his captains sailed past Cape Bojador, and voyages further and further south followed soon afterwards. By 1471 the Portuguese had crossed the Equator and had established a lucrative West African trade in slaves and gold.

In 1481 Henry's nephew, who had been in charge of Portugal's Africa trade, was crowned King João II. He encouraged further exploratory voyages and their territorial claims were marked with 2-m-high limestone columns with small crosses at the top. As the Portuguese explorers sailed further south they reached the Zaïre River in 1483 and then, in 1486, reached Cape Cross in present-day Namibia.

In August 1487 Bartolomeu Diaz de Novaes set out from Portugal with two caravels and a supply ship which he used to restock his two vessels mid-voyage. On Christmas Day they reached Lüderitz (in Namibia) and sailing south saw the Cedarberg mountains of the Cape, near Clanwilliam. For 13 days they then headed out to sea, in the direction south-southwest, and after sailing north-east they eventually reached land at the Gouritz River, near Mossel Bay. Despite threats of mutiny, they sailed further east, landed on today's St Croix Island near Port Elizabeth and then finally erected a cross at Kwaaihoek, west of the Bushman's River mouth where the officers refused to go further east.

On their homeward voyage they entered a small bay near Cape Point where on 6 June 1488 they set up a cross. Diaz called the place 'Cabo de Boa Esperança' – the Cape of Good Hope. Diaz's party spent a month in the south of the Cape Peninsula, which was at that time inhabited by Khoi (Hottentot) people. After his return to Portugal, Diaz's voyage of discovery was treated as a state secret and nautical maps of Africa used by other countries did not show his discoveries until 1502, when a secret Portuguese nautical map of Africa was obtained by an Italian spy.

In 1497 a second fleet under command of Vasco da Gama rounded the Cape after taking on fresh water, about 150 km north of Cape Town, at St Helena Bay where they skirmished with the Khoi. In 1503 another fleet, under command of Antonio da Saldanha, became separated from the fleet and, as a result of a navigational error, he entered what we now know as Table Bay, where they found fresh-water streams and explored Table Mountain. For more than a century present-day Table Bay was known as Aguada de Saldanha ('watering place of Saldanha'). (Today's Saldanha Bay, 105 km to the north, was named in 1601 by Joris van Spilbergen, who thought he was in Table Bay.)

In 1580, Sir Francis Drake wrote:

'We ran aboard the Cape, finding the report of the Portuguese to be most false, who affirm that it is the most dangerous cape in the world, never without intolerable storms and present danger to travellers who came near the same. This cape is a most stately thing, and the fairest cape we saw in the whole circumference of the earth and we passed it on the 18th June.'

By 1600 Dutch, English and French vessels had begun to journey to the East for spices and had eclipsed Portugal's supremacy at sea. In 1647 a Dutch ship, *De Nieuwe Haerlem*, ran aground in Table Bay and about 60 crew, under the command of a junior merchant, Leendert Janszen, spent a year fending for themselves and interacting with the Khoi, while the two accompanying ships sailed back to Holland. Janszen's party was eventually rescued and, on their return to Holland, Janszen and Matthys Proot advised the ruling Council of Seventeen of the Dutch East India Company as follows:

'If the proposed fort is provided with a good commander, who treats the natives with kindness, and gratefully pays for everything bartered from them, then nothing whatever would need to be feared. The soil in the said valley is very good and fruitful, and in the dry season all the water one could wish for could be led through the gardens with a little toil. Everything will grow there as well as anywhere in the world. Daily experience teaches us what can be done at the Cape, both for the sick and fit of the crews of the ships bound for the Indies, even with only some sorrel (*) and sometimes two or three cattle, since everything is to be had there in sufficient quantity. Fish, eland and steenbok are abundant. At some seasons of the year there is a quantity of whales, and hundreds of seals. Behind and on the slopes of the Table Mountain there is wood enough available.'

[* Sorrel provides vitamin C, without which sailors suffered from scurvy.]

One of those on the ship that transported Janszen's party back to Holland was Jan van Riebeeck, who was returning from the East. After receiving their report the Council of Seventeen persuaded Van Riebeeck to return to the Cape as commander of a settlement.

On Christmas Eve 1651 Jan van Riebeeck sailed from Holland with his wife, Maria de la Queillerie, and their four-month-old son, with a fleet consisting of the *Drommedaris*, *Goede Hoope*, *Reijger*, *Walvis* and the *Oliphant*. Late in the afternoon of 6 April 1652 the first two ships anchored in Table Bay. Their commission was to establish a 'rendezvous and garrison' – a replenishment station for ships calling on their way to the East. They were to build a fort large enough for 80 men, to erect a flag pole for signalling to ships, to cultivate the land, to barter for livestock and to become financially self-sufficient.

The first few months were a nightmare for the 80 people left on shore who had to stay in tents – at the onset of winter – until they had built an earth fort. By the time they moved into the earth fort in early August, nearly a quarter of their party had died. Van Riebeeck's main interest then became the development of vegetable gardens and the completion of the fortifications, but he had insufficient labour to do this work. After trying unsuccessfully to persuade the Khoi to assist them, he requested a detachment of sailors from a passing ship and arranged for slaves to be brought from Java and Madagascar.

In October 1653 lime was produced from Robben Island shells and stone was quarried from the lower slopes of Lion's Head near Signal Hill. In May 1654 the first kiln of 60 000 bricks was fired and a small plot was sown experimentally with wheat, rice and oats. Later that year tobacco was planted and work began on a timber-framed jetty about 5 m wide and stretching 150 m into Table Bay. In February 1657 the first 'free burghers' were granted rights to farm their own land in the vicinity of present-day Mowbray and Rondebosch, and at the beginning of 1659, when the settlement consisted of about 190 European people, the first wine was produced from Cape grapes.

From the start, relationships with the nearby Khoi were not good and there were several skirmishes. By 1662, when Van Riebeeck left the Cape for Malacca in the Far East, the Dutch had built a fence with four small fortifications and an almond hedge to demarcate the territorial separation between their settlement and the Khoi. The hedge still flourishes in present-day Kirstenbosch Garden and at Klaassens Road, Bishopscourt.

Cape Town's history is now told in the context of *Walking Cape Town*.

In 1662 Zacharias Wagenaar succeeded Jan van Riebeeck as Commander at the Cape. Despite his 'poor health and advancing age' (he was 48 years old!) he energetically implemented improvements for the servicing of the ships and fortifying Van Riebeeck's earth fort. (His reservoir for filling barrels with freshwater is visited on pg 19). He also arranged for construction of the Castle of Good Hope, which started in 1666.

In 1679 Simon van der Stel was appointed Commander at the Cape. He was an outstanding leader and applied himself to developing the agricultural resources of the settlement. He founded the farming district and town of Stellenbosch in 1680, opened the Drakenstein farming district in 1684, went prospecting for copper in Namaqualand in the following year and vigorously assisted Huguenot settlers who had arrived in 1688. His endeavours included establishing his own farm at Groot Constantia (*see* pg 107), upgrading the Company's Gardens (*see* pg 23), extensive tree planting, establishing schools and even attempting to colonise the then Natal. In 1699 Van der Stel was succeeded as Governor by his son Willem Adriaan, whose personal farming endeavours at Vergelegen near the Hottentots Holland Mountains led to his recall in disgrace to the Netherlands.

At the beginning of the 18th century there were only 200 houses in Cape Town, but its strategic importance to the European powers was already beginning to become apparent as more foreign vessels began to call at the Cape. During the Seven Years War (1756–63), which involved all the major European powers, Cape Town's position as a neutral port, which could be accessed by all nations, gave it great importance. By 1775 Cape Town had over 1 200 houses and expansion was occurring outside the original boundaries of Buitengracht and Buitenkant streets.

In 1781, during the American War of Independence, a French fleet arrived at the Cape with a garrison to assist the Dutch in defending it against the English. The arrival of the French was accompanied by a boom in building and commerce in the town. The settlement had outgrown many of the controls of the Dutch East India Company. By 1782, rule by the company was in real decline and there was an increasing spirit of rebelliousness in the Colony. This was fuelled by events in Europe and wars between the settlers and Xhosa peoples on the eastern frontier.

Following the start of the French Revolution in 1789 and the establishment of a Batavian Republic in the Netherlands, a British fleet was sent to occupy the Cape. The forces arrived in False Bay on 11 June 1795 and, following some fighting as the British advanced from Simon's Town to Muizenberg, the Commissioner-General of the Dutch East India Company capitulated to the British on 16 September 1795. The Cape Colony now came under the rule of the British Colonial Office in London. (This was the First British Occupation of the Cape.) At this time it is estimated that there were between 16 000 and 20 000 Europeans, 17 000 and 25 000 slaves and about 15 000 Khoi.

In 1803, under conditions imposed by the Treaty of Amiens, the Cape was placed under the rule of the Batavian Republic in the Netherlands (in accordance with the ideas of the French Revolution), who supported the French. A few years later, the British sent a fleet to re-take the Cape. On 7 January 1806 a fleet of 61 British ships, carrying 6 654 men, anchored off Blouberg. The Cape's governor, who had only 2 000 men, capitulated on 18 January 1806 at what has become known as the Battle of Blouberg. The Second British Occupation was confirmed under the Convention of London when the Colony was formally ceded to Britain, a few years later.

Under a succession of governors the British abolished slavery, tried to control press freedom, gave full citizenship to the Khoi, brought thousands of European settlers to the eastern frontier and tried to anglicise the colony. English became the only language used by government and the courts. With the abolition of slavery there was a need for banking facilities for the new wage-earners and commerce was greatly stimulated. The Municipality of Cape Town was created in 1840, resulting in many improvements to the roads, drainage and civic affairs of the town.

In 1849 the British Government decided to establish a penal settlement at the Cape for convicts from the British Isles. A ship with 282 convicts on board was sent to the Cape, but there was such a public outcry that the ship eventually sailed on to Tasmania (see pg 17). The cause of the Cape colonists, in opposing the introduction of convicts, was taken up in the House of Commons of the British Parliament by Charles Adderley. Largely as a result of Adderley's efforts and the expressions of the public opinion in respect of the convicts, the British Government formally recognised the need for self-government and elections for a Cape Parliament were held in 1853.

A rapid upsurge in agricultural and mining developments, and the need for safe berthing facilities for the vessels using the Cape sea route, led to the construction and opening of the Alfred Dock, South Africa's first enclosed harbour, in 1870 (see pg 48). The first rail link between Cape Town and Wellington was completed in 1858, but it was not until 1892 that Cape Town was finally linked by rail to Johannesburg.

From the end of the 19th century rapid urban and industrial expansion took place around the city. Because of constraints imposed by the mountain, the coastline and the shifting sand dunes and vleis of the Cape Flats, expansion of Cape Town was generally restricted to the environs of the central business district (CBD) and a ribbon development along the lower slopes of Table Mountain. In 1938, to alleviate the lack of space in the CBD, reclamation of the Foreshore area north of Strand Street and construction of the Duncan Dock began. By July 1945, roughly 194 hectares had been reclaimed from the sea.

During the 1960s and 1970s, the road system was substantially upgraded and many elevated highways were built. The problem in upgrading Cape Town's road system included a need to provide major roads in an east-west direction because previously, as Cape Town had evolved between the mountain and the docks, the major roads (such as Buitenkant, Adderley and Buitengracht streets) were all aligned north-south. De Waal Drive and the Eastern and Western boulevards were constructed to solve this problem.

Cape Town has matured as an interesting and lively city that combines a rich historical heritage with many delightful places to visit. Its mountains, beaches, vleis and forests are easily accessed from the residential areas, and its many walks are part of a fabric that makes Cape Town a most attractive place to live in.

GEOLOGY OF THE CAPE PENINSULA

The geology of the Cape Peninsula is a dramatic story of mighty forces, earthquakes, fire, water and ice which have produced four main soil and rock types:

* The Table Mountain Group, which consists mainly of sandstone and forms the highest part of the Peninsula mountain chain.
* The Cape Granite, which forms the foothills of the mountains.
* The Malmesbury Group rocks, found in the city to the north of Table Mountain.
* The sands which cover the lowest areas and valleys.

About 560 million years ago the earth's crust split apart to form a new ocean in the area that was to become the Cape Peninsula and over vast periods of time, clays and sands settled on the ocean floor.

Then tremendous forces deep below the earth's surface began to close the ocean, squeezing, contorting and burying the muds and sands on the ocean floor. Some was carried deep into the earth's mantle where it became molten magma which, being less dense than the mantle, 'floated' up to within 10 km of the surface. The magma cooled and crystallised to form huge granite bodies, called plutons. The surrounding rocks were metamorphosed by the pressure and high temperature to form the hard slatey greyish rocks of the Malmesbury Group. These are the underlying rocks to the north of the face of Table Mountain in Cape Town's City Bowl, the rocky outcrops along the Sea Point and Green Point beachfronts, Robben Island and the beachfront rocks at Bloubergstrand. In the Tygerberg Hills they are quarried for building stone and road aggregate. The walls of the Castle of Good Hope are built of this material.

The Cape Granite formed about 540 million years ago from a molten magma. It can best be seen along the coast of False Bay from Simon's Town to Smitswinkel Bay, and on the Atlantic coast below the coastal road from Llandudno to the contact with the Malmesbury Group just north and south of Queen's Road in Sea Point (*see* pg 62).

After formation of the Malmesbury Group and the Cape Granite, a period of about 20 million years followed when these deeply buried rocks were forced towards the surface. They were then weathered and eroded to a fairly smooth surface (peneplane) which can be seen at the level of the upper contour path below Table Mountain (about 500 m above sea level) and at the level of the road on Chapman's Peak Drive.

After the granite peneplane had been smoothed off, there was a period of about 150 million years, starting about 520 million years ago, when layers of mainly sandy sediments were deposited on top of the granite. This sediment formed the rocks known as the Table Mountain Group, which is the sequence of layered rocks you can see on the face of Table Mountain and above Chapman's Peak Drive.

11

From the bottom upwards you will first see the maroon-coloured mudstones and thinly-bedded light brown sandstones of the Graafwater Formation and then very thin layers of mudstone and the thickly bedded whitish sandstones of the Peninsula Formation, up to 700 m thick in places. At the top of Table Mountain are pebbly mudstones of the Pakhuis Formation, which were laid down under glacial conditions. Right at the top of Table Mountain, between Maclear's Beacon and Platteklip Gorge, geologists have found small pebbles with scratch marks caused by a continental ice sheet about 450 million years ago, when the African Plate drifted over the South Pole.

About 250 million years ago the rocks of the Cape Peninsula were squeezed again and the sandstones bowed upwards forming an arch (anticline) over False Bay. You can see evidence of this bowing in the westward dip of the sandstone beds at Smitswinkel Bay (on the west coast of False Bay) and in the eastward dip of the beds on the other side of the bay. At this time much of the landmass of the world was concentrated in the southern hemisphere, forming the supercontinent of Gondwana.

About 130 million years ago, Gondwana started breaking up and the continental masses drifted apart very slowly to form Africa, South America, Australia, Antarctica, Madagascar and India. There were great earthquakes as the continental crust rifted and sheared along fault planes. Some of the faults are clearly visible along Chapman's Peak Drive where they appear as offsets in the sandstone bedding. A very large fault line from Fish Hoek to Noordhoek also exists where the two sides of the valley moved relative to one other. Old faults are occasionally reactivated in modern times and when this occurs the movement releases tremendous stresses that are felt as earthquakes. Many Capetonians will recall the earthquake (magnitude 6.5 on the Richter Scale) in 1969, due to movement, centred in the Tulbagh-Ceres area, of the 130 million-year-old Worcester Fault.

During the millions of years of erosion that followed the break-up of Gondwana, the continents have drifted apart at a speed of a few centimetres per year. The steep cliffs of Table Mountain, Lion's Head and the other Cape mountains have been worn back by weathering, rockfalls and stream erosion. Initially the climate was tropical and dinosaurs walked the land. During this time the Cape Granite was chemically weathered to form high-quality china clay (kaolin), mined today in Sun Valley and at Noordhoek. The Malmesbury Group rocks have weathered to form reddish clays used for brick-making.

The sands in the Peninsula relate mainly to changing sea levels in the last few million years. At some times the sea has been high enough to flood the Cape Flats and the Fish Hoek valley, but for most of this period the sea has been about 130 m below its present level and dunefields have extended across the areas of present-day False Bay and Table Bay. At this time the northern hemisphere experienced the Ice Ages and in the Peninsula freeze-thaw cycles in winter and spring caused substantial mechanical weathering of the mountain rocks. Huge blocks of sandstone broke off the cliffs to form cone-shaped talus fans spreading over the slopes below (e.g. immediately above Tafelberg Road, beyond the Cableway Station). Abrasion of rocks under the forces of waves and sand-laden wind has produced the sands that form the beaches, cover the Cape Flats and fill the valleys.

CAPE FLORA – A UNIQUE PLANT HERITAGE

The Cape Flora is the natural vegetation that occurs in the Cape Floral Kingdom – in undisturbed areas of the Western Cape, from the Olifants River in the north-west to the Swartberg in the north and Port Elizabeth in the east. The Cape Floral Kingdom is tiny compared with the other five of the world's floral kingdoms:

* Boreal Kingdom (the northern hemisphere)
* Palaeotropic Kingdom (Madagascar and most of Africa)
* Neotropical Kingdom (South America and the Caribbean)
* Australian Kingdom
* Antarctic Kingdom (including New Zealand).

Notwithstanding its minute size, the Cape Floral Kingdom contains more than 8 500 plant species – more plants per unit area than any other region in the world – and as such is the location of the world's greatest plant diversity. The centre of this is in the Kögelberg, near Caledon. In the Cape Floral Kingdom 68% of the plant species, 20% of the genera and six entire families are found nowhere else in the world.

FYNBOS VEGETATION: About four-fifths of the Cape Floral Kingdom comprises the vegetation type dominated by shrubs unique to this area, known as the Cape Fynbos. Fynbos is a hard, leathery, fine-leaved vegetation type. It grows in nutrient-poor soils and is dominated by three botanical families, namely the protea (*Proteaceae*), the heath (*Ericaceae*) and the reed families (*Restionaceae*).

Many species have clearly defined distribution ranges and some are confined to specific geographical areas, such as a single mountain range. You may be surprised to notice how many different communities of plants grow within metres of each other. The reason for this is that the landscape is a patchwork of microhabitats that are entirely distinct from each other in terms of their geology, climate, slope and aspect. Each habitat is ideal for certain groups of species. Another striking feature of fynbos is the lack of trees and the abundance of fragrant species, evident when you crush a leaf.

Most fynbos species have adapted to the harsh conditions in the Cape, and particularly to the lack of nutrients and water. While doing the walks in this book, notice how plants are either divided, channelled, needle-like, hard and shiny on the upper surface, covered by a dense layer of silver hairs or waxy scales, tightly folded or clasped close to the stem. All these features protect the plant from excessive waterloss.

Fynbos is adapted to be burnt by fires every seven to 35 years. In fact, many species are dependent on fire for their flowering and seed germination – and thus their very existence. Many plants, presumed to be extinct, have been rediscovered after the heat and chemicals in the smoke of a fire caused their soil-stored seed to be brought back to life.

Many species of fynbos have been cultivated as garden plants and cut flowers. On mountain walks you are likely to see the wild forms of ericas, freesias, geraniums, gladioli, nerinas and other fynbos flowers that are now sold by horticulturists throughout the world. We are indeed fortunate to be the custodians of this rich heritage.

WALKS IN ORDER OF LENGTH

	LENGTH	DISTANCE
Arderne Gardens	0.5 km	40 mins
Bo-Kaap	1 km	20 mins
Hout Bay Beach	1 km	45 mins
Lion's Head	1.6 km +	1.75 hours +
Fish Hoek Beach and the Catwalk	1.7 km	1.75 hours
Government Avenue and the Company's Gardens	2 km	1 hour
Kalk Bay Harbour and Clovelly	2 km	1 hour
Kirstenbosch National Botanical Garden	2 km	1.5 hours
Adderley Street, St George's Mall, Greenmarket Square and Strand Street	2 km	2 hours
The Victoria and Alfred Waterfront	2 km	2 hours
Peers Cave	2 km	2.5 hours
Skeleton Gorge and Table Mountain Plateau	2 km +	4 hours +
Newlands Forest	2.5 km	1 hour
Muizenberg to St James Coast	3 km	1.5 hours
Grand Parade, Buitenkant Street and Parliament	3.5 km	1.5 hours
Rhodes Memorial and the Contour Path	4 km	1.5 hours
Zandvlei	4 km	1.5 hours
Groot Constantia	4 km	1.75 hours
Muizenberg Beach	4 km	2 hours
Simon's Town	4 km	2 hours
Milnerton Beach	4 km +	1.5 hours +
Constantia Nek to Table Mountain Plateau	4 km +	3.5 hours +
Liesbeek River	4.5 km (x2)	1.5 hours (x2)
Boyes Drive	5 km	2 hours
Table Mountain Pipe Track	5 km	3 hours
Three Anchor Bay to the Waterfront	6 km	2 hours
Three Anchor Bay to Saunders Rocks	6 km	2 hours
Noordhoek Beach	6 km +	2.5 hours +
Cape of Good Hope Nature Reserve	7 km	2.5 hours

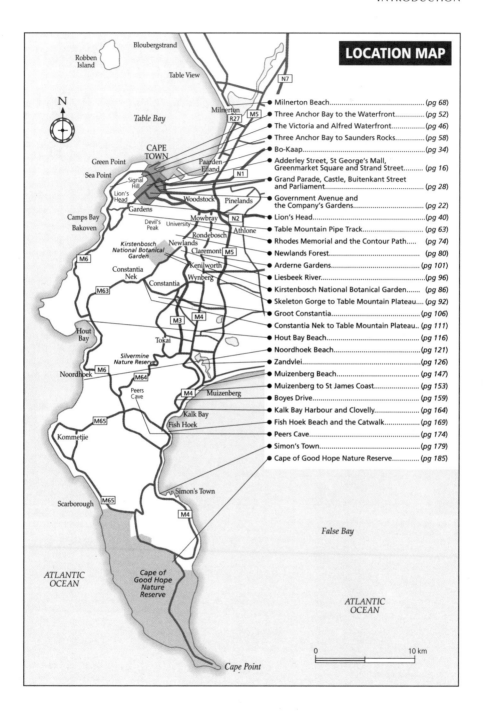

LOCATION MAP

Milnerton Beach... (pg 68)

Three Anchor Bay to the Waterfront.............. (pg 52)

The Victoria and Alfred Waterfront................. (pg 46)

Three Anchor Bay to Saunders Rocks.............. (pg 58)

Bo-Kaap... (pg 34)

Adderley Street, St George's Mall,
Greenmarket Square and Strand Street......... (pg 16)

Grand Parade, Castle, Buitenkant Street
and Parliament.. (pg 28)

Government Avenue and
the Company's Gardens.................................... (pg 22)

Lion's Head..(pg 40)

Table Mountain Pipe Track............................. (pg 63)

Rhodes Memorial and the Contour Path..... (pg 74)

Newlands Forest.. (pg 80)

Arderne Gardens.. (pg 101)

Liesbeek River..(pg 96)

Kirstenbosch National Botanical Garden....... (pg 86)

Skeleton Gorge to Table Mountain Plateau.... (pg 92)

Groot Constantia.. (pg 106)

Constantia Nek to Table Mountain Plateau.. (pg 111)

Hout Bay Beach... (pg 116)

Noordhoek Beach.. (pg 121)

Zandvlei...(pg 126)

Muizenberg Beach... (pg 147)

Muizenberg to St James Coast....................... (pg 153)

Boyes Drive.. (pg 159)

Kalk Bay Harbour and Clovelly....................... (pg 164)

Fish Hoek Beach and the Catwalk................. (pg 169)

Peers Cave.. (pg 174)

Simon's Town.. (pg 179)

Cape of Good Hope Nature Reserve............. (pg 185)

Adderley Street, St George's Mall, Greenmarket Square and Strand Street

Glimpses of the Past

This walk through central Cape Town weaves a thread through 350 years of history when the first Dutch settlers arrived at the Cape in 1652. At that time, the shore was covered in low bush, which gradually sloped up towards the towering crags of Table Mountain, and the bay consisted of small beaches with occasional rocky outcrops.

If you had been here when the first Dutch settlers arrived in 1652, your ship would have been one of three anchoring offshore of the beach which was on the line of present-day Strand Street. Soon after their arrival, Jan van Riebeeck, Commander of the Cape of Good Hope, built an earth fort but, from the start, it proved to be a disaster – rain collapsed its walls. In 1665 the Company ordered Commander Wagenaar, who replaced Van Riebeeck, to build a new stone fortress – the Castle of Good Hope (see pg 29) – which now stands to the east of the Grand Parade.

One hundred years later, in 1752, the settlement had become a thriving town of about 12 500 people. Today's Adderley Street was the main road and was called the Heerengracht – 'Gentleman's canal' – from about 1731, named after a canal in Amsterdam. This should not to be confused with the present-day Heerengracht on the Foreshore, which is an extension of Adderley Street on ground that was reclaimed from the sea shortly before World War II. The original Heerengracht ran from today's entrance to the Company's Gardens at the top of Adderley Street to the shore at Strand Street, where there was a jetty and reservoirs for filling barrels with fresh water. (By 1670 the streams from Table Mountain had been channelled into a network of canals, one of which ran along the east of the Heerengracht and brought fresh water to the shore reservoirs.)

In the 1750s both residential and commercial parts of the settlement lay within the boundaries of present-day Buitengracht, Buitenkant and Buitensingel streets ('Buiten' means 'outside'). The Castle was defence headquarters, centre of all administration, and was where the governor had his offices.

At the top of the Heerengracht, to the east of the entrance to the Gardens, there was a Slave Lodge where many Company slaves were housed. On the other side of the road was the Company's hospital which, from 1699 to 1784, stood in large gardens that extended between today's Adderley Street, St George's Street, St George's Cathedral and Longmarket Street.

From 1703 the Dutch Reformed Church's Groote Kerk (meaning 'large church') stood to the east of the Heerengracht facing the hospital entrance. This building, which is now dwarfed by offices, was for many years by far the highest building in the town. The present steeple, which dates from the first church building of 1703, was retained when the Groote Kerk was rebuilt in its present form in 1837. Despite this being a Dutch Reformed Church, it was also used for church services of the Church of England in South Africa from 1749 until 1833.

The change in name from Heerengracht to Adderley Street marks one of the most momentous events in the country's history. On 21 February 1850 the British government was coerced by the people of Cape Town to divert a convict ship destined for the Cape to the convict settlement in Van Diemens Land (Tasmania). Sir Charles Adderley, a member of the British parliament, championed the cause of the Cape colonists. As a token of gratitude the Municipality of Cape Town presented him with the considerable sum of £100 and the name Heerengracht was changed to Adderley Street.

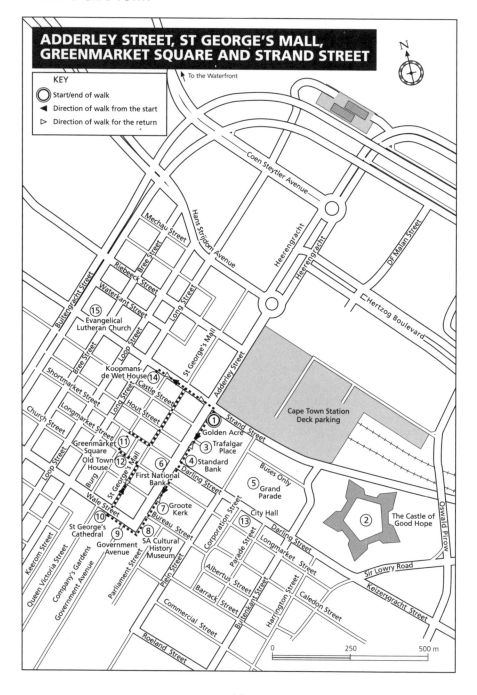

ADDERLEY STREET, ST GEORGE'S MALL, GREENMARKET SQUARE AND STRAND STREET

KEY

◯ Start/end of walk

◀ Direction of walk from the start

▷ Direction of walk for the return

18

Walk along Adderley Street, St George's Mall, Greenmarket Square and Strand Street

The walk starts in the basement of the Golden Acre shopping centre **(1)**, which marks the line of the beach at the time of the Dutch landing. Here you can see the remains of the fresh-water shore reservoir – Wagenaar's Reservoir – that was built in the time of Commander Zacharias Wagenaar. The building of the Castle **(2)** was started under his command in 1665.

Now walk out of the Golden Acre into Adderley Street. Immediately in front of you, on the opposite side of the road, are two elegantly gabled commercial buildings from the 1860s. Continue up Adderley Street towards the mountain. On the left, beyond the OK Bazaars' building, is a small lane called Trafalgar Place **(3)** where flower sellers have created a colourful scene since the early 1860s. At one time it was called Trafalgar Square!

In the next block stands the magnificent Standard Bank building **(4)** designed by Charles Freeman. The Standard Bank was built in 1880 on part of the Grand Parade **(5)** and was extended in 1890. This is Victorian opulent construction at its best and, if the bank is open, have a look inside.

Now cross over to the west side of Adderley Street where, slightly further on, is the First National Bank building **(6)**, designed in 1936 and the last of hundreds that the famous architect, Sir Herbert Baker, designed in South Africa. About

this building he is said to have remarked *'I really do not feel that I much want to do the work except for a rather natural longing to attempt to remove some of the squalor of Adderley Street'*. If you are passing during banking hours also examine the grandeur of this building's interior.

At the corner of Church Street cross back to the east side of Adderley Street to the rear of the Groote Kerk **(7)**. On the Bureau Street side of the church is a statue of Rev Andrew Murray, one the country's most outstanding religious leaders, and the minister here from 1864 to 1871. Born in 1828 at Graaff-Reinet in the Karoo, and after studying theology at Aberdeen University in Scotland, he became a most influential leader in the Dutch Reformed Church. His books are widely read and are still reprinted in South Africa, America and England. He died in 1917.

Continuing up Adderley Street, cross Bureau Street to the green-shuttered SA Cultural History Museum **(8)** which incorporates the foundations of the old Slave Lodge, built by the Dutch East India Company in 1679. In 1807, after the Second Occupation of the Cape by the British, the building was used to house their administration which was too large to be accommodated in the Castle. From 1815 until 1914 it became the Supreme Court. In 1840 the first South African post office was opened here. The Cultural History Museum, which illustrates Dutch,

FIELD MARSHALL (GENERAL) SMUTS

Jan Christian Smuts is one of South Africa's most remarkable sons. He grew up on a farm near Riebeek West and had no school education until he was 12. He was a brilliant scholar at school, Stellenbosch (Victoria College), the University of Cape of Good Hope and Cambridge University. He achieved distinction in degrees in literature, science and law.

Smuts was prominent as a guerrilla leader in the Anglo-Boer War, and in the government of unity that followed. He led the campaign in East Africa in World War I and in 1917 was part of the British Government's War Cabinet. He was twice Prime Minister of South Africa, and was largely responsible for the establishment of the Royal Air Force and the League of Nations (which later led to the formation of the United Nations). He drafted the Covenant of the United Nations, was a close confidant of Winston Churchill and played a prominent role in World War II. Smuts was also a Fellow of the Royal Society and Rector of St Andrew University (Scotland). He wrote several books, one of which is a philosophical work, *Holism and Evolution*. Honours that he received in Europe and America are unprecedented.

His love of Table Mountain is recorded in the official naming of the walk up Skeleton Gorge as 'General Smuts' Track' (*see* page 93).

created by Anton Anreith in 1810 and humorously shows an exhausted lion leaning over the cornice – a representation of the worn-out British government at the end of the Napoleonic wars.

At the top of Adderley Street you come to the entrance to Government Avenue **(9)** and the Dutch East India Company's Gardens (*see* pg 22). The Edwardian building on the other side of the road is on the site of the former Company's hospital.

On your left, facing the Company's Gardens, is a statue of Field Marshall (General) Smuts (1870–1950) undertaken by Ivan Mitford-Barberton and erected in 1974 (*see also* pg 25).

As you face the mountain, St George's Cathedral **(10)** is on your right. This imposing stone building, dating from 1901, was designed by Sir Herbert Baker and his partner Francis Masey. It replaced an earlier cathedral building based on the St Pancras Church in London that was demolished because it was said to 'resemble a pagan temple'.

Cross Wale Street and walk down St George's Mall north-eastwards in the direction of the docks. Along the way you will pass the stone-carved memorial to Bishop Robert Gray, first Anglican Bishop of Cape Town (*see also* pg 25).

British, Malay and oriental cultural influences at the Cape, was opened in 1966. If you make a short detour to your left down Bureau Street to Parliament Street, you will see an unusual triangular pediment high on the back of the SA Cultural History Museum. This was

20

Close to Gray's memorial, and also further down St George's Mall, are mounted panels of old photographs. In the first panel, notice the monumental appearance of the first Anglican cathedral in 1898. At that stage most buildings had only two storeys and the roads had not yet been surfaced. Adderley Street was first surfaced in 1908 with woodblocks placed on sand, on top of a concrete base.

Further down St George's Mall, you pass the old newspaper office area of the city, where the two main English newspapers are still printed. Journalists for the *Cape Times* work late into the night for a printing start at 1am. The *Cape Argus* is printed from about 11am.

At Longmarket Street turn to the left, and you will see the Old Town House **(12)** on your left as you enter Greenmarket Square **(11)**. Visualise the scene in 1761 when the Town House was the centre of civic affairs and a gong was tolled when pronouncements were read from the balcony. The Town House was the centre of Cape Town until the City Hall **(13)** was built in 1905. Distances indicated on slate milestones along suburban main roads were measured from the Town House. In 1913 the Old Town House was refurbished to house the private collection of 17th century Dutch art that had been donated to the public by Sir Max Michaelis, a well-known financier. The restaurant in the courtyard is a good place to stop for refreshments.

As you cross Greenmarket Square, spend a little time exploring the market. This area was originally called Burgerwagtsplijn ('Burgher Watch Square') and only in the 19th century was it called by its present name when it became a market. Then, as Cape Town's civic centre, it was also a popular venue for the *'eating, drinking and romancing of soldiers, sailors and visitors'*. In 1967 this square, and the area around it, was paved with cobbles. In the 1980s, together with St George's Mall, the area was made into a pedestrian precinct, creating a friendly shopping environment in the city.

From Greenmarket Square walk down Shortmarket Street and turn left along St George's Mall into Strand Street. Then turn left again and walk up the hill to the Koopmans-de Wet House **(14)**, mid-way between Burg and Long streets. This building dates between 1771 and 1793. It was bought by Hendrik de Wet in 1806 and was the private home of his granddaughter, Mrs Maria Koopmans-de Wet, until her death in 1906, and that of her sister in 1911. The museum is furnished with their collection of antiques and *objets d'art* from the 18th and 19th centuries.

Further up Strand Street, you can see the spire and clock tower of the Evangelical Lutheran Church **(15)** on the horizon. This is beyond the limit of the walk, but it is an interesting landmark. In 1771, when Governor Ryk Tulbagh died, permission was granted for Lutherans to hold services in a Strand Street 'barn'. As religious tolerance increased, this was converted into the present church.

To return to the start, walk back down Strand Street and use the underground route across Adderley Street to the Golden Acre. As you walk under Adderley Street you will be under two large pipes that, despite 350 years of change, still carry streams of fresh mountain water to the sea.

Useful Information

- DISTANCE: 2 km

TIME TAKEN: 1 hour

PARKING: In Queen Victoria Street

START: Top of Adderley Street, at entrance to Government Avenue

ROUTE: Government Avenue and back through the Company's Gardens

REFRESHMENTS: Informal restaurant in the middle of the Gardens

AMENITIES: Public toilets and numerous benches

WEATHER: Protected from wind

TERRAIN: Paved

SUITABLE FOR: Walkers of all ages, push- and wheelchairs

Government Avenue and the Company's Gardens

Squirrels and Shady Paths

When Jan van Riebeeck and his small band of men and women landed in Table Bay in 1652, their primary commission was to establish a settlement that could provide vegetables and other provisions for the Dutch fleet trading with the East. Soon the Dutch East India Company's Gardens were being laid out in the shelter of Table Mountain.

On the long voyages between Europe and the East many sailors died of scurvy, a debilitating disease caused by lack of vitamin C which occurs in fresh vegetables and fruit. Jan van Riebeeck's journey from Holland to the Cape took just over three months – during this time they lived on meat preserved in brine, limited fruit and vegetables and water had to be carefully rationed. On arrival at the Cape, Van Riebeeck's main task, therefore, was to supply Dutch ships with fresh provisions.

At the beginning of July 1652 experimental patches of wheat and barley were sown and at the end of the month Jan van Riebeeck recorded:

'During these fine warm days, we have again prepared some soil and have sown peas, turnips, carrots and other potherbs close to the fort on high, dry, soft, sandy ground. The turnips and carrots sown at the same place at the beginning of the month are coming up very well. Hope that Almighty God will grant good fruit in due course and will in future protect the crops from the bad weather. Amen.'

During 1653 the Dutch East India Company's Gardens were systematically laid out to the west of the fort. The chosen site had fertile soil, was protected from the wind and had an abundance of fresh water from a mountain stream which was also led into a moat around the fort. The stream still runs down the length of the Gardens and then disappears into a canal under present-day Adderley Street, entering the sea at the docks.

Two years after landing at the Cape, Van Riebeeck requested slaves to be brought from the East to assist the settlers as he could not persuade the local Khoi to work for the Company. By 1679, at the time of Commander Simon van der Stel, there were so many slaves at the Cape that a slave lodge was constructed at the entrance to the Gardens. Van der Stel also ordered the planting of oak trees on the sides of a broad path that bisected the gardens and was known first as Company's Avenue and later, at the time of the British, as Government Avenue. This Avenue became the favourite promenade for the whole community of Cape Town.

A map of the 'Caabse Vlek' ('hamlet of the Cape') drawn in 1751 shows the Gardens lying between present-day Wale, Parliament, Orange and Queen Victoria streets. On the Table Mountain side there was a museum (the main exhibits were stuffed animals) and a menagerie.

In 1800, at the time of the First British Occupation and despite public outrage, Governor Sir George Yonge gave instructions to close the Avenue to the public and visitors had to sign their names at a guardhouse. A year later Yonge was dismissed as governor after he had been accused of corruption and other malpractice.

In the past century, the most radical change has been the Company's Garden's remodelling as an English garden under the direction of Sir Herbert Baker and his architect partner E K Kendall. It now has large areas of lawn and shady walks and is a place where city workers, tourists and holidaymakers can relax.

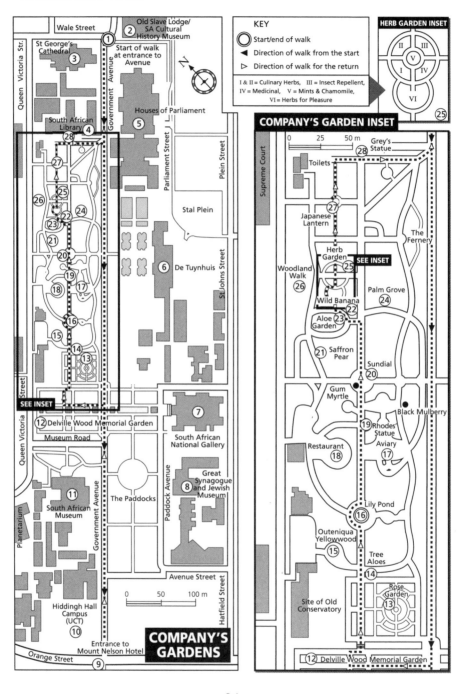

Company's Gardens Walk

Before entering Government Avenue from Adderley Street at the start of the walk (1), notice the old Slave Lodge (2) which housed slaves from 1679 to 1807 (sometimes as many as 400 to 1 000 slaves at a time). It is the second oldest building in South Africa, the oldest being the Castle of Good Hope (*see* pg 29). Towards the end of the 18th century it was used as a mental asylum and a jail for petty criminals and political exiles. After the Second British Occupation this building housed the Supreme Court and, in 1854, the Legislative Council. The façade was reconstructed when Adderley Street was widened in the 1920s. It is now the South African Cultural History Museum (*see also* pg 19).

As you enter the Avenue, you will pass the statue of Field-Marshal (General) Jan Smuts (*see also* pp 20 and 26) by Ivan Mitford-Barberton, erected in 1974 (*see also* pg 119). Ahead is the 1-km-long oak avenue first planted by Simon van der Stel. The original gardens covered an area of 18 hectares (equivalent to about 36 rugby fields), but today only a small three-hectare section has been preserved (to the west, on your right).

The first building on your right is St George's Cathedral (3), dating from 1901 and designed by Sir Herbert Baker and Francis Masey. It was designated a cathedral in 1848 when Bishop Robert Gray arrived at the Cape (*see* pg 20).

At the entrance to the Avenue you can usually buy peanuts to feed the surprisingly tame American grey squirrels that abound in the Gardens. These were introduced from Europe by Cecil Rhodes (*see* pg 75) around 1900.

Over 25 species of wild bird are also found here, the most common being pigeons, red-winged starlings and European starlings (the latter are also reputed to have been introduced by Rhodes). Indigenous birds include laughing doves, Cape turtle doves and red-eyed doves.

Several types of oak line the Avenue, many with identification plates. Van der Stel probably planted European oaks but, because these suffer from powdery mildew, they were replaced with Turkey oaks, which also suffered mildew. Most recently water oaks, which are a lighter green than other oaks, have been planted. They seem to be resistant to mildew.

Beyond the cathedral, on the extreme right, is the South African Library (4) which houses an outstanding collection of Africana, as well as illuminated mediaeval manuscripts, first editions of Shakespeare and Spencer, and an original manuscript of Dante from the 14th century. It is one of five libraries where all South African publications must, by law, be deposited. The SA Library was opened in 1860 and designed by William Kohler.

To the south of the Library is a statue of Governor Sir George Grey, whose priceless collection of manuscripts and books formed the basis for the start of the Library (*see* pg 47).

As you continue up the Avenue, the Houses of Parliament (5), completed in

1884, is the stately building on your left (*see also* pg 33). The original design was by Charles Freeman, but, as a result of construction problems, Freeman's role as Resident Architect was replaced by Henry Greaves, a British architect.

The next building is De Tuynhuis (6), now the President's city home where receptions for ambassadors and other formal functions are often held. From 1700 this building was used to accommodate visiting dignitaries who were not housed at the Castle. After the First British Occupation it was converted to Government House, and, in the time of Governor Lord Charles Somerset (1814-27), it was extensively renovated. Since about 1975 there have been other modifications.

During the summer, and periodically at other times, open-air exhibitions and a sale of contemporary paintings take place in this part of the Avenue.

About 500 m from the start, the road widens at the Delville Wood Memorial Garden (12) designed by Sir Herbert Baker. It commemorates a terrible five-day battle in France during World War I. Of 121 officers and 3 032 men in the South African Brigade, only five officers and 750 men escaped injury.

The South African National Gallery (7) is on your extreme left. This building, whose monumental approach incorporates the Delville Wood Memorial Garden, was opened in 1930. It houses works of art by South African, English, Flemish, Dutch, Spanish, French and other artists. The collection started in 1871 and now has many outstanding bequests including those of Sir Max and Lady Michaelis (15th to 17th century paintings and drawings) (*see* pg 21) and Sir Abe Bailey's 18th and 19th century portraits, watercolours and prints (*see* pp 151 and 157).

In front of the SA National Gallery stands Sydney Harpley's statue of Field-Marshal (General) Jan Smuts, which was unveiled in 1964. Its representation of Smuts has been widely criticised as being an inadequate likeness. This resulted in the commissioning of the other statue of Smuts, at the entrance to Government Avenue (*see* pp 20 and 25).

The buildings on the mountain side of the gallery include the Great Synagogue, designed in the baroque tradition, and the Jewish Museum (8), designed in an Egyptian style. It is housed in the Old Synagogue – the first synagogue in South Africa – opened in 1863.

Continuing further up the Avenue you pass an open area on your left, once used as horse paddocks. The oldest oaks in the gardens are in this area. At the top of the Avenue on the right is where the Dutch East India Company's menagerie stood until about 1800. Buildings of the University of Cape Town's Hiddingh Hall campus (10), which were once the South African College, stand on this site.

At the top of the Avenue, across the road, are huge columns marking the entrance to the Mount Nelson Hotel (9). This prestigious establishment was built in 1899 by the Castle Steamship Company, and was the unofficial headquarters of the British army during the Anglo-Boer War. The Mount Nelson estate had previously been the townhouse of Hamilton Ross (1774–1853), a wealthy merchant and property owner.

To reach the remaining section of the Company's Gardens, retrace your steps through the Memorial Garden and walk west towards Queen Victoria Street. On your left you will pass the buildings of the South African Museum **(11)**, and to the west, the Planetarium. The SA Museum houses outstanding collections of historical, natural history and other unique material. A fascinating display is of engraved 'post office' stones, dating from times, before there was any settlement at the Cape, when the captains of passing ships bound for the East, left letters to be carried back by others heading for Europe.

You should now walk away from the mountain and take the path towards the rose garden **(13)**. These are at the top of the remaining section of original gardens. Along the way you will pass several fish ponds stocked with overfed goldfish whose diet includes a plentiful supply of school sandwiches.

On your right, beyond the rose beds, are enormous tree aloes **(14)** (*Aloe bainesii*) named after the famous English explorer and artist, Thomas Baines, who explored southern Africa from about 1842. They are more than 100 years old. About 30 m to your left is an Outeniqua yellowwood tree **(15)**, thought to have been planted here in the late 1700s.

Take the centre path in the direction of the lily pond **(16)**, which is stocked with Japanese koi. About 30 m further on is an aviary **(17)** where the birds are separated into four compatible groups. The easiest birds to identify are the golden and silver pheasants and the rosy-faced lovebirds.

On your far left is a restaurant **(18)** with informal seating under the trees.

Over weekends it is particularly popular with locals who play chess here (chessboards are supplied by the management).

As you walk along the central path, in the direction of the SA Library, you will pass Henry Pegram's well-known statue of Cecil John Rhodes **(19)** with his arm held up in the direction of the north. Rhodes had an enormous influence on the history of Africa (*see* pg 75).

The sundial at **(20)** is dated 1781. The original brass style was broken off and stolen in 1980 but has been replaced by an exact replica. Close by is a saffron pear tree **(21)** that was planted in the time of Van Riebeeck. This is the oldest tree in the garden and is probably the oldest cultivated tree in South Africa. Despite major tree surgery in 1980 and its great age, the tree still bears fruit.

After passing an aloe garden **(23)** you will see a huge clump of wild bananas **(22)**, thought to have been brought here in about 1772, and on the other side of the main path at **(24)** is a palm grove.

Ahead of you is the herb garden **(25)**, replanted in much the manner that it was at the time of the Dutch East India Company. At **(26)** the garden has been planted as a woodland walk, and at the centre of the next block of beds is a Japanese lantern **(27)**, donated by the Japanese government in 1932 in appreciation for hospitality given to Japanese citizens on their way to South America.

As you turn to the right along the path towards Government Avenue, you pass the statue of Sir George Grey **(28)**, in front of the façade of the SA Library.

At any time of year, this shady walk is a pleasant escape from the city's bustle.

Useful Information

DISTANCE: 3.5 km

TIME TAKEN: About 1.5 hours

PARKING AND START: On the Grand Parade in front of the City Hall

ROUTE: Circular route from Grand Parade to Castle, along Buitenkant Street to Rust en Vreugd, then along Roeland Street to the Houses of Parliament and back to start via Spin and Corporation streets

REFRESHMENTS: Cafés en route

AMENITIES: Toilets at Golden Acre and Rust en Vreugd

WEATHER: No protection from wind

TERRAIN: Paved

SUITABLE FOR: Walkers of all ages. Kerbs and steps at buildings difficult for push- and wheelchairs

SAFETY: As in any large city, be vigilant and only walk here when there are many people about. Do not display valuables

Grand Parade, Castle, Buitenkant Street and Parliament

Settlers to Settlement

The Grand Parade, the large open area in front of Cape Town's City Hall, has been the centre of the town's celebrations for more than 300 years and it remains a hub of the city's activities. It was initially an area of dunes and low bush next to a beach, on the line of present-day Strand Street.

Soon after his arrival at the Cape in 1652, Jan van Riebeeck constructed an earth fort at the north-west end of today's Grand Parade. Unfortunately the earth walls of the fort were built far too steep for stability and so, after rain, parts of the embankments often collapsed. Commander Zacharias Wagenaar, who succeeded Van Riebeeck, was instructed by the Dutch East India Company's Council of Seventeen in the Netherlands to build a new stone fortress, which was begun on 2 January 1666.

In April 1679, the Castle was complete and the five bastions were named for the titles of the Stadholder of the Netherlands, Prince William of Orange: Buren, Nassau, Catzenellenbogen, Oranje and Leerdam. At the main entrance, an elaborate gateway was built incorporating the coats of arms of the six major Netherlands' cities which made up the Dutch East India Company. On each side of the gateway was the monogram of the V.O.C. (Vereenigde Oostindische Compagnie – United East India Company). Overlooking the entrance was the heraldic lion of the Netherlands. A brass bell, cast in Amsterdam in 1697 and large enough to be heard throughout Cape Town, was later mounted high above the entrance.

In 1697 the area we know as the Grand Parade was levelled as a parade ground for the soldiers stationed at the Castle. At this time it was about twice its present size and extended to where Adderley Street is today. It was called the 'Grand Parade' to distinguish it from the 'Little Parade' (later named Caledon Square after the Earl of Caledon who was Governor of the Cape Colony from 1807 to 1811 and is remembered for his opposition to slavery).

In addition to its military function, the Grand Parade was where the town celebrated with fireworks, parades and processions. But, in early 1849, the huge crowds that assembled there were incensed by a British Government announcement that they were sending convicts to the colony from England. By 19 September, when the convict ship *Neptune* arrived, virtually the entire town had pledged not to supply the convicts with food, water or assistance. The protests continued until 21 February 1850, and the *Neptune* was forced to sail on to Van Diemen's Land (Tasmania) (*see pg 17*).

In 1822 a Commercial Exchange was built on the west of the Parade. This became the centre of commercial activity and served as the focus of Cape Town's social life and grand balls. It was demolished in 1892 (Cape Town's General Post Office now occupies this site).

In 1863 the wedding in England of Prince Albert, Queen Victoria's eldest son, was celebrated on the Grand Parade with all the jubilation the colony could muster. (In 1902, using his second name, he was crowned Edward VII.) There was rejoicing, too, for Queen Victoria's two birthday jubilees: her Golden Jubilee (50 years) in 1887 and Diamond Jubilee in 1897. Huge crowds also assembled here at the end of World War I and World War II.

More recently, in 1990 when Nelson Mandela was released after 27 years in prison, he addressed the nation from the City Hall balcony as a jubilant crowd of tens of thousands cheered from the Parade.

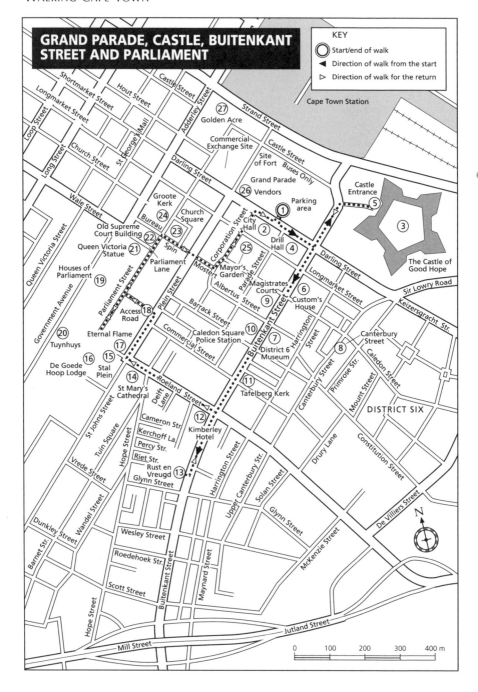

GRAND PARADE, CASTLE, BUITENKANT STREET AND PARLIAMENT

KEY

○ Start/end of walk

◄ Direction of walk from the start

▷ Direction of walk for the return

30

Walk from Grand Parade to the Castle, Buitenkant Street and Parliament

The walk starts at the Grand Parade (1) in front of the City Hall of Cape Town (2), then leads along Darling Street towards the Castle (3). The City Hall was originally intended as a tribute to Queen Victoria on her Golden Jubilee (1887), but it was not completed until 1905 because of the Anglo-Boer War and other delays. It was the last major Victorian structure to be built in Cape Town – the interior of this elaborate building can be examined at the end of the walk. The hall is now principally used for symphony concerts and the City's Library occupies part of the building.

The road running between the City Hall and the Parade was originally called Keizersgracht ('Emperor's Canal'), but was renamed Darling Street in honour of Lieutenant Governor Sir Charles Darling, who convened the first Cape Parliament in 1854 when he was Acting Governor of the Cape Colony.

To the east of the City Hall a long building (4) extending to Buitenkant Street houses the administrative offices of the City's Library service. This was originally the Volunteer Drill Hall, built for volunteer military units to drill in bad weather.

From Buitenkant Street corner, follow the road round to the Castle entrance (5) where you will see the moat that has been restored as a water body after being filled with soil for many years. Notice the bell tower and coats of arms above the gate.

Now retrace your steps back to Darling Street and walk up Buitenkant Street in the direction of the mountain. Buitenkant Street ('outside street') formed the eastern boundary of the town until the second half of the 18th century. It is a good idea to walk on the pavement nearest the City Hall so that you can see the façades on the other side of the road. The first building of interest is the Custom's House (6), built around 1814 and recognisable by the remarkable detail in the plaster mouldings of the Royal Coat of Arms. The façade is by Anton Anreith, Louis Michel Thibault and Herman Schutte.

On the south-eastern corner of the crossing with Albertus Street is an old building that has been renovated and converted into the District Six Museum (7). In the 18th century this was a wine store and more recently it has been used as a church by the Central Methodist Mission.

The name 'District Six' applies to the area east of the Castle and Canterbury Street (8), and stems from when Cape Town was sub-divided in 1867 into 12 municipal districts. (See also pg 35.) District Six was an appalling slum without proper sanitation or drainage but, despite poverty and disease, a wonderful community spirit prevailed until the 1960s and 1970s, when it was bulldozed flat under apartheid legislation. Its destruction is seen as one of the worst examples of apartheid tyranny, as the inhabitants were forcibly removed to live in areas far from the city centre.

Continuing up Buitenkant Street you pass the Magistrates Courts **(9)** and Caledon Square Police Station **(10)**, on the site of the former Little Parade. On the opposite side of the road, just before Commercial Street, stands the Dutch Reformed Church's Tafelberg Kerk **(11)**, dating from 1892.

Cross over Roeland Street and continue up past the Kimberley Hotel **(12)** to the imposing Rust en Vreugd **(13)** ('Peace and Happiness'). Walking up the drive you can easily imagine how, in 1778 when this elegant home was built for Willem Boers, he had a superb view of the bay with the ships anchored just north of the Castle. Fiscal to the Dutch East India Company, he is reputed to have been thoroughly corrupt. His home now houses the watercolour paintings, maps, prints and drawings of the William Fehr Collection. Fehr was a wealthy wholesale merchant who was involved in many aspects of preservation of natural and cultural objects. His oil paintings, antique furniture and *objets d'art* are housed at the Castle.

The large gardens at Rust en Vreugd have been carefully planted with herbs and old varieties of plants that are likely to have grown here in the 18th century.

Now retrace your steps to Roeland Street and then turn to the left (towards Signal Hill). Roeland Street was named in 1790 after Jacob Rohland of Obercassel who came to the Cape to assist in improving the quality of the wines. It became a fashionable area in the early 1800s.

At the end of Roeland Street you pass St Mary's Cathedral **(14)** on your left (its full name is St Mary's Cathedral of Our Lady of the Flight into Egypt). Built from 1840, this is the oldest existing Roman Catholic church in South Africa.

The open area to the west of the Cathedral is Stal Plein **(15)** ('Stable Square'), where the Dutch East India Company kept stables from 1705 until 1791. The statue on Stal Plein is of General Louis Botha, the first Prime Minister of the Union of South Africa in 1910. He was one of the Boer leaders during the Anglo-Boer War and was largely responsible for the negotiations that led to the Peace Conference and Treaty at Vereeniging in 1902. After World War I, Botha was the South African signatory to the Treaty of Versailles.

On the mountain side of Stal Plein, behind the security railings, lies the historic Freemason's Lodge, De Goede Hoop **(16)**, which was built in 1803 by Thibault, Anreith and Schutte. This is one of the most magnificent buildings in Cape Town but unfortunately is not open to the public as it is now used by the Office of the President.

Behind the railings you can see the *'Eternal Flame* **(17)**, *burning in memory of those who have laid down lives for their beliefs and ideals in wars within and beyond the frontiers of our country'*.

Walk down Plein Street and pass the government office building called '120 Plein Street' until you come to a small road leading to the left **(18)**. After reporting to the security official, continue into Parliament Street. The Houses of Parliament **(19)** are immediately in front of you.

This enormous red brick building was designed by Charles Freeman (*see* pg 26).

To have a look at the exterior of the Tuynhuis **(20)**, walk up Parliament Street for about 200 m towards the mountain. Beyond Parliament you will come to the Tuynhuis, an elegant white building used by the Dutch East India Company as a guest house from 1700 and now by the President of South Africa (*see* pg 26).

Now retrace your steps down Parliament Street to the northern end of Parliament **(19)**. Parliament Lane is the small path leading to the left and halfway along is a statue of Queen Victoria **(21)** by British sculptor, Sir Thomas Brock. Return to Parliament Street and the Old Supreme Court Building **(22)** (*see also* pg 25), which was designed and built by Anreith, Thibault and Schutte in 1810.

The road in front of you leading to the right is Spin Street, a memory of unsuccessful endeavours to introduce a silkworm industry to the Cape in 1704 by Governor William Adriaan van der Stel and in 1753 by François Guillaume.

Church Square **(23)** is to the north of Spin Street. Its name relates to the Dutch Reformed Church's Groote Kerk **(24)**, to the west of the square. This was the only church that was allowed in Cape Town until the death of Governor Ryk Tulbagh in 1871 (*see* pg 21). The statue at the centre of the square is that of Jan Hendrik Hofmeyr, popularly known as 'Onze Jan' ('Our Jan'). As editor of the *Zuid Afrikaan*, he became an important Afrikaner leader and was largely responsible for the recognition of equality for Dutch and English languages. He was also involved in drafting the 1909 South African Constitution.

As you continue round to the right, Spin Street becomes Mostert Street. When you reach Corporation Street, turn to the left towards the Grand Parade. You will see a remarkably fine plaster detail in the façade of Number 5 Corporation Street. These are the offices of the Wooltru Group who built the large modern ochre-and-black building that you pass further on. This building was constructed on a site behind the City Hall previously known as the Mayor's Garden **(25)**. During World War II there was a canteen and centre here for the thousands of men and women in the armed forces who passed through the city. Dances were held here every evening.

Corporation Street, named in 1904, replaced the name Zieke Street ('Sick Street') which referred to a Dutch East India Company's hospital that stood to the east of the City Hall in the 18th century.

Further down Corporation Street you will pass one of the entrances to the City Hall **(3)**. If you want to look at the interior of this grand building, here is the place to make enquiries.

Now cross over to the Grand Parade **(26)** and enjoy another colourful scene, unique to Cape Town. In the south-west corner of the Parade, herbs, roots and other traditional medicines are for sale. Nearby are flower sellers and closer to the Golden Acre **(27)** are stalls selling refreshments, spices and interesting commodities such as sour fig jam. On Wednesday and Saturday mornings the regulars are joined by other vendors and an extraordinary array of goods are sold in a vibrant market scene. (Be particularly aware of pickpockets and opportunists here.)

Bo-Kaap

Malays, Mosques and Muezzin

This short walk through the Bo-Kaap (meaning 'Above Cape Town') will give you a glimpse of Cape Town as it was in the early part of the 19th century. It will also bring you close to the traditions of the Malay community who have made this their home.

The Bo-Kaap can be broadly defined as the area on the slopes of Signal Hill above Buitengracht Street. It is bounded by Carisbrook and Strand streets and most of its built-up area is below Chiappini Street. There are also two higher sections that were originally market gardens: Schotse Kloof, at the top of Wale Street, and Stadzicht at the top of Longmarket Street. In 1952, under apartheid legislation, this entire area was declared the exclusive domain of the 'Cape Malay Group' and all people of other races and origins were required to leave. Although this legislation has now been revoked it is now ironically a far more Malay area than it was in the past.

Records suggest that most of the houses constructed in the Bo-Kaap were specifically built for the purpose of being let. They appear to have been occupied mainly by artisans and tradesmen who arrived in great numbers from Europe (from about 1780 onwards). Up to that time the artisans were Malay slaves and soldiers of the Dutch East India Company.

The Malays of Cape Town were brought to the Cape by the Company as political exiles, company convicts and slaves in the period from 1657 to 1794. They came mainly from parts of the Indonesian Archipelago such as Java, Bali, the Celebes, Timor, Buton and Tambora, as well as Bengal in India, Sri Lanka, Malaysia and Madagascar. Most were Suni Muslims.

As the Dutch discouraged the practice of Islam, no mosques were permitted at the Cape until, in 1797, during the First British Occupation, the new government allowed a freed prisoner, Tuan Guru (see box pg 39), to establish the Auwal Mosque in a converted warehouse in Dorp Street. At this time, the 20 000 Europeans living at the Cape were outnumbered by about 24 000 slaves.

A few years later, in 1804, when control of the Cape had been handed back to the Dutch (Batavian Republic) under the Treaty of Amiens (see Historical Background, pg 11), the Dutch government endeavoured to buy the loyalty of the Cape Town Muslims. As motivation for the formation of a special artillery unit to defend the Cape against the threatening British invasion, they granted land for a Muslim cemetery on the slopes of Signal Hill and guaranteed their religious freedom. The Second Occupation of the Cape by the British in 1806 (see also pg 11) brought significantly more religious tolerance for Muslims.

By 1832 there were two mosques, five prayer rooms and 12 Muslim schools in the vicinity of the Bo-Kaap (Palm Tree Mosque in Long Street was founded in 1807). Following the abolition of slavery at the Cape in 1834 many more Muslims moved into the area. In 1867, when Cape Town was divided into six 'districts' and the Bo-Kaap was part of District Two, it had a clear identity, but was becoming so neglected that the buildings were being demolished as a way of controlling smallpox and other diseases. (The well-known District Six to the east of the Castle was another subdivision of the town. See also pg 31.)

By the early 1930s, areas of the Bo-Kaap had become so derelict that the City Council was systematically expropriating and demolishing the buildings on the grounds of safety and hygiene. As buildings were demolished many were replaced by commercial and light industrial activities.

In 1943, a group of concerned citizens motivated for the preservation of the Bo-Kaap's historic buildings and the retention of the area as the centre of the Malay way of life. As a result, in 1951 the City Council, with the support of the Historical Monuments Commission, restored 15 houses in the block bounded by Chiappini, Longmarket, Rose and Shortmarket streets.

Fifteen years later the houses between Rose and Chiappini, Wale and Longmarket streets were declared National Monuments and plans were drawn up to restore 52 houses that were in a bad state of repair.

Restoration of the Bo-Kaap has been undertaken with the clear objective of rehabilitating the area and restoring it to its original character. Houses that had been demolished have been rebuilt, many of the old façades have been restored, stone road cobbles have been re-laid and much of the original character has been regained.

Walk through the Bo-Kaap

The Bo-Kaap Museum (1) is a particularly appropriate place to start as it houses artefacts relating to the area and has displays of cultural and religious traditions that are still observed by the Malay community. You are likely to find interest in those relating to brides, furniture, language, weddings, funerals, architecture of the neighbourhood and kalifa (an exhibition of swordplay as a proof of faith, similar to rites also practised in Bali).

The building, which is distinctive in having an elegant curvilinear parapet with plaster details somewhat similar to a Dutch gable, is thought to be the oldest house in Cape Town that survives in its original form. It was built between 1763 and 1768 as part of a block of *huurhuisies* ('houses for rent') by Jan de Waal, sexton (administrator) of the Groote Kerk in Adderley Street (*see* pg 19).

From the museum walk up Wale Street for about 90 m and then turn to the right into Chiappini Street (2). This name was first shown in a street directory of 1830 as a replacement for the name 'Schotse Kloof'. It was named after Antonio Chiappini, a local businessman. The name Wale Street was originally 'Waale', meaning 'comes from Wallon', the French-speaking part of Belgium. In the middle of the 18th century, some Wallon families had settled in this area.

Ahead of you, on both sides of the road, you will see the rows of small multi-coloured houses that have made the Bo-Kaap distinctive. Although the paint colour chosen by the residents remains a local controversy, the architectural forms are of considerable interest and certain elements of material and design recur in almost every building.

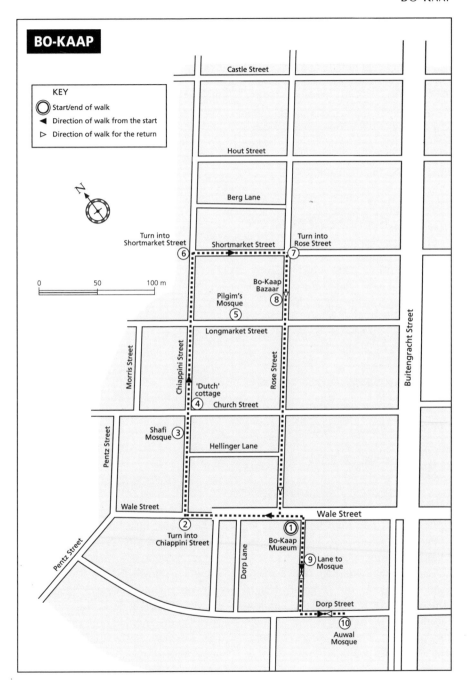

BO-KAAP

KEY

⬭ Start/end of walk

◀ Direction of walk from the start

▷ Direction of walk for the return

Castle Street

Hout Street

Berg Lane

Turn into
Shortmarket Street

Shortmarket Street

Turn into
Rose Street

⑥

⑦

0   50   100 m

Bo-Kaap
Bazaar

Pilgim's
Mosque

⑤

⑧

Longmarket Street

Morris Street

Chiappini Street

Rose Street

Buitengracht Street

'Dutch'
cottage

④

Church Street

Shafi
Mosque ③

Hellinger Lane

Pentz Street

Wale Street

②

Turn into
Chiappini Street

①

Bo-Kaap
Museum

Wale Street

Pentz Street

Dorp Lane

⑨ Lane to
Mosque

Dorp Street

⑩

Auwal
Mosque

The width of most houses is about half that of the average house in the old part of the city. The narrow frontage has resulted in a layout where the rooms are stacked from the front, one after another, and are linked by a long passage. The few 'double width' houses have central passages. The centre of activity is generally in the kitchen-dining room at the back of the house adjoining a small

HEAD COVERINGS

Along the walk you are likely to see many different head coverings worn by Malays. Large flattish conical hats, similar to those worn in Indonesia and China, were once popular in Cape Town; so were bright red and black fezzes worn by men (introduced from Turkey by Abu Bakr Effendi). A tassle on the fez signified that it was worn by a hadji who had been to Mecca. As an anti-Turkish political response the fez is now seldom seen here. Wearing of 'under-fezzes' and small distinctive Muslim caps are a recent recognition of a more international identity.

At the Bo-Kaap Museum you will see several striking head coverings including the medora, or gold crown, which is worn by a woman hadji or by a bride.

stone-paved courtyard. Children play in community courtyards that are also unfortunately used for parking.

As you walk, you may find it interesting to identify the common design details. You will notice that the building façades include distinctive forms where the parapets, doors, windows, steps and low stoep walls are unified by a single style.

The fine details in the windows, doors and fanlights include attractive features that are distinctive of their times of construction. In the Dutch period (before 1805) the frame is flush or nearly flush with the outside of the wall and there are no window-sills. After the arrival of the British, the Georgian sash window was introduced in which both top and bottom portions of the window slide. The frames are set back in a recess behind the front of the wall, which relates to a 18th century London by-law, intended to increase fire protection.

The Dutch front doors are divided horizontally so they can be opened in two halves. The Georgian doors are elegantly panelled and are sometimes vertically split.

After the first block of houses, you will pass on your left the Shafi Mosque (3), which is in an elegant, almost neo-Gothic, church-style. It has a simple distinctive minaret from where the Bilal (muezzin) calls the faithful to pray five times each day.

On your right, at the corner of Chiappini and Church streets, you can see an example of a 'Dutch' cottage (4) without window-sills.

Further along Chiappini Street, look down Longmarket Street towards town. The Pilgrim's Mosque (5) is on your left. This was built in the 1930s in a traditional Eastern style. Before the advent of air travel to Mecca, this mosque was the base where the community gathered before the procession set off for the docks.

A block further on (6), turn down Shortmarket Street where you will notice several other 'Dutch' cottages. When you reach Rose Street (7) turn to the right. You will be facing towards Table Mountain. On your right is the Bo-Kaap Bazaar (8) where you can enjoy refreshments and try Malay specialities. In addition to the dish of the day, there is other excellent Malay cuisine to choose from: vegetable or meat samoosas (triangular pastry savoury cakes), tasty chilli-bites that will surprise you, koeksisters (traditional Malay sweet-cakes) and delicious pastries.

As you walk towards the Bo-Kaap Museum, look up Longmarket Street. This is an excellent photo opportunity with the elegant Pilgrim's Mosque set against the background of Signal Hill. There are also good views up Helliger Lane, two blocks further on. At the end of Rose Street you will see the museum (1), slightly to your left.

MUSLIM LEADERS

Two Muslim leaders that have had significant impact on the Cape are Tuan Guru and Abu Bakr Effendi.

Tuan Guru (Imam Abdulullah ibn Qadi Abd al-Salam) was incarcerated on Robben Island in 1780 after being banished from Tidore (a small island in the Indonesian Archipelago) for conspiring with the British against the Dutch. At the Cape he assumed leadership of the Muslim community and wrote several books detailing Islamic jurisprudence (laws) and introducing Shafi orthodoxy. Tuan Guru inscribed the Qur'an in phonetic Afrikaans using Arabic characters at a time when this language was virtually unknown outside the slave community.

Abu Bakr Effendi, a learned man of Kurdish origin, was sent to the Cape by the Turkish government in 1863 at the request of the British. His role was to assist in settling religious differences that had arisen between different congregations. He established a Muslim school at 71 Wale Street (now the Bo-Kaap Museum) and also wrote a book on Islamic jurisprudence in phonetic Afrikaans using Arabic characters. Although his arrival greatly increased Islamic interest at the Cape, he also created some controversy by introducing the Hanafi creed into the predominantly Shafi community and by declaring that snoek and crayfish were unacceptable for Muslim consumption.

If you want to have a peep at Cape Town's first mosque, walk down the narrow lane (9) that leads (on the Buitengracht Street side of the museum) into Dorp Street. The Auwal Mosque (10) is in front of you on the opposite side of the road. Return back along the lane to the start in Wale Street.

Lion's Head

A Bird's Eye View of the City

From the first days of Dutch occupation at the Cape, the slopes of Lion's Head and Signal Hill, the ridge immediately to the north, were important as vantage points for sighting approaching ships. Archaeological finds suggest that they were also used for religious activities by Khoi, San and maybe even earlier inhabitants.

A walk up Lion's Head, the peak to the right of Table Mountain as you look from the sea, is a rewarding activity with outstanding views in all directions. The optional climb up to the beacon at the top of the rock face (669 m) affords even more stunning views, often featured on postcards and in travel films showing the beauty of the Cape.

In 1620, at a time when there was intense rivalry between the English and the Dutch, two English sea captains, Humphrey Fitzherbert and Andrew Shillinge, commanders of English East India Company trading fleets, formally annexed the shores of Table Bay in the name of King James of Great Britain. (This is the same king who 'authorised' the translation of the Bible into English.) They named Lion's Head as 'Ye Sugar Loafe', present-day Signal Hill as 'King James Mount' and Devil's Peak as 'King Charles Mount'. Notwithstanding the annexation, King James took no further steps to assert the claim and Table Bay continued to be freely visited by trading fleets from other countries until the arrival of Jan van Riebeeck and the first Dutch settlers.

Van Riebeeck's Journal tells of their momentous arrival on board the *Drommedaris.*

'*5th April 1652: At about 5 glasses of the afternoon watch, praise God, we saw the land of Cabo de Boa Esperance, namely the Table Mountain, E and E by S about 100 km from us. It was first seen by the chief mate, to whom we accordingly presented four Spanish reals in specie, the reward for first sighting this land. We pointed it out to the Reijger and the Hoope (being further to windward) by hoisting the flags and firing a gun.*

'*As the dog-watch was drawing to its close, we discerned the Reijger and the Hoope close to us and together we turned towards the land.'*

6th April 1652: 'Calm weather with variable wind. It was on account of this that we were unable to make much progress, but as we were quite close inshore, we sent the sloop with the bookkeeper, Adam Hulster, and second mate, Aernt van Jeveren, to the tail* of the Lion Mountain with instructions to go round the corner of the mountain and find what ships – and how many – might be lying at anchor in the roadstead in the Table Bay. They could do it easily without even showing themselves and their sloop to the ships they might find there. This was done so that we, after receiving notification, might prepare ourselves for defence or offence.

'*They returned on board about 2 hours before dark and reported that there were no ships, so we stood in, notwithstanding the calm. We had, God be praised, a fine southerly breeze at the last moment, so that we as well as the yacht Goede Hoope came to anchor safely, shortly after sunset, in the Table Bay in 5 fathoms, sandy bottom, off the Fresh River** .'*

* Probably present-day Camps Bay
** The Fresh River referred to here crossed the beach close to today's Golden Acre in Adderley Street.

In addition to the Dutch referring to present-day Lion's Head as 'Lion Mountain', a name that relates to its sphinx-like appearance when viewed from the Castle, they also extended this description to several nearby features. Present-day Kloof Nek was called 'Lion's Kloof', Three Anchor Bay was 'Lion's Cove', Camps Bay was 'Lion's Tail' and Signal Hill was known as 'Lion's Rump'.

The Dutch East India Company maintained a lookout and signalling station at the top of Lion's Head, where there was a signalling cannon and flagmast that were used to warn of approaching ships. A shot was fired for each vessel approaching. When the British took over the Cape for the second time in 1806, the signal station at the top of Lion's Head was moved down to the Lion's Rump, which then became known as Signal Hill.

Cape Town's noon gun, which is fired each day (except Sunday) from an old muzzle loader at the Lion Battery on Signal Hill, derives from a Dutch East India Company practice that continued for over 200 years when a gun was fired at 6 am and 9 pm, to signal the start and end of each day. In 1807 this was changed to the firing of a time-gun from the Imhoff Battery, situated on the seaward side of the Castle. From 1865 it was fired at 1 pm. Since 4 August 1902 the signal has been fired from the Lion Battery at noon. During World Wars I and II the boom of the noon gun signalled a two-minute pause during which activity in the Mother City came to a halt and all bowed their heads in remembrance of those fighting at the front.

LION BATTERY

In 1891, due to fears of war with Russia, two 9-inch rifled muzzle-loading guns were mounted at the Lion Battery on the eastern slopes of Signal Hill. The fortification was remodelled in 1911 and 9.2-inch guns were installed during World War I. These caused considerable damage to windows in the city when they were fired. The calibre was reduced to 6-inch during World War II.

The natural vegetation types that occur on Lion's Head and the adjacent Signal Hill are different, relating directly to a difference in their soils and geological origin. The soils on Lion's Head are derived mainly from weathered granite and sandstone favoured by certain fynbos species. At most times of the year you are likely to find fynbos flowering on Lion's Head, but the best show is in spring and early summer (August–November) when the purple watsonias are most striking. Throughout the year there are thousands of shimmering silvertrees on the slopes above and below the path.

The soils on Signal Hill are derived mainly from decomposed slates of the Malmesbury rocks (see pg 12) and support the renosterbos (*Elytropappus rhinocerotis*), a grey-green bush that occurs all over the slopes. Renosterveld, which is the veld-type, is distinguished from fynbos by an absence of restioids (reed-like plants), there are few proteoids (protea shrubs with large leaves), and the clay-rich soils are less sandy and more fertile than fynbos soils (see pg 15).

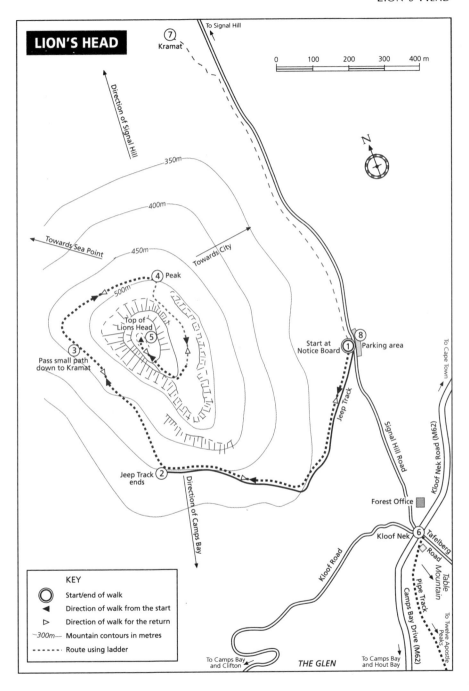

Walk up Lion's Head

From the start **(1)** walk up the jeep track towards the south-west. As the road slowly bends clockwise round the peak you are treated to constantly changing mountain and sea views. The silvertrees, which favour these granitic soils, are very striking. About 200 m from the start the towering buttresses of Kloof Corner on Table Mountain and the Upper Cableway Station are ahead, but slightly to the left. If you look carefully you may see some of the main features of the Pipe Track walk (*see* pg 65). Near Kloof Nek **(6)** you can see the tops of the two buried reservoirs. The pipeline leads round the mountain on the far side of the kloof, and the huge buttresses of the Twelve Apostle peaks run towards Llandudno in the distance.

The jeep track ends at **(2)** as you turn the corner and look down on Camps Bay beach, where a row of palm trees lines the Main Road. Fourth Beach Clifton is on the far right. The path then narrows and rises to fairly level ground from where, high above you, there are sheer rock cliffs that present a challenge to serious rock climbers. The steps on the path have been built with unusual square 'logs', made of recycled plastic.

About 400 m beyond the jeep track you pass a small path **(3)** which leads down the valley to a green-roofed Kramat **(7)** (Muslim burial shrine) that you can see about 1 km to the north. Near you and on the slopes below are

LION'S HEAD FYNBOS SPECIES

Dozens of fynbos species flower on Lion's Head and other parts of Table Mountain. Professor W P U Jackson's book *Wild Flowers of Table Mountain* mentions these species for Lion's Head in spring: *Euryops, Adenandra, Muraltia, Podalyria calyptrata, Erica baccans, Polygala* spp., *Lobelia* spp., *Leonotis, Oxalis* spp., *Senecio elegans, Chrysanthemoides, Felicia fruticosa, Leucospermum conocarpodendron, Cyphia, Lobostemon, Lampranthus, Struthiola, Salvia, Aristea spiralis, Spiloxene, Arum (Zantedeschia), Ixia scillaris,* dubia, white cotton (*Eriocephalus*), sundew (*Drosera*), silvertrees (*Leucadendron argentum*), *Scabiosa, Arctopus,* Wolharpuisbos (*Euryops pectinatus*), *Bulbine, Babiane, Atistea africana,* chincherinchee (*Ornithogalum*) and crimson suurkanol (*Chasmanthe*). After fires, which stimulate the growth of certain fynbos species, Lion's Head is splashed by pink and white March lilies (*Amaryllis belladonna*) and crimson fire lilies (*Cyrtanthus ventricosus*).

hundreds of silvertrees (*Leucadendron argentum*), which are endemic to these slopes. They are the largest of the proteas. This tree is also called the witboom and the suburb Wittebome was named after them. In spring you will also see masses of purple watsonias, pink and purple pelargoniums, pale blue salvia and many other fynbos species. The Signal Hill slopes ahead of you are covered by grey-green renosterbos.

Carry on round the northern face of the peak to **(4)** where there is a notice board showing the recommended route up to the top of the mountain. This is the suggested turning point for the walk if you are not going to climb up the rocks.

From here the view is outstanding. On the left is Sea Point and to the far right is the city with its many skyscrapers. The large rectangular water area in the Oranjezicht area above the city is the Molteno Reservoir, which was completed in 1886 after nine years of difficult construction, and was named after the first Prime Minister of the Cape, Sir John Molteno. In 1882 there was a major failure of the dam and water flowed like a tidal wave into the city. The level area immediately below you is part of the sports fields of Jan van Riebeeck High School, which was once a large rock quarry. This is one of the places where there is a distinct contact between the Malmesbury Group slatey rock and the Cape Granite (see pp 13 and 62).

Steeper walk to top of Lion's Head

If you are going to the top of the mountain, follow the arrow showing the recommended route to the right up the first set of rocks. A few paces on you will see a steel ladder, which takes you up to a higher level. Follow the signboards, arrows, chains and yellow-painted footprints. Be careful to follow the recommended route, and always stay on the widest path where there are alternative routes. You will come to another ladder near some pine trees and eventually your reward is the most spectacular view of all, from the top **(5)**.

On the way down, remember to face the mountain when the going is awkward, and always keep a firm grip. If you are confused about the route at any stage wait for others to pass you. This is a very popular walk and you should have no difficulty in finding someone to show you the way.

The Victoria and Alfred Waterfront

Harbour Lights and Holidays

The historic Victoria and Alfred Waterfront, one of South Africa's most popular tourist spots, is the original harbour of Cape Town. It was named after Queen Victoria and her son Alfred, who was sent to the Cape in 1860 to tip the first load of rock for the construction of the breakwater. The Waterfront offers the unique combination of a working harbour, and excellent shops and entertainment.

For over 300 years preceding the harbour's construction, ships anchoring in Table Bay were entirely exposed to the winter north-west wind, and the loose slatey-rock seabed covered with only a thin layer of sand provided poor anchorage. In May 1692, 40 years after Jan van Riebeeck's arrival at the Cape, a storm struck 11 ships at anchor in Table Bay. These consisted of eight Dutch vessels, two British ships and an old frigate being used as a hospital ship. Between 2 am and dawn, four of the Dutch and one of the British vessels were blown onto the shore near the Castle. Most aboard were drowned and valuable cargo was lost.

In the winter of 1728, three more fully laden Dutch vessels were wrecked. On 21 May 1737 a fleet of 10 homeward-bound Dutch vessels were at anchor in the bay when a gale struck and eight vessels were wrecked. The losses of 1737 were such a financial disaster for the Dutch East India Company that the directors ordered that in future, between 15 May and 15 August, all vessels were to anchor in the wind-protected area of Simon's Bay (next to Simon's Town) until a harbour had been built in Table Bay.

Five years later, in 1742, a 700-m-long breakwater was started on an offshore reef near Green Point. By May 1747, when only 100 m of the breakwater had been constructed, it was badly damaged by a storm. When locusts devastated the settlers' crops, resources were limited and the breakwater project had to be abandoned. The site of this first breakwater is called Mouille Point, the first rocky promontory to the west of the Waterfront ('Moelje' is old Dutch for a narrow breakwater).

SIR GEORGE GREY

In 1854, Sir George Grey arrived at the Cape after governorships in New Zealand and Australia. He is considered by many to be the most outstanding Cape governor. On his travels through the Cape, former Orange Free State and Natal, he established good relationships with leaders of all communities. He encouraged the start of the first railways at the Cape, gave large sums of money to found Grey College in Bloemfontein and other schools, erected hospitals for blacks to combat the influence of witchdoctors, and donated his personal library as the start of the South African Library in Queen Victoria Street, Cape Town (see pg 27). He was recalled to England in 1859 for having encouraged a scheme for the unification of the whole of South Africa, without authority, but was later restored to office. He is buried at St Paul's Cathedral in London.

The problems of using Table Bay as a winter anchorage continued with the transfer of control from the Dutch to the British at the beginning of the 19th century, and in subsequent storms many more vessels were lost. In the winter of 1822 nine ships were wrecked in only two weeks which resulted in an urgent call to the British government for a new breakwater and an enclosed harbour. While the plans were being discussed, in

47

1831 a further six ships were lost. Plans for a protected harbour continued to be discussed for many years, but these were not implemented because the cost was considered to be excessive (costs of up to £300 000 were estimated, comparable to the total annual revenue of the colony).

Eventually, at the instigation of the governor Sir George Grey (see also pp 25 and 47), on 17 September 1860 as 20 000 people lined the shore with bands playing and cannons firing, Prince Alfred ceremonially tipped the first load of broken rock into the sea. The construction of the Alfred Basin (4.5 hectares) and breakwater (550 m long) had begun. Convicts built the breakwater and the most dangerous men were chained. It was terrible work and for more than 50 years hard labour on the breakwater was a dreaded sentence.

In May 1865, while the breakwater was under construction, a storm struck the bay and, as if to prove the need, over the next 24 hours 15 ships were lost. One of them was the Union mailship, Athens, which attempted to steam out of the bay to safety. As it was passing Mouille Point a huge wave washed over the deck and extinguished the boilers. All 29 crewmen were drowned. The remains of this vessel are still visible at low tide about 200 m west of Granger Bay, which is on the Sea Point side of the Victoria and Alfred Waterfront (see pg 56).

Eventually, on 4 July 1870, Prince Alfred, by then the Duke of Edinburgh, officially opened the Alfred Basin and the breakwater. Despite potential competition from the opening of the Suez Canal (1869), which enabled shipping between Europe and the East to bypass the Cape, the new harbour brought considerable trade and prosperity to Cape Town. In particular, it became the port of entry as people and equipment streamed from all over the world to the diamond fields of Kimberley. By 1878 this town had over 40 000 inhabitants. Within a few years there was an urgent need to extend Cape Town's harbour.

Improvements at the harbour included the construction of the huge Robinson Graving Dock, completed in 1882 ('graving' is the process of removing barnacles from the bottom of ships); a 34-hectare basin west of the Alfred Dock; an extension of the breakwater; and the Victoria Basin, completed to the north of the Alfred Dock in 1895.

With the start of the Anglo-Boer War (1899–1902), the harbour became the focus for mobilising forces from all parts of the British Empire. Troops and supplies were landed here and at Simon's Town. In 1900, nearly 1 500 vessels visited Table Bay.

By the beginning of World War II, the harbour facilities of the Victoria and Alfred basins had become inadequate and a new harbour for Cape Town was under construction. A new 126-hectare basin, the Duncan Dock, was being built to the east of the Victoria Basin. (It was named after Sir Patrick Duncan who, in 1936, was the first South African-appointed Governor-General of the Union of South Africa.) The Sturrock Graving Dock – the largest drydock in the world at the time and capable of accommodating a battleship – was also under construction. The new harbour and Foreshore were by far the largest public works undertaking in the history of South Africa.

By the 1970s the need for the V&A basins had waned and they were only being used by small vessels such as fishing boats and tugs. But in the early 1980s,

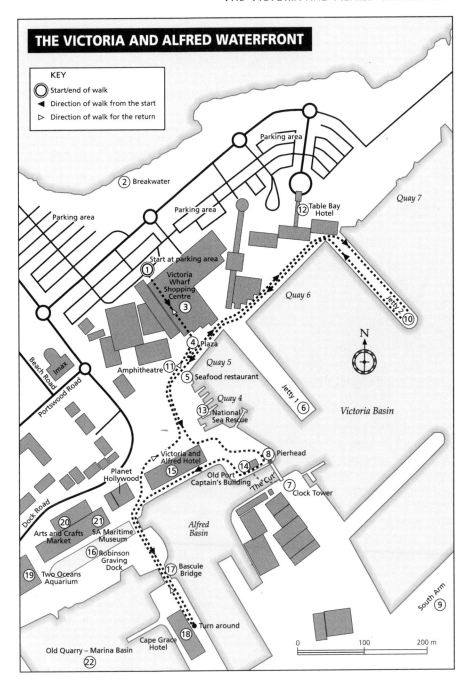

THE VICTORIA AND ALFRED WATERFRONT

KEY
○ Start/end of walk
◀ Direction of walk from the start
▷ Direction of walk for the return

② Breakwater

Parking area

Parking area

Parking area

Quay 7

⑫ Table Bay Hotel

① Start at parking area

Victoria Wharf Shopping Centre ③

Quay 6

Jetty 2 ⑩

④ Plaza

N

Amphitheatre ⑪

Quay 5

⑤ Seafood restaurant

Beach Road

Imax

Portswood Road

Jetty 1 ⑥

Quay 4

⑬ National Sea Rescue

Victoria Basin

▽ Victoria and Alfred Hotel

Planet Hollywood

⑮

⑧ Pierhead

⑭

Old Port Captain's Building

"The Cut"

⑦ Clock Tower

Dock Road

⑳ ㉑

Arts and Crafts Market   SA Maritime Museum

⑯ Robinson Graving Dock

⑰ Bascule Bridge

Alfred Basin

⑲ Two Oceans Aquarium

▷ Turn around

⑱

South Arm ⑨

Old Quarry – Marina Basin

Cape Grace Hotel

㉒

0   100   200 m

discussions on how to redevelop them began. Redevelopment of old harbour areas such as those at Boston and San Francisco had shown that they could be given a completely new and attractive character by exploiting their Victorian style and refurbishing their dilapidated warehouses.

In November 1988, the Victoria and Alfred Waterfront Company was formed. The whole area was subdivided into 14 separate precincts, and each subsequently planned in increasing detail by a team of enthusiastic architects, planners, engineers and other specialist consultants. The director of this remarkable achievement, David Jack, was also the leader of the planning group in 1970 that created Marina da Gama at Zandvlei near Muizenberg (*see* pg 127).

Waterfront Walk

At the start (1), outside the Victoria Wharf Shopping Centre, large boulders mark the line of the breakwater (2) on the far side (northwest) of the parking area.

The first part of the walk meanders through the shopping centre (3) to the edge of the plaza (4) overlooking the Victoria Basin. As you walk through the building, notice the outstanding attention to detail, combining modern elements such as lighting and escalators in the context of exposed steel elements reminiscent of a Victorian warehouse.

From the plaza overlooking the Victoria Basin's Quay 5, look out towards Table Mountain and enjoy the colourful scene before you – on the right is a seafood restaurant (5) serving excellent fish in a box; below the plaza are other speciality restaurants and tour operators offering near-shore boat trips. To your left is the base for service boats taking supplies to ships passing the Cape 'off port limits'. Further left on Jetty 1 (6) is the shore office for ferries to Robben Island.

Because of its isolation, Robben Island came to be used as a place of banishment for society's unwanted, including lepers, the mentally ill and political prisoners (*see* pg 55). Jetty 1 is where the prisoners embarked. The passenger ferry leaves in front of the historic clock tower (7) on the far side of Victoria Basin.

For many years you could, for one penny, be rowed across to the other side of 'The Cut' that separates the Pierhead (8) from the clock tower (7). A water taxi that leaves from the quay in front of you now offers this service at a somewhat more realistic cost.

During the Anglo-Boer War the British Army used the South Arm (9) on the far side of Victoria Basin for offloading troops, horses, fodder and war materiel.

To reach the next section, walk down the stairs or the ramp next to the amphitheatre (11) to the edge of Quay 5, then stroll past Quay 6 to the impressive Table Bay Hotel (12). On the base of the seal statue in front of this hotel, you will see plaques marking visits by heads of state, entertainers and sporting stars such as Michael Jackson and Boris Becker.

From the hotel, turn to the right and walk to the end of Jetty 2 **(10)**, which is a good place for photographing the harbour and city with Table Mountain forming an imposing backdrop. The moorings around Jetty 2 are used by all types of interesting vessels including round-the-world yacht fleets, square-rigged sailing vessels, motor yachts and the *SA Agulhas*, which services the South African scientific base in Antarctica and the weather stations on offshore islands.

When you pass the amphitheatre **(11)**, where open-air entertainment is regularly held, turn to the left behind the buildings on Quay 4. You will then pass the National Sea Rescue boat station **(13)**, one of six stations serving the area between Cape Point and Saldanha Bay.

Wind your way to the Pierhead **(8)** where a swing bridge gives access to the clock tower area **(7)**. Victorian architectural elements in these buildings are very striking. Notice in particular the fine detail in the old Port Captain's Building **(14)**, which now houses the administration offices of the V&A Waterfront.

From the Pierhead walk along the quay of the Alfred Basin, past the Victoria and Alfred Hotel **(15)**. This was previously an area of warehouses that were once used by Union-Castle mailships and have been elegantly transformed. At the corner, turn to the left and cross the bridge formed by the gate to the Robinson Graving Dock **(16)**. This enormous structure is still used for ship repair.

About 150 m beyond the Robinson Dock and after crossing a 'bascule' (lifting) bridge **(17)** you come to the elegant Cape Grace Hotel **(18)**, designed in the French provincial style. Celebrities who have stayed here include President Clinton, Yasser Arafat and Fidel Castro.

ROBINSON GRAVING DOCK

The dock usually accommodates two vessels – within limits of 152 m long and 17.2 m wide – at a time for periods of about 12 days. Before ships can enter the dock, huge blocks are accurately positioned on the bed in the empty dock to take the profile of each vessel. This preparation takes about half a day. Water is allowed to flow in until the level equalises inside and out. The huge dock gate is then floated away from the entrance. Vessels to be repaired move into the dock under power or by winching and then the gate is closed. Finally, the water is pumped out until the dock is dry, which takes another three hours.

This is the turning point for the walk and a good place to stop for a cup of coffee.

On the return to the start, notice on your left some of the special features of the Waterfront which are worth a separate visit: the Two Oceans Aquarium **(19)**, Arts and Crafts Market **(20)** and the SA Maritime Museum **(21)**. The old quarry **(22)**, where rock was removed for building the breakwater, is now a yacht marina basin with residential development.

Three Anchor Bay to the Waterfront

Cape Town's

Original Waterfront

Although the area around the Victoria and Alfred Docks is known as 'The Waterfront', for more than two centuries the term was used to describe the entire area of this walk, which lies west of Cape Town harbour. If you had walked along this route at the turn of the 19th century, you would have seen a rocky coast with small sandy beaches, backed by low dunes.

At the turn of the 19th century, on the route of this walk, were several houses and a gun battery, known as 'Kyk-in-die-Pot' (literally 'look in the pot') set in the dunes on the landward side of a dusty road. On the mountain side there was a large flat area, running for nearly a kilometre towards the slopes of Signal Hill, where flags fluttered on high masts at a prominent naval signal station. The flat area was used as a military camp and there was the occasional public display of flogging and execution near today's Traffic Department, at Gallows Hill (south-east of Portswood Road).

By the middle of the 18th century there had been so many shipwrecks caused by the north-west wind, that for three years (from 1743) the Dutch East India Company attempted to build a protective breakwater at Mouille Point, about 2 km from the start of the walk. This was unsuccessful and vessels using the bay remained at risk until the middle of the 19th century, when a breakwater was constructed to the west of the present-day Victoria and Alfred Waterfront (*see* pg 47).

Walk from Three Anchor Bay to the Waterfront

Walk from the parking area **(1)** at the two Putt-Putt (miniature golf) courses which have successfully operated here since 1966, along the promenade in the direction of Cape Town. About 300 m further on **(2)** is a miniature railway loop that has been run since the late 1950s by the charitable service organisation, Cape Town Round Table. Huge logs edge the path. Despite their immense size they are sometimes moved when the waves wash over the promenade. If you look around you can see kelp and seabed pebbles dropped on the walkway by waves.

Further along the promenade, the sunken building at the corner **(3)**, which is called Green Point, houses a pumping station that discharges waste water into a large submarine outfall that runs over 1.7 km offshore. In the mid-1990s the residents of nearby flats felt the shudder of underwater blasting when the trench was cut into the seabed rock. An earlier 'weighted' pipeline had been destroyed by storm waves in May 1984.

A few metres on, as the path turns the corner, the bright red-and-white Green Point Lighthouse **(4)** is on your right. Built in 1824, this was the first lighthouse in southern Africa and produced a rather feeble light from two lanterns burning whale oil. In 1865 it was raised to its present height of about 20 m above high water. The light has been upgraded several times. The lighthouse building also serves as the headquarters of the South African Lighthouse Service.

For many years there was also a floating bell near this lighthouse, that

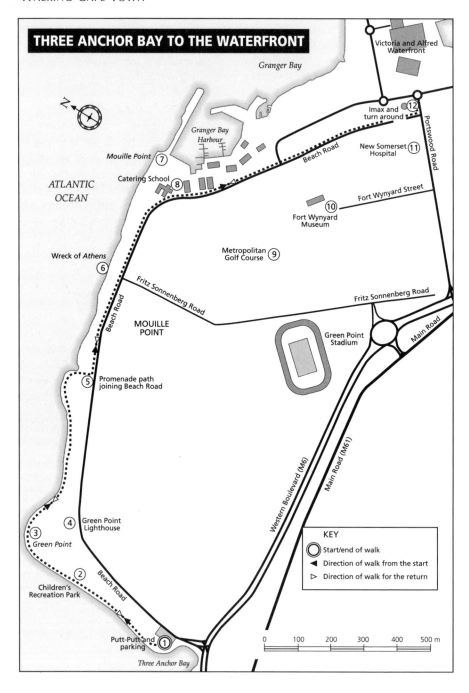

THREE ANCHOR BAY TO THE WATERFRONT

Granger Bay

Victoria and Alfred Waterfront

Imax and turn around (12)

Portswood Road

Granger Bay Harbour

Beach Road

New Somerset Hospital (11)

Mouille Point (7)

Catering School (8)

Fort Wynyard Street

ATLANTIC OCEAN

(10)

Fort Wynyard Museum

Metropolitan Golf Course (9)

Wreck of *Athens* (6)

Fritz Sonnenberg Road

Fritz Sonnenberg Road

Beach Road

MOUILLE POINT

Green Point Stadium

Main Road

Promenade path joining Beach Road (5)

Western Boulevard (M6)

Main Road (M61)

Green Point Lighthouse (4)

(3) Green Point

(2)

Children's Recreation Park

Beach Road

KEY

◯ Start/end of walk

◀ Direction of walk from the start

▷ Direction of walk for the return

Putt-Putt and parking (1)

Three Anchor Bay

0   100   200   300   400   500 m

sounded with the movement of the sea. In 1926 it was replaced by an air-driven foghorn which was connected to huge air tanks that sounded a deep (150 Hz) 'boo-oop', whenever there was coastal fog. Sixty years later, as a result of the high maintenance cost and not a few complaints from the neighbours, this foghorn was replaced by a somewhat softer and higher pitched (300 Hz) electro-mechanical 'nautophone'. You can see it mounted on a pole in front of the lighthouse.

Notwithstanding the 'softening' of the noise, its range is still impressive and, unless the wind is blowing adversely, it can be heard more than 14 km away. On occasion it can even be heard in Wynberg, on the other side of Table Mountain, about 12 km away. Coastal fog occurs here on about 30 days a year – mainly during the change of seasons (April/May and September/October).

The importance of this lighthouse was shown just after midnight on 1 July 1966 when the residents of the nearby flats woke to the sound of a ship's whistle and the impact of the cargo vessel, *SA Seafarer* (7 800 tons), striking the rocks directly in front of the Green Point Lighthouse. After a terrifying night on board, and unsuccessful attempts to use rocket apparatus to fasten rescue lines from the shore, the *Seafarer* broke in half at 04h45. From

ROBBEN ISLAND

Although the island (*see also* pg 50) had previously been visited by the Khoi, the landing in 1488 by João del Infanto, second-in-command to the Portuguese explorer, Bartholomeu Diaz, is thought to be the first by a traveller from Europe. In 1614 the English East India Company put 10 convicts ashore to establish a settlement, and mutineers were banished to the island in 1636. Rock corner stones for the Castle of Good Hope were cut there at the time of Commander Zacharias Wagenaar on 22 January 1666. The Castle was constructed by soldiers while slaves cut stone and prepared the lime.

By 1671, when the Dutch constructed a formal prison on the island, it had also been used for farming, isolating lepers and for banishment. In 1681 political prisoners from Malaysia, India, Sri Lanka and Indonesia were brought by the Dutch to Robben Island. Under British rule it continued as a penal settlement until 1844 when Sir John Montagu, Colonial Secretary, ordered the removal of all prisoners and had lepers and the mentally ill transferred there.

The island continued to be used for the mentally ill until 1913, and lepers remained there until 1931 when they were relocated to Pretoria. During World War II the island was fortified with large naval guns as part of the defence of Table Bay. In 1960 its role as a prison was re-established, and this was upgraded to 'maximum security' in 1964, when many political prisoners, including Nelson Mandela, were moved there. The last prisoners and warders left in December 1996.

55

first light it took three helicopters about two-and-a-half hours to rescue the crew and all 12 passengers.

From 1652, the earliest days of the Dutch settlement, fires were maintained on Robben Island to assist navigation. The island can be seen nearly 10 km away in the distance. In addition to its well-known role as a political jail and leper colony, the island has played an important role in providing lime, stone, seals, eggs, birds and pasturage. 'Robbe' is Dutch for seals.

Beyond the Green Point Lighthouse, to the south-east, you can see the level terrace below Signal Hill. This is what geologists call a 'wave-cut platform', formed by the sea about 2 million years ago (Early Pleistocene) when the sea level was much higher than at present. The highest edge of the terrace, which is about 18 m above present mean sea level, is near the Western Boulevard freeway. Smaller wave-cut platforms at the same level can be seen on walks in other parts of the Peninsula (e.g. Kalk Bay harbour pg 168).

At (5), the path along the promenade now joins Beach Road and about 400 m further along the coast, you can see the remains of the steamship, the *Athens* (6) at low tide. This ran aground in a tempestuous storm on 16 May 1865 and all 29 on board were drowned. During this storm, 17 of the 28 vessels that had been at anchor in Table Bay were lost.

About 300 m beyond the wreck of the *Athens* lies Mouille Point (7) ('break-water point' in Dutch), where the first breakwater construction was attempted (*see* pg 47).

Opposite Mouille Point, Beach Road turns slightly to the right and on the seaward side you will see buildings constructed in 1966 for the SA Merchant Navy Academy 'General Botha' (8). These are now operated by the Cape Technikon, who use the nearest buildings as a catering school. Survival training in life rafts is taught to seamen from the small Granger Bay harbour to the east. Around the harbour, hotel and residential development have replaced buildings of the Nautical Academy.

Granger Bay is named after Captain Robert Granger, who was a merchant involved in shipping in the mid-1850s. His house was just behind a lighthouse that stood on the lawn in front of the present-day catering school. The base of this lighthouse, which was built in 1842, can still be seen.

On the mountain side of Beach Road, beyond the buildings at Granger Bay, lies the Metropolitan Golf Course (9) and then the high earth embankment of 'Kyk-in-die-Pot Battery'. The barrels of several large guns project over the edge. This is now called Fort Wynyard (10). It was built in 1795 at the request of Colonel R J Gordon, who commanded the Dutch forces at the time of the First British invasion of the Cape (*see* pg 11) and supplemented a line of 18 batteries around Table Bay. Each of the batteries had an oven that could be used to heat the cannon balls for setting fire to wooden enemy ships. A total of 450 cannon balls could be heated in 14 minutes. Lieutenant-Engineer L M Thibault, who was responsible for some of the reconstruction of

SOMERSET HOSPITAL

In 1819 the first hospital to serve the non-military community of Cape Town was built near the present-day Provincial Administration buildings in Alfred Street. It was named the Somerset Hospital after Lord Charles Somerset, Governor of the Cape from 1814 to 1826. The project was the initiative of a Dr Samuel Bailley, who had been a naval surgeon. In 1862 the New Somerset Hospital, which is the building overlooking the Victoria and Alfred Waterfront at the turning point of the walk, was opened. The old hospital remained in use for the chronically ill until the 1930s.

Westervoort Bridge on the Liesbeek River (see pg 100), Groot Constantia (see pg 109) and many other significant buildings, was involved in the construction of these fortifications.

After the British occupation of the Cape in 1795, Kyk-in-die-Pot was upgraded many times with improved armaments. In December 1810 it was fortified with four 24-pounder brass guns. During the American Civil War (1861) it boasted six 32-pounders and one year later, on Lieutenant-General R H Wynyard's recommendation, it was armed with five 68-pounders. During World War I it had some importance when it was used to fire a warning shot across the bows of a Japanese light cruiser entering the bay. During World War II it sported 6-inch guns with a range of about 13 km and was additionally equipped for protection against aircraft and torpedo boats. (The larger 9.2-inch guns on Robben Island had a range of about 33 km and could reach targets well south of Hout Bay.) Unfortunately the museum and fortifications at Fort Wynyard are no longer open to the public.

For the next 500 m you will pass the buildings of the New Somerset Hospital (11) on your right. The first section of this hospital was built in 1862. It was constructed to supplement an earlier Somerset Hospital that had been built in 1819 which was the first hospital at the Cape to be constructed for non-military personnel. The New Somerset Hospital was the first South African hospital used for training doctors. It continues to serve the medical needs of all communities.

The turning point of the walk is where Beach Road meets Portswood Road, near the Imax Theatre (12). From here you can return to the start on the Waterfront bus or retrace your steps.

BREAKWATER 'PRISON'

Breakwater Lodge (13), the imposing turreted former prison building in Portswood Road (near the turning point for this walk), where the University of Cape Town's Graduate School of Business is now located, was built between 1896 and 1901. It was the first prison in the Cape where artisan training was undertaken.

USEFUL INFORMATION

DISTANCE: 3 km each way

TIME: 1 hour each way – this can be shortened

START AND PARKING: Parking area at Three Anchor Bay near Putt-Putt or along route

ROUTE: Along beachfront walkway

TERRAIN: Flat, paved

PUBLIC TRANSPORT: On Beach Road, the bus from the Victoria and Alfred Waterfront stops along whole route

REFRESHMENTS: Available at start and along route

AMENITIES: Public toilets and plenty of benches

WEATHER: Protected from south-easter wind, exposed to north-wester

SUITABLE FOR: Young and old, push- and wheelchairs, roller-bladers, joggers, dogs

Three Anchor Bay to Saunders Rocks

Along the Beachfront Promenade

Between Green Point and Sea Point, high above the water's edge, a wide beachfront promenade runs for about 3 km. This is where a cosmopolitan group of young and old Capetonians stretch their legs. The walk crosses an area where, in the 19th century, many of the most affluent and influential people of the Cape lived in beachfront mansions.

long this route you see walkers, joggers, roller-bladers and, over the weekends and holidays – particularly on hot summer evenings – a holiday spirit prevails. In the 1860s the area was served first by horse-drawn trams running on rails connected to Cape Town station and then from 1890, by a private railway. After the financial failure of the railway company, a second railway was established by the government in 1905 at the request of the Municipality of Sea Point. In 1929, when this service also proved to be uneconomical, the railway was removed and a condition was imposed that at no time were any buildings to be erected on the land occupied by the track. It is because of this far-sighted thinking that there are now more than 2 kilometres of continuous lawn alongside the promenade.

The whole area of the walk was initially called Green Point. This name appears on an English map dated 1675. In about 1810 the name Sea Point was given to a farm near Saunders Rocks and this name gradually came to be applied to the section west of Three Anchor Bay. The 1-km-wide strip of level ground to the east of the start of the walk, which includes Green Point Common and the Metropolitan Golf Course, was called 'De Waterplaats' ('Waterfront') by the Dutch in the 18th century.

This pleasant walk has much to commend it. Sheltered from the south-easter wind that prevails in summer, there are lots of benches and restaurants nearby, and access is easy by car or bus. On the continuous green lawn to the landward side of the walkway there is plenty of room for picnics and ball games, and there are also swings, climbing frames and roundabouts for children. The exercise circuits are popular with the nearby flat-dwellers. On the sea-side, the rolling Atlantic Ocean stretches to the horizon.

At Three Anchor Bay you will find an amusement park with Putt-Putt (miniature golf), model train rides, climbing frames and other children's activities.

Seawards of the promenade, an endless procession of vessels rounding the Cape can be seen, for this is one of the main shipping routes of the world. It was the way all ships travelled from Europe to the East until the opening of the Suez Canal in 1869. Keen observers will identify tankers, cargo ships, ocean tugs and occasionally oil drilling rigs on the horizon. Almost due north, the coast of Robben Island (*see* pp 50 and 55) is also clearly visible. This has become famous as the prison where many members of the present South African Government were once imprisoned, notably Nelson Mandela.

Walk from Three Anchor Bay to Saunders Rocks

alk westward from the parking area (1) – near the Putt-Putt courses (2) – towards Sea Point. About 100 m from the start, the promenade overlooks Three Anchor Bay (3). In the summer and over weekends

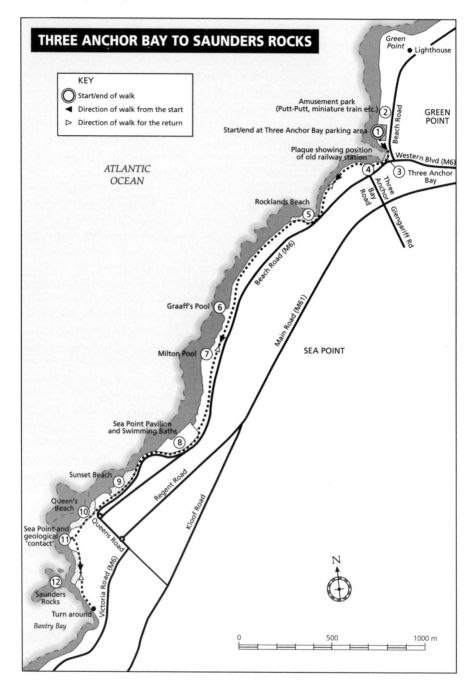

THREE ANCHOR BAY TO SAUNDERS ROCKS

Green Point ● Lighthouse

KEY

◯ Start/end of walk
◀ Direction of walk from the start
▷ Direction of walk for the return

Amusement park
(Putt-Putt, miniature train etc.) ②

GREEN POINT

Start/end at Three Anchor Bay parking area ①

Beach Road

ATLANTIC OCEAN

Plaque showing position
of old railway station

Western Blvd (M6)

④

③ Three Anchor Bay

Three Anchor Bay Road

Glengariff Rd

Rocklands Beach

⑤

Beach Road (M6)

Graaff's Pool ⑥

Main Road (M61)

SEA POINT

Milton Pool ⑦

Sea Point Pavilion
and Swimming Baths

⑧

Sunset Beach ⑨

Regent Road

Queen's Beach ⑩

Kloof Road

Sea Point and
geological
'contact' ⑪

Queens Road

⑫

Victoria Road (M6)

Saunders Rocks

Turn around

Bantry Bay

N

0   500   1000 m

you can watch small boats and jet-skis being launched into a deep channel that leads between treacherous rocks to the open sea. Three Anchor Bay was named after three anchors originally used to hold a defensive chain across the inlet, which is one of the few natural landing spots on this part of the coast.

Immediately after Three Anchor Bay, cross the lawn towards Beach Road (away from the sea) and you will see a small plaque (4) just before you come to the intersection with Three Anchor Bay Road (the continuation of Glengariff Road). This marks the position of a railway station on the line that ran between Cape Town and Sea Point until 1929.

Cross the lawn back to the seaside promenade and continue for about 400 m where you will come to Rocklands Beach (5). This is named after 'Rocklands', the home of Captain James Smith which, from about 1833, was set in large grounds that extended from the beach to the Main Road, about 200 m away. A map of 1839 shows a flagstaff erected on the promontory on the Sea Point side of the beach. In 1955 the studios of the South African Broadcasting Corporation (SABC), on the far side of Beach Road, were built where the Rocklands home once stood.

Continuing along the promenade for about 600 m beyond Rocklands Beach you will see a curious wall, on the seaward side, which discretely hides Graaff's Pool (6). Until 1998 this was an exclusively male sunbathing and swimming venue where nudity was allowed – it is no longer reserved for males only. The pool was built in the 1870s for use

by the invalid wife of Mr Pieter Marais, who from 1865 owned an enormous property and mansion called Bordeaux, which was landwards of the pool. (In 1959 the block of flats of the same name was built on a small part of this property.) Marais was a wine merchant and member of the Cape Legislative Assembly.

The pool is named after the Graaff family who purchased Bordeaux in 1893. David Graaff and his brother, Jacobus, (both of whom were knighted) were prominent businessmen. David was largely responsible for introducing mechanical refrigeration to South Africa at a time when ice was being imported from countries such as Canada. He was one of the original developers of Milnerton (see pg 69). In 1890 Graaff's Pool was enlarged by blasting to provide stone ballast for the Cape Town–Sea Point railway.

About 250 m on you will pass Milton Pool (7), a tidal pool named after a nearby Graaff family home, which in 1912 was known as Milton Manor.

The Sea Point Pavilion (8) is about 500 m further along the promenade. Here there is a large seawater swimming pool complex with restaurant, change rooms and an ice-cream hatch. This is a good place to buy cool drinks and ice-creams dunked in hot chocolate. The temperature of the water in the pool is several degrees above that of the sea and the whole complex is a popular holiday destination in summer. The sea temperature on this side of the Peninsula is seldom above about 15 °C, so swimming in the ocean is only for the very hardy. The Sea Point Pavilion, which replaced small wooden structures built around the original baths, was constructed in 1914. It was modernised in the 1950s and extensively renovated in 1996.

The pavilion stands on an area which was once part of Clarensville, a vast estate belonging to Saul Solomon, one of the most influential people at the Cape in the 19th century. Solomon, who had dwarfed legs, was born in St Helena in 1817 and distinguished himself in many ways. He was the most brilliant scholar at the South African College, a member of the first Cape Parliament, the owner of the *Cape Argus* and an outstanding leader of the community. The grounds of Clarensville covered some 8 ha (about 16 rugby fields) between Regent Road, Clarens Road, Cassell Road and the sea.

Continue along the pavement for about half a kilometre, and soon you will pass a long office complex on your left, which is the research laboratory of the Division of Sea Fisheries. Stroll on past Sunset Beach (9) and Queen's Beach (10) until you reach a large car park (11), about 200 m beyond the intersection between Beach and Queen's roads. This is where you will find a famous geological 'contact' on the seaward side of the parking area (*see* pg 13). The promontory here is known as Sea Point. You will also see a conspicuous concrete pedestal with a vane at the top. This survey beacon was placed here for use by land surveyors to determine their position, using trigonometry.

The contact is the boundary where two rock-types once interacted. Over 540 million years ago, an injection of molten granite squeezed upwards from beneath thick layers of mudstone. Incredible pressure and high temperatures converted the softer rocks to change to the hard blue-grey rocks that we now quarry in the Western Cape for building and road aggregate. These rocks are known as the Malmesbury Group.

At the contact geologists can identify the quartz, biotite mica and feldspar of the Granite, and the greywacke, hornfels, phylite, mudstone, shale, slate and minor volcanic rocks of the Malmesbury Group, which are predominantly blue-grey. The top surface of the rocks is generally whitish from salt and guano.

If you are interested, climb down to the shore and inspect the unusual mineralogy. At the car park a distinctive National Monuments Commission plaque commemorates the visit to this spot by Charles Darwin in 1836. Nearby, on a pedestal, the Geological Society of South Africa has provided a detailed explanation of the geological significance of the 'contact' (*see* pp 13 and 71).

From here the walk continues for about another 10 minutes towards the south when you will reach Saunders Rocks (12), the turning point of this walk. To reach this spot constitutes about an hour's easy walk from Three Anchor Bay. Now relax on a bench and enjoy the view. You can return to the start by bus or on foot.

This walk is particularly attractive in the late afternoon when there are often spectacular sunsets. For those interested in photography, the walk provides a great opportunity to capture the waves, the shimmering sea and the swooping gulls on film.

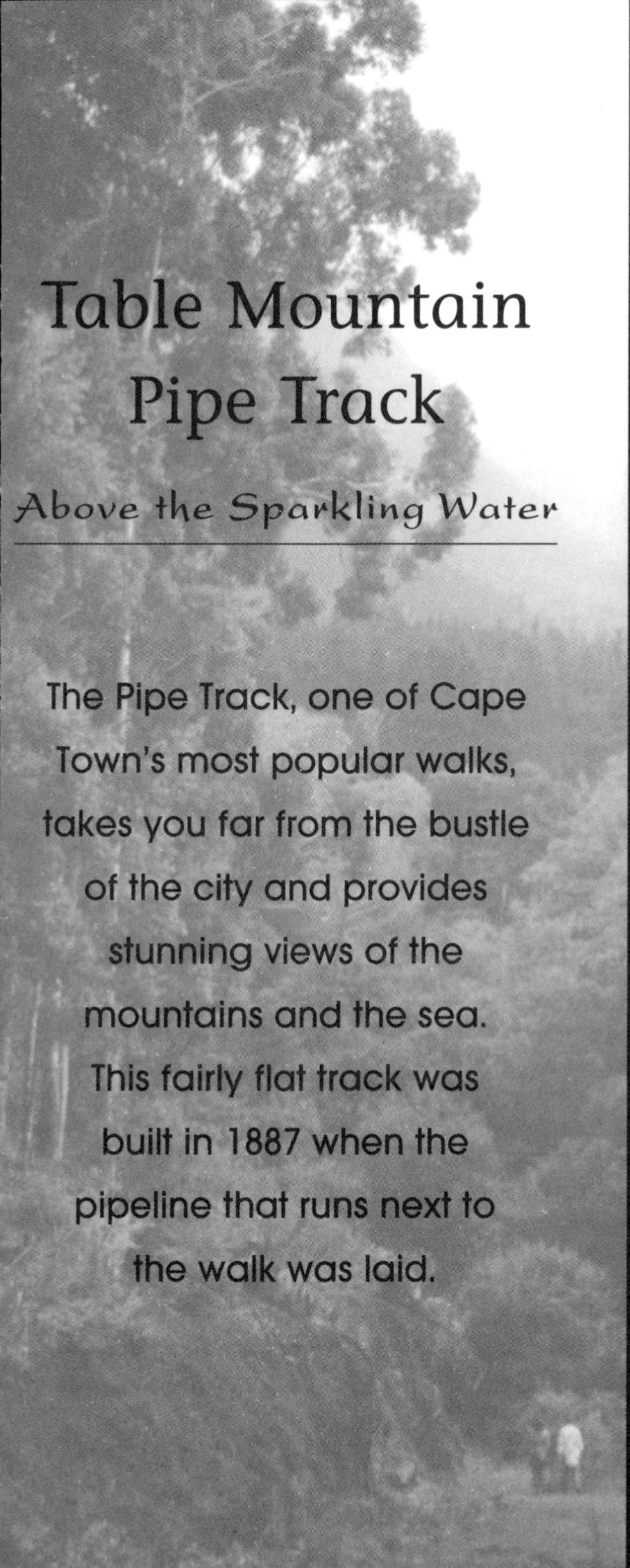

Table Mountain Pipe Track

Above the Sparkling Water

The Pipe Track, one of Cape Town's most popular walks, takes you far from the bustle of the city and provides stunning views of the mountains and the sea. This fairly flat track was built in 1887 when the pipeline that runs next to the walk was laid.

USEFUL INFORMATION

DISTANCE: 3 km each way

TIME: 2 hours for a slow walk

PARKING: At start of Tafelberg Road near Kloof Nek traffic circle

START: Steps on Table Mountain side of parking area

ROUTE: Along Pipe Track towards Kasteelspoort Path and back

TERRAIN: Gravel path

REFRESHMENTS: Water tap at start; take water

AMENITIES: Toilets at start

WEATHER: Sheltered from south-easter but exposed to north-wester. Limited shade. Can be very hot on summer days so take water, hats and suntan lotion

SUITABLE FOR: Walkers of all ages and dogs

SAFETY: Stay on Pipe Track. Do not explore ravines as some paths look easy but become dangerously steep (e.g. Blinkwater Ravine)

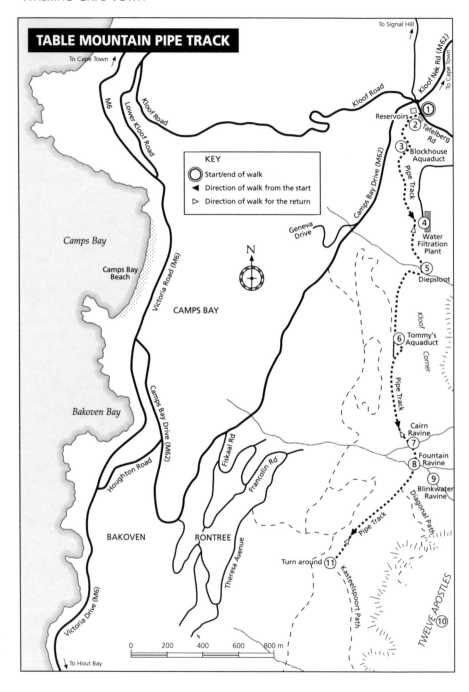

TABLE MOUNTAIN PIPE TRACK

To Signal Hill

To Cape Town

Kloof Nek Rd (M62)

To Cape Town

M6

Lower Kloof Road

Kloof Road

Kloof Road

Reservoirs

①

② Tafelberg Rd

③ Blockhouse Aquaduct

Camps Bay Drive (M62)

Pipe Track

④ Water Filtration Plant

Geneva Drive

⑤ Diepsloot

KEY

◯ Start/end of walk

◀ Direction of walk from the start

▷ Direction of walk for the return

Camps Bay

Camps Bay Beach

Victoria Road (M6)

N

CAMPS BAY

Kloof Corner

⑥ Tommy's Aquaduct

Pipe Track

Bakoven Bay

Camps Bay Drive (M6)

⑦ Cairn Ravine

⑧ Fountain Ravine

⑨ Blinkwater Ravine

Houghton Road

Fiskaal Rd

Francolin Rd

Diagonal Path

BAKOVEN

RONTREE

Theresa Avenue

Turn around ⑪

Pipe Track

Kasteelspoort Path

TWELVE APOSTLES ⑩

0   200   400   600   800 m

Victoria Drive (M6)

To Hout Bay

64

The pipeline alongside the Pipe Track channels water from two large dams (Hely-Hutchinson and Woodhead) on the Table Mountain plateau to the filtration plant that you pass about 650 m from the start. Water is piped from here to the Kloof Nek Service Reservoir, at the beginning of the walk, and then on to the higher sections of Cape Town and Camps Bay.

From 1888 this pipeline brought water from the dams through the Woodhead Tunnel, which ran from Disa Gorge on the plateau, through the mountain, to a portal in Slangolie Ravine, about 1.6 km south of the turning point for the walk. From the portal, the pipeline ran on the Pipe Track route to the Molteno Reservoir in Oranjezicht, above the city. As a result of problems with the original tunnel, a new structure – the Apostles Tunnel – was built in 1964. This brings the water through the mountain in an open channel and discharges it through a bulkhead into the pipeline, just to the south of Kasteelspoort, about 800 m north of the original portal.

Walk along the Pipe Track

From the start (1), walk up the steps past some municipal buildings. On your left is the large (13.6 megalitre) Kloof Nek Service Reservoir (2) which was constructed in 1908. The adjacent small (0.9 megalitre) Mocke Reservoir, completed in 1900, is no longer used. These reservoirs were built to balance the water flow requirement, i.e. to provide extra flow at times when the water demand from Cape Town is greater than the amount that can be delivered directly from the filtration works.

About 100 m further on you pass the Blockhouse Aqueduct (3), a small bridge built specifically to carry the pipeline across a small gully. It is named after a blockhouse that stood here from about 1781 to the time of the World War I, and was built by a French garrison working for the Dutch East India Company. Soldiers protecting the wagon route over Kloof Nek occupied the blockhouse.

The route then runs past a cluster of large boulders, including a most prominent feature on the left called Baboon Rock. It passes Granite Aqueduct and crosses a small bridge until you are below the Water Filtration Plant (4), a large building with an impressive façade resembling a residential mansion. This was built in 1938 for purification purposes to remove the natural brown colour of the mountain water, and followed the construction of an experimental plant at Constantia Nek in 1936.

The colour of mountain water is caused by organic acids, such as humic and fulvic acids, which are absorbed as the water runs through peaty vegetation. At the filtration plant the mountain water is treated with chemicals (e.g. aluminium sulphate) that form a floc (a jelly-like liquid), which is then filtered to remove small particles and its natural brown colour. The water is also stabilised with lime and carbon dioxide to reduce its acidity and is treated with chlorine gas to deal with any pathogen contamination that may have occurred. The floc and fine debris are removed by sand filters which are cleared by occasional backwashing. The backwash water runs down a stream to the shore, east of Camps Bay, and residents intercept some of it for use in their gardens.

Although the 16-megalitres/per day capacity of this filtration works was once considered impressive, compared with Cape Town's (1999) peak requirement of about 1 400 megalitres/per day this is now relatively small. Most of the city's bulk water treatment is now undertaken at Faure (500 megalitres/per day) and Blackheath (400 megalitres/per day), and the water is supplied from the enormous Theewaterskloof Dam in the mountain to the north, near Villiersdorp.

The increase in Cape Town's water requirement can be gauged from the sizes of the pipes used. The diameter of the pipeline along the Pipe Track is 375 mm – slightly bigger than a wheelbarrow wheel. The delivery pipeline bringing treated water from Faure to the city is 2.4 m in diameter – large enough for a small car to drive through.

The brown colour of some borehole water in the Cape Peninsula is not caused by organic acids. It is due to dissolved iron compounds in the water which come from the ground. The brown colour of such ground-water can be removed by spraying the water into the air, which causes the iron compounds to precipitate as a sludge. Staining of walls when untreated borehole water is used in gardens is due to precipitation of the iron compounds.

The path now drops down into a tree-lined gully called Diepsloot (5) and then rises up again to the level of the pipeline which runs at approximately 310 m above sea level. As you emerge from the trees, dramatic mountain features soon appear on your left. Immediately above you is the enormous Kloof Buttress, which is part of a line of dozens of peaks and ravines that make up this side of the Table Mountain massif. There are many famous rock climbs on this Kloof Corner side of the mountain and you may be able to see rope climbers on these faces.

Further along the Pipe Track, the path turns sharply towards the mountain at Tommy's Aqueduct (6) and then about 500 m further on you enter a wooded area where the path crosses the deep gullies of Cairn (7), Fountain, Grotto and Blinkwater ravines. The Upper Cableway Station is visible from here.

Fountain Ravine (8), the second gully that you cross here, is of particular interest as it runs right up to the edge of the Western Table where, since 1928, water has been drawn from a spring at the top of the ravine for use at the Upper Cableway Station. Unfortunately this spring does not run through the summer and additional water is needed. Since the upgrading of the cableway in 1997, a water tank has been fitted under the new cable car which can take four tonnes of water to the top on each trip.

Near the top of Fountain Ravine is a cave where, from 1799, Joshua Penny, a deserter from the Royal Navy vessel *HMS Sceptre*, lived for 14 months until he was able to escape to Europe on a Danish ship. He lived on dassies, small buck, honey and edible mountain plants such as sorrel. Penny had been captured by a press gang and forced to join the British Navy in Jamaica. He had taken part in the Battle of Muizenberg in 1795 (*see* pg 148).

Blinkwater **(9)** (meaning 'sparking water'), the next ravine, is aptly named because along much of the route you look down on a shimmering ocean, with the lines of waves sparkling to the horizon in a spectacular panorama. On windless days it is very quiet here and you will be aware of the natural beauty of fynbos, birds and an abundance of lizards sunning themselves on the rocks.

From Blinkwater, which was, for unknown reasons, originally called 'Stinkwater', a line of gigantic mountain buttresses stretches for about 4 km to Llandudno Corner. Although as a group they are known as the Twelve Apostles **(10)**, there are far more than 12 if you count them on the different levels. The names of some of the most prominent buttresses (which were probably named by mountain climbers) are, from north to south: Porcupine, Jubilee, Barrier, Valken, Kasteel, Postern, Wood, Spring, Slangolie, Corridor, Grootkop Peak and Separation. At a higher level are the Frustration, Orange and Bosky buttresses.

Jan van Riebeeck referred to the Twelve Apostles as 'De Gevelbergen' ('gable mountains') and his Journal mentions his intention to quarter and trap the Khoi in the Hout Bay Valley beyond the Gevelbergen. His Journal records:

'The Commander told them (the Khoi) that he had come to look at the pasture in the veld, and as he had observed that it had been largely consumed by their animals and those of the Company and the freemen, he requested them kindly to look for other pastures beyond the Gevelbergen or in the Hout Bay Valley, leaving the pastures hereabout to the Hollanders alone, as these were insufficient to support both their animals and ours. They promised to do this and said that they would break camp early tomorrow morning for that purpose and move to the Hout Bay Valley, where they will then be nicely caught and confined until the Hon. Company shall decide their fate.'

The track continues for about 700 m to a signboard showing a side path up the mountain to Kasteelspoort **(11)**. The signboard is the suggested turning point for the walk although the Pipe Track continues for about 1.5 km to Slangolie ('snake oil') Ravine. This ravine has had a curious name change, which appears to have been due to a misunderstanding by map makers. The area is still known to many by its earlier name, Slang Gully (or 'snake gully') which has been corrupted to Slangolie.

Take your time returning to the start (on the same route) as the views are outstanding and the atmosphere serene.

Milnerton Beach

Sandy Shores and City Skyli

USEFUL INFORMATION

DISTANCE: 2 km each way along beach for short walk; can be extended for over 9 km to rocks at Bloubergstrand

TIME: 1.5 hours (for short walk) or up to 6 hours if you walk to Bloubergstrand and back

START AND PARKING: From Otto du Plessis Drive at Milnerton, cross the bridge (at the bottom of Loxton Road) to Woodbridge Island; drive to the end of the road and park at the lighthouse

ROUTE: From the lighthouse walk northwards (away from Table Mountain) along the beach towards Bloubergstrand and back

TERRAIN: Sandy beach

REFRESHMENTS: Available at shops and restaurant at lighthouse

AMENITIES: Toilets at lighthouse

WEATHER: Exposed to wind; best in morning and early evening when wind has dropped

SUITABLE FOR: Walkers of all ages, joggers, dogs, kite-flying

At the turn of the 20th century the town of Milnerton was planned to be the new marine suburb of Cape Town. In 1908 a full page advertisement in the Cape Gala declared: 'Milnerton the Magnificent: Three miles from Cape Town. Reasonable fares. Good Roads. The Killarney of South Africa. Racing, Rowing, "Rugger", Recreation, Relaxation and Rural Rambles. Unsurpassed as a Health and Pleasure Resort. See you get there.'

Milnerton lies to the east of the Diep River, which flows from a large catchment (1 400 sq km) and enters Rietvlei, a marshy wetland of about 900 ha (9 sq km) some 11 km north of the start of the walk. From Rietvlei the river flows to the sea through the tidal lagoon that you cross near the walk's starting point. The western river bank is a narrow peninsula with a golf course and an area of densely-packed housing known as Woodbridge Island. For most of the year the river mouth is blocked by sand.

The developers of Milnerton, who included many of the most prominent people of the day, spared no cost in developing amenities for the area and in selling the plots. In addition to providing normal municipal services, they also laid a railway line connecting to the suburban rail system. Several bridges were built, the river was dredged for a 3.2-km rowing course and a weir was built to control the water level of the river. As part of the sales campaign there were regattas, a shooting gallery and skittles. Military bands and concerts accompanied auction sales and the razzmatazz was quite unprecedented. Travelling salesmen were dispatched to sell the plots in other parts of South Africa and one plot offer even included free life assurance. As land sales succeeded, a rugby field and racecourse were also built.

Milnerton did not develop as quickly as its promoters had hoped because of the economic downturn in the country. During World War I parts of Milnerton were used as a military camp and training area. During World War II its military role was extended and Ysterplaat, about 1 km inland of the lagoon, was developed as an important military airfield. Since World War II the town has expanded greatly and, with the development of adjacent suburbs, it has now merged with surrounding areas such as Table View in the north and Montague Gardens industrial township to the east. The railway to Milnerton operated until 1938 but was eventually demolished in 1956. The station was on the open ground next to the river opposite Woodbridge Island.

Descendants of Sir David de Villiers Graaff (see pg 61), one of the original developers of Milnerton, are still linked with the town. The family farm, De Grendel, which is situated on the mountain behind Milnerton, is still run by the Graaff family.

Milnerton Beach Walk

As you walk down to the beach from Milnerton Lighthouse (1), on your left (south-west) is a spectacular view of Table Mountain across Table Bay. The highest point on the mountain, Maclear's Beacon (1 085 m), is 11 km away. Table Mountain is flanked by Devil's Peak on the left and Lion's Head to the right; Signal Hill is the low peak to the right of the docks. Robben Island (see pg 55) is 12 km away to the north-west. Facing the sea, on your right the

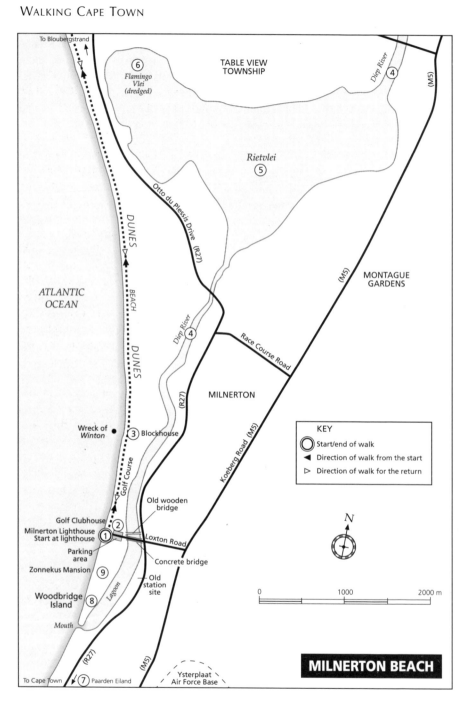

MILNERTON BEACH

beach runs northwards for about 9 km to the rocks at Bloubergstrand and then for a further 8 km to Melkbosstrand village.

On a clear day, particularly in the morning until about 11 o'clock when the wind generally starts, there is often a wonderful stillness on this beach. The scene is most impressive at low tide – a shimmering sea, gulls and the hush of the waves on the sandy shore. It is also very beautiful in the early evening and you can expect striking sunsets when there is light cloud.

As you walk towards Bloubergstrand from the lighthouse, you will notice, to your right, the remains of the old coastal road in front of the golf clubhouse (2), on the edge of the dunes. This road, which has been severely eroded by the sea, was built to serve a military blockhouse (3) about 1.2 km further up the coast. Over the past 150 years, this coast has been eroded by more than 70 m.

The erosion has resulted mainly from the construction of the harbour in Table Bay which has interrupted the natural flow of sand round the bay, and has introduced wave action that tends to take beach sand offshore. Unfortunately, sources of beach sand replenishment that would have reduced the impact of the harbour construction have been lost as a result of dredging, shoreline revetments, canalised rivers and the removal of coastal dunes. Unless remedial measures are implemented, the erosion is likely to continue until a further 20 to 30 m of beach is lost. Groyne structures, which could be constructed across the beach to reduce the erosion, would unfortunately spoil the character of the beach.

You may notice that, on the seaward side, the beach slopes slightly more steeply than elsewhere on the Western Cape coast – this is symptomatic of the erosion. In places there are also small offshore sandbars.

As you walk along the tide line, all sorts of interesting things can usually be found – shells, strange pieces of gnarled driftwood, jetsam from passing ships and the chalky internal shells of cuttlefish. Cuttlefish are squid-like molluscs with ten tentacles, two of which are much longer than the others. These are rapidly shot out to catch small fish. Occasionally, fossilised shark teeth that have been eroded from the cliffs and the hard sedimentary layers in the nearshore, are also found on the beach.

A wide variety of different coloured pebbles line the water's edge as this area is close to the geological contact between two different rock types. The 'contact' runs across the bay towards Sea Point (see pp 13 and 62). At the lowest tide you will find brick-red (jasper), slate-grey and black pebbles of the Malmesbury Group rocks and milky-white quartz pebbles from the quartz veins in the Malmesbury Group.

Dozens of sailing ships have been wrecked along this coast, and divers still sometimes find cannons and other artefacts offshore. In the 18th century the Dutch East India Company occasionally erected gallows on this beach to discourage looters from stealing valuable cargo from the wrecks.

As you walk along the beach you will see to the north the high buildings of Bloubergstrand where the battle fought between British and Dutch forces in 1806 marked the Second British Occupation of the Cape (see pg 11). It was at the time when the Napoleonic wars were raging in Europe and the Dutch government (the Batavian Republic) was sympathetic to the French. Britain sent 6 654 troops and 61 ships to the Cape. They arrived in Table Bay on 5 January 1806 in bad weather and some of the ships were sent northwards to disembark at Saldanha Bay. After a small brig had been run aground to form a breakwater at Melkbosstrand, the remaining troops were landed. The Dutch Governor of the Cape, Lieut-General Janssens, formed up his defending troops at Blouberg and after a short skirmish, in which the British lost 204 men and the Dutch 347, the Dutch retreated to the Hottentots Holland Mountains near Somerset West. Cape Town was virtually unprotected and the Dutch capitulated a few days later.

On your right (the landward side) are small dunes that form a barrier between the sea and the Diep River (4). Old maps show that, in the past, the river broke through to the sea at several different places along this section of the coast during times of flood. Changes in the position of the river mouth have now been prevented by canalising sections of the river bank on the far side of the dunes.

Flooding of low areas of Milnerton from the river is a problem when there are heavy rains in the river catchment and either the river mouth is silted up or there is a high tide. During the winter of 1941 the weir sluices, that had been built south of the lighthouse to facilitate boating, jammed during a flood and the army

had to blast a section of the weir. To avoid a recurrence the weir was later demolished. Other major floods occurred in 1954, 1961, 1974 and 1983.

In the 1960s a harbour mouth was planned across the beach ahead of you. This was to be the entrance to a large inland fishing harbour at Rietvlei (5). To make it possible for ships with a deep draught to enter the harbour, the entrance was located on the line of a deep underground channel that was cut into the rock by an ancient river at a time when the sea was much lower than at present. The Rietvlei harbour plan was abandoned because of a downturn in the South African fishing catches as a result of over-fishing.

In the 1970s parts of Rietvlei were dredged to provide sand for the reclamation of the container berths in the Cape Town harbour. This dredged area, Flamingo Vlei (6), is now used for sailing. As a result of public protest Rietvlei is now a conservation area with statutory protection and it is one of the most important natural areas in the Cape. Although there are many thousands of birds from over 50 species in the nearby Milnerton Lagoon and at Rietvlei, along this coast there are relatively few.

On the walk you are most likely to see Hartlaub's gulls (about 35 cm long) which come from a large breeding colony on Robben Island. They have pale grey backs and wings, dark brown eyes and maroon-red bills. The young birds have brown flecks on the upper wings. You may also see kelp gulls, which are much larger (about 60 cm long) with a distinctive black back and wings edged with white. They have large yellow bills and their undersides are white.

On the way back along the beach you can see, to the left of the docks, the industrial area known as Paarden Eiland ('Island of Horses') **(7)**. Before the 20th century, where the Diep River flowing from the Milnerton Lagoon joined the Liesbeek and Black rivers, this was a marshy area used for grazing. Since World War II these rivers have been canalised and the swamps filled. Where there was once a sandy shore the coast is now lined with concrete blocks.

As you return to the Milnerton Lighthouse you may be interested to learn that it was built as a result of an accident. In July 1934, the *Winton*, a 4 388-ton British vessel carrying a cargo of Australian wheat to Britain, was accidentally beached about 1.3 km north of the lighthouse. The captain had mistaken the aircraft warning lights on nearby 76-m-high radio masts for the navigation lights of the Cape Town harbour. Three years later, in the Cape Supreme Court, the owners of the vessel failed to claim compensation from the SA Railways and Harbours Authority who were responsible for navigation warnings. The court ruled that the 'stranding of the *Winton* was due solely to the grossly negligent manner in which she was navigated'. The lighthouse was built to prevent a recurrence. Shortly after World War II, a small Brazilian vessel went ashore close to the wreck of the *Winton*, but could, fortunately, be re-floated.

Woodbridge Island **(8)** is an attractive housing development to the south of the lighthouse. In the middle of the houses you can see the imposing Zonnekus Mansion **(9)** that was a Graaff family home long before there was any development here.

Apart from the coastal erosion, Milnerton beach remains one of the most unspoilt beaches in the Peninsula with a spectacular view of Table Mountain from across the bay.

Rhodes Memorial and the Contour Path

Legacy for the Nation

Rhodes Memorial commemorates Cecil John Rhodes, Prime Minister of the Cape Colony from 1890 to 1895, and mining magnate after whom Rhodesia (now Zimbabwe) was named. The memorial, designed by Sir Herbert Baker, is built of huge blocks of granite and was modelled on the form of a temple at Paestum, Greece.

In 1870, at the age of 17, Cecil Rhodes came to South Africa to join his brother, Herbert, who had started to farm cotton near Pietermaritzburg. When the crop failed they moved to the recently discovered diamond diggings at Colesberg Kopje (later called Kimberley), where they acquired claims and became involved in the diamond business. A few years later, the two brothers undertook a long journey by ox-wagon to the highveld, north of present-day Gauteng. The attractiveness of the countryside gave Cecil the vision for extending British influence from the Cape to Zimbabwe and beyond. When he returned to Kimberley he made a will in which he expressed this dream – all his possessions were to go to the Secretary of State for the Colonies in trust 'for the extension of the British Empire'. A remarkable vision for a 24-year-old.

For the rest of his life Rhodes applied himself to this goal and, when he died at the age of 49 in 1902, he had added nearly two million square kilometres to Britain's possessions in Africa and become by far the richest and most influential industrialist on the continent. Between 1873 and 1881 Rhodes managed, by periodically commuting between Kimberley and England, to 'keep his terms' at Oriel College, Oxford, and he successfully completed his degree.

In 1880 Rhodes formed De Beers Mining Company, which made him rich enough to pursue his goals. (De Beers has become the largest diamond-trading organisation in the world.) To further his ideas he entered politics and became the representative for Griqualand West (where Kimberley is situated) in the Cape House of Assembly. Rhodes then progressively facilitated expansion of the Colony northwards. He secured the rights to mine, trade and settle colonists in Bechuanaland (Botswana), Matabeleland (southern Zimbabwe) and Mashonaland (northern Zimbabwe). In 1890 he became Prime Minister of the Cape Colony and by the end of that year, at a time when he had already suffered two heart attacks, he was working towards scores of other ambitious plans. These included an extension of the Cape Railway to Johannesburg, and then to Zimbabwe; a telegraph from Cape Town to Cairo; and the purchase of Maputo in Mozambique from the Portuguese.

Rhodes envisaged a federation of states of South Africa under the British flag and attempted unsuccessfully to persuade President Kruger of the then Transvaal Republic to share this vision. In 1895 Rhodes' close confidant, Dr Leander Jameson, who had been a medical practitioner at Kimberley, became involved in an unsuccessful attempt to take the Transvaal by force, in what became known as the Jameson Raid. Rhodes' association with Jameson became a subject of much controversy and led to his resignation as Prime Minister, effectively ending his political career.

Rhodes' industrial undertakings were pursued with great vigour. Among many significant endeavours he was responsible for establishing the South African dynamite industry, Goldfields of South Africa (later Consolidated Goldfields), De Beers Consolidated Diamond Mines, Rhodes Fruit Farms at Groot Drakenstein, as well as farming activities in other parts of southern Africa.

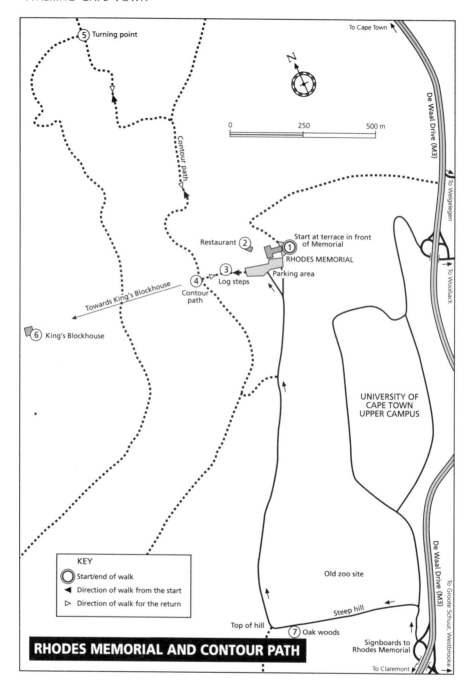

RHODES MEMORIAL AND CONTOUR PATH

He died in 1902 at his seaside cottage at St James (see pg 155). His estate was valued at six and a half million pounds – most of which was left to the service of the public. He asked to be buried in a simple grave in the Matobo Hills near Bulawayo in Zimbabwe, and that the surrounding area be developed into a public pleasure ground and farm. Rhodes' will envisaged a British-American alliance that would eventually dominate the world and, towards this end, he provided scholarships for the education of outstanding young British colonists and Americans at Oxford University.

The memorial to Rhodes, high up on his Groote Schuur estate, is a tribute to a most remarkable man.

Walk at Rhodes Memorial

From the start at the lowest terrace level in front of the memorial (1), look north-east over the northern suburbs of Cape Town towards the Tygerberg. This is a wonderful panorama at any time of day. Rhodes' estate included the land covered by Groote Schuur Hospital and the game paddocks higher up on the mountain (on your far left), as well as the land spreading across to the University of Cape Town (immediately below and to the right).

He owned several mansions below you, which he had built for himself and friends. These include Welgelegen (a red-tiled gabled building) and Woolsack (out of sight, slightly to the right). His mansions at Westbrooke and Groote Schuur are behind the University, further to the right. To the south of the University, and next to the steep road from De Waal Drive, are game paddocks that housed Rhodes' private zoo, which was closed in the 1970s.

The Woolsack (which is in the middle of a university residence, with the same name) was built for the author, Rudyard Kipling, and is where he composed the well-known poem *If*. Welgelegen was built for John Blades Currey, who was Rhodes' friend and secretary. The mansion, Groote Schuur, which was Rhodes' private home, was originally a Dutch East India Company barn. It was bequeathed by him to be used by future prime ministers of a united South Africa. (The union of South Africa's provinces occurred eight years later, in 1910.) Westbrooke was part of the original Groote Schuur estate and was named after Judge William Westbrooke Burton who bought it in 1800.

As you look out across the immense panorama of the sprawling city extending to the Tygerberg Hills and the Hottentots Holland Mountains to the east, it is not difficult to envisage how this view inspired Rhodes. One of his close friends described his enormous enjoyment of this part of his estate and in particular how he used to gallop his horse in the early morning along a path which he had built between his home at Groote Schuur and a field immediately below you. Of Table Mountain Rhodes wrote: *'We people here broaden in our ideas and in our sympathies because we are always looking at the mountain.'*

In the foreground of the memorial is the famous statue 'Physical Energy' by G R Watts, who donated it to the memorial. It once stood at Burlington House in London where it has been replaced by a replica. From the statue, climb the enormous granite steps to the bust of Rhodes and again enjoy the panorama.

The eight enormous bronze lions flanking the steps were inspired by the sphinxes of ancient Egyptian temples and were created by the English sculptor, J M Swan. Swan's charge for travelling to Cape Town for two months and modelling the lions was £315. After two years of construction the monument was officially opened in 1912.

Before undertaking their commission, Sir Herbert Baker and other members of the design team travelled to many parts of Europe for inspiration.

At the back of the memorial a small path leads to a cosy restaurant (2) where delicious lunches and teas are served.

Walk along Contour Path

Several routes lead to the upper parking area where, on the right-hand side as you go up, there is a clearly defined track with log steps (3) straight up the mountain. Walk up these steps until you come to a wide gravel road (4) that runs along the mountain contour at about 200 m above sea level. Turn to the right towards Cape Town and for the next 30 minutes or so you walk along the contour path at more or less the same level.

There are wonderful views along this walk and as you round each corner you will enjoy an ever-changing panorama until the vast expanse of Table Bay and Robben Island appears in the distance.

The natural fynbos seen on both sides of the contour path is of the renosterveld type, which occurs on the drier parts of these mountains. It is characterised by grasses; renosterbos (*Elytropappus rhinocerotis*), a small grey leafed bush with no visible flowers; and the kapok-bossie or wild rosemary (*Eriocephalus africanus*), which, from May to September, has tiny grey-green fleshy aromatic leaves and white flowers. On the slopes you will also see many silvertrees (*Leucadendron argenteum*) which favour the soils deriving from granite rocks on these mountains. Their silvery look is due to a sheen of fine hairs that cover the leaves to prevent moisture loss in dry weather.

There are also many alien plants on this walk. Stone pines (*Pinus pinea*) are well established near the memorial and parking area. They have a distinctive 'umbrella' canopy and large cones with edible nuts. The cluster pines (*Pinus pinaster*), which are more bushy, have invaded the fynbos areas. They were planted by broadcasting seed in 1894 to stop soil erosion at a time when the slopes were scarred by deep erosion channels. The plantation pines (*Pinus radiata*), which are used for building timber, are tall single-trunked trees with regular branches. Surprisingly, in a deep ravine below the path you can also see a plantation of tall Californian coastal redwoods (*Sequoia sempervirens*). The game paddocks above the Groote Schuur hospital, which were once pristine renosterveld, are unfortunately now grassed.

Near the memorial and along the contour path you may also see fallow deer, which Rhodes brought to the Cape from Europe.

On the mountainside of the contour path youcan see road cuttings where the underlying silt-, mud-, and sandstones of the Graafwater Formation are exposed (Graafwater is a small village near Clanwilliam where the formation is also visible). These rocks were laid down in a deep ocean about 560 million years ago and were folded and metamorphosed by intrusive granite lava about 540 million years ago (*see* pg 13). This dating was determined, using advanced technology, in 1998 by a South African scientist working in Australia.

The suggested place to turn back is where the road splits at (5), because the paths become much steeper further on.

If you want to explore further, it is strongly recommended that you obtain the excellent hiking map, *Approved Paths on Table Mountain*, that is published by the Mountain Club of South Africa. The road links, which are complex here, connect to three old blockhouses where there were fortifications for the protection of Cape Town, two centuries ago. They were built during the First British Occupation of the Cape in 1795 to prevent invading infantry, landing in False Bay, from circumventing a line of fortifications which had been built further down the slopes of Devil's Peak. From the contour path it is also possible to reach Tafelberg Road which runs past the Lower Cableway Station, about 7 km away.

As you retrace your steps, look up towards the top of Devil's Peak (1 000 m) and you will see the highest fortification, the King's Blockhouse (6) (431 m above sea level). It offered an excellent vantage point and was used for signalling between ships in Table Bay and False Bay. At this blockhouse there are two cannons on wheels dated 1792. At the beginning of the 20th century and until 1920, the blockhouse was used as a prison for convicts who were working on forestry projects.

After your return to the start and as you drive down the steep hill towards De Waal Drive, you will see Rhodes' beautiful oak woods (7) on your right, which is an excellent place for a picnic. On your left are the remains of the old animal paddocks of Rhodes' private zoo. The Groote Schuur mansion is straight ahead of you behind the trees on the other side of De Waal Drive.

USEFUL INFORMATION

DISTANCE: 2.5 km

TIME: About an hour

PARKING: Park below the Newlands Forest Station on mountain side of Union Avenue (M3), signposted 'Municipal Depot – Parks and Forests'. Do not confuse this entry point with one closer to the University that leads to a picnic area (13)

START: At the Forest Station

ROUTE: Circular route along jeep track and footpaths

TERRAIN: Jeep track and forest footpaths

REFRESHMENTS: Taps at start and picnic area. Do not drink from streams on the mountain; they may be contaminated

AMENITIES: A few benches and many picnic places, but no fires allowed. Toilets at start and at picnic area

WEATHER: Protected from wind

SUITABLE FOR: Walkers of all ages and dogs

SAFETY: Women should not walk here alone

Newlands Forest

An Old Forest Trail

Newlands Forest is a cool, peaceful place to walk. It is made up of pine plantations and the remains of a very large indigenous forested area that once extended over the lower slopes of Table Mountain between present-day Rondebosch and Constantia Nek. On this walk there is the chance to identify several of the indigenous tree species that once were common here.

N ewlands Forest was one of the first areas that was found by the Dutch settlers to have timber suitable for construction, and many of the paths that cross the forest were used by woodcutters more than 300 years ago.

On 26 May 1653, a year after the first Dutch settlers' arrival, it was recorded in Jan van Riebeeck's Journal: *'The Hon. Riebeeck in person, with some Hottentots, went to the forest behind the Table Mountain where the carpenters are busy cutting beams and poles for building the fireproof magazine. His Honour went to encourage the said Hottentots to bring the beams to the fort, to which end they were liberally entertained with food, drink and a little tobacco, until we managed to carry a fair sized beam. They arrived with this at the fort towards evening.'*

Four years later, in 1657, the rights to fell trees and to saw them into planks in the forest south of Rondebosch were granted to Leendert Cornelissen and the forested area, which included present-day Newlands Forest and Kirstenbosch, became known as Leendert's Bosch. It was used to supply timber for a palisade fence and fortifications running between the present-day Castle (*see* pg 29) and the mouth of the Salt River, about 4 km to the east. As the forest was cleared it was ploughed for agricultural lands and, by 1660, the fields nearest to Rondebosch were referred to as the 'new lands' from which the present-day name 'Newlands' derives. Slightly further to the south, on the north-facing slopes in the area of present-day Bishopscourt, a farm called Bosheuvel was established for the Commander, Jan van Riebeeck.

As the trees near the settlement were felled it became necessary to search for other forested areas, and, by the time Simon van der Stel arrived as Commander of the settlement in 1679, little accessible timber remained on the eastern side of Table Mountain. Van der Stel had the road to Bosheuvel extended over Constantia Nek to Hout Bay to reach the forests on the other side of the mountain. When these forests were also cleared, timber had to be sourced from much further afield and eventually trees were felled in the Hottentots Holland Mountains (about 60 km away near present-day Somerset West), near Riviersonderend (200 km away) and even in the Langeberg mountains more than 300 km away.

The decimation of the forests of the Western Cape continued until 1883 when the need to replant the forests was recognised by the government in 'Regulations for Working of Crown Forests', which required the planting of new areas of forest equiv- alent to those felled. This policy led to the establishment of pine plantations in Tokai in 1893 and later on the slopes of Devil's Peak and at Newlands Forest. The oldest pines that are presently growing in the Newlands Forest are at the picnic spot nearest to the University. These were planted in the period 1920 to 1925.

Today, although much of the Newlands Forest still consists of pine plantations (mainly Monterey pines, or *Pinus radiata*), after these trees mature and have been felled, the indigenous forest is now being allowed to return. Areas where you are likely to see indigenous species are shaded on the map.

81

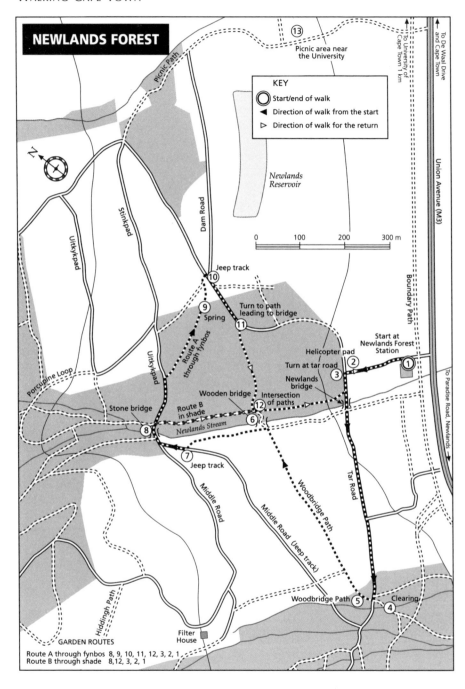

NEWLANDS FOREST

Picnic area near
the University

Picnic Path

To De Waal Drive
and Cape Town

To University of
Cape Town 1 km

To Cape Town 1 km

Union Avenue (M3)

KEY

◯ Start/end of walk
◀ Direction of walk from the start
▷ Direction of walk for the return

Newlands
Reservoir

N

Stinkpad

Dam Road

Uitkykpad

0   100   200   300 m

Jeep track

⑩

⑨
Spring

Turn to path
leading to bridge

⑪

Route A
through fynbos

Porcupine Loop

Uitkykpad

Start at
Newlands Forest
Station

Boundary Path

Helicopter pad

Turn at tar road   ②   ①

③

Newlands
bridge

Wooden bridge   Intersection
of paths

Stone bridge   Route B
in shade   ⑫

⑥

⑧   Newlands Stream

⑦
Jeep track

Middle Road

Woodbridge Path

Middle Road (Jeep track)

Tar Road

To Paradise Road, Newlands

Hiddingh Path

Filter
House

Woodbridge Path ⑤   Clearing
④

GARDEN ROUTES
Route A through fynbos 8, 9, 10, 11, 12, 3, 2, 1
Route B through shade 8, 12, 3, 2, 1

⑬

82

Newlands Forest Walk

From the start at the Forest Station, **(1)** the road slopes upwards for about 150 m while passing the Municipal Parks and Forests buildings and an area **(2)** where helicopters for fighting mountain fires are based. These helicopters scoop water from the sea and dams and pour it directly onto the flames. In recent years many potentially devastating mountain fires have been controlled in this way.

At the tarred road **(3)** turn left and continue for about 300 m when you will come to a clearing **(4)** where open-air functions are occasionally held. On the way you will cross a small bridge, and then pass a curious 'house' on your left that appears to be half-buried. It is actually a small reservoir with a rotting roof. At the clearing there is a freshwater tap and ablution block, half-hidden by trees on the left. Several curious old structures are also in the vicinity, which relate to bygone forestry activities. If you look carefully you can find an old horse drinking trough and earth-filled dam with curved buttress walls.

From here take Woodbridge Path to the right **(5)** which brings you into a cluster pine forest (*Pinus pinaster*) planted in 1979. You will see that the shape of the cluster pines, which originate from France, are substantially different from those in the vicinity of the clearing at **(4)**, which are Monterey pines planted in 1957. Monterey pines originate from California and are the type now generally grown for timber in South Africa, because of their long straight trunks and few, regularly spaced branches. Huguenot settlers are thought to have brought cluster and stone pines (*Pinus pinea*) to the Cape in about 1690. Stone pines, which have a distinctive umbrella-shaped form, were often planted to provide shade at farmhouses. You can see them growing on the slopes near Rhodes Memorial (*see* pg 79).

It is easy to differentiate between the three common pines from their cones. The stone pines have large rounded cones with edible pine 'nuts', the cluster pines have smaller, more rounded cones with small inedible nuts on a flat papery surface, and the Monterey pines have tapered cones.

As you walk through this section of pine forest you will notice that there is very little ground vegetation here other than ferns. This is because only ferns can tolerate the conditions created by the shade and the acidic pine needles.

The path eventually comes to a narrow wooden bridge **(6)** that crosses the deep ravine of the Newlands Stream. Although you may wish to have a look at this bridge and the spectacular way that the stream has cut into the bed, do not cross the river at this stage. Rather continue up the southern river bank towards the jeep track at **(7)**, which will take you through parts of the indigenous forest. Be careful not to allow children too close to the steep river bank.

Between the wooden bridge and the jeep track are dozens of large wild almond trees (*Brabejum stellatifolium*) growing near the stream. This is the same species that Jan van Riebeeck used to make his barrier hedge (*see also* pp 87, 95 and 97) that stretched from Kirstenbosch to the Liesbeek River. Wild almond trees are easily recognised by their long yellow-green leaves growing in whorls.

At the jeep track turn to the right and follow the path for about 75 m down to the stone bridge at **(8)**. Here you will find a large shady wild peach tree (*Kiggelaria africana*) casting its shadow over a delightful picnic spot near the stream, where there is a bench offering a welcome rest. Wild peach-tree wood was once used for the construction of wagon wheel spokes. If you look carefully at the leaves you are likely to see some hairy caterpillars which find these leaves delicious. They turn into beautiful orange butterflies.

Just below the bridge is a delightful paddling pool where children may enjoy swimming in the summer.

On the mountain side of the bridge is an area of mature indigenous forest. You can see how dense the bush is here and how the branches of many of the trees are interlocked. Without even considering the presence of wild animals such as lions, one can imagine how difficult it was for the early settlers to move through this type of undergrowth.

At the bridge and at several other places in the forest you will see notices warning against 'bark stripping' of the trees. This practice, which unfortunately kills the trees, is carried out by those making traditional medicines, and it has become one of the biggest threats to the survival of South Africa's indigenous forests.

If you examine the map you will see that, close to the bridge at **(8)**, a network of paths offer several other routes back to the start.

ROUTE 'A' BACK TO START

The path marked 'A' on the map is a particularly interesting route as it crosses an area where the pine forest has been cleared and the indigenous forest, bush and fynbos (*see* pg 15) are beginning to return. Despite nearly 100 years of pine cover, enough fynbos seed has survived in the ground and been broadcast from other areas to enable the ground to be covered in just a few years. The first plants to recover (for example, the keurbooms) are termed 'pioneer' species and their appearance is somewhat different from those of the mature indigenous forest seen further up the mountain near the stone bridge.

To follow route A, walk for about 90 paces along the track from the wild peach tree at **(8)** towards the north until you come to a bench. About 100 paces further on, take the path to the right and continue down the hill.

On the way you should be able to recognise the following trees which are common here: keurboom (*Virgilia oroboides*), with lilac pea-shaped flowers and compound leaves which are composed of pairs of small leaves; assegaai tree (*Curtisia dentata*), with shiny green leaves shaped like assegaai blades and which are coarsely serrated; and rooi els or red alder (*Cunonia capensis*) – the young shoots are distinctively reddish and it has compound, finely toothed leaves and unusual spoon-shaped stipules (small appendages at the base of the leaf stalk).

At a clearing in the fynbos, you will have a good view of the Claremont business area in the distance. The large green-roofed building is Cavendish Square, one of the largest shopping malls in this part of the Peninsula. On its left you can see the high mast lights at the famous Newlands Cricket Ground and, further to the left, the green tanks of Ohlsson's Breweries (see also pg 99).

Further along the clearing you will come to a spring in the middle of the path where the water bubbles out of the ground (9). This water joins the Newlands Stream that flows to the south of the forest station and eventually forms part of the Liesbeek River. Springs are found all along the lower slopes of the mountain. The Albion Spring, which is below the Main Road near Groote Schuur (the President's residence) was once used by the Schweppes Company for making mineral water and cool drinks and is now pumped into the municipal water supply. The Newlands Spring, which is close to Newlands Avenue below the forest station, is still piped to Ohlsson's Breweries. The breweries also use very pure water from deep boreholes that is filtered by the sandstone and granite rocks in this area.

When you reach the jeep track at (10) continue down the hill for about 100 m until you reach the path on your right at (11) that takes you back towards the wooden bridge (6). Just before you reach this bridge turn to the left and walk down next to the stream on the path between (12) and (3).

You will pass a wide variety of beautiful trees and shrubs including striking silvertrees (*Leucadendron argenteum*) and other proteas, that are indigenous to this part of Table Mountain. On very hot days the silvertrees look particularly 'silvery' when the fine hairs on their leaves lie flat to restrict the loss of moisture.

ALTERNATIVE ROUTE 'B' BACK TO START IN SHADE

If it is mid-summer and very hot you may wish to return to the start from the stone bridge (8) in the shade of the trees on the northern side of the stream. This brings you directly back to the road above the forest station, a short distance from the start.

Newlands Forest is one of the most popular walking areas in the Peninsula and offers the chance to explore many other walking routes besides the ones described here. Parts of the forest are isolated and women should not walk here on their own.

Kirstenbosch National Botanica Garden

Our Unique Botanical

Heritage

The origin of the name, Kirstenbosch, is not certain but it probably relates to Johann Kirsten who was a Dutch East India Company's stores manage in Cape Town and the official in charge of the southern part of th Cape Peninsula. The suffix '-bosch' means 'forest' or 'bush'.

At the time of the Dutch settlement at the Cape in 1652, the area occupied by Kirstenbosch National Botanical Garden was part of the dense forest which had great importance to the settlers for supplying timber for building construction, fencing and ship repair (see pg 81). Within a few years much of this forest had been felled and agricultural lands had been extended from present-day Mowbray to the crest of Wynberg Hill, east of Kirstenbosch. Jan van Riebeeck established his farm, Bosheuvel, on the north-facing slopes below Kirstenbosch, which later became known as Bishopscourt.

By 1660, plundering by the local Khoi had become such a problem for the Dutch settlers that a line of fortifications was planned from the mouth of the Salt River in Table Bay, along the line of the Liesbeek River to the slopes above Kirstenbosch. Where there were gaps in the natural barrier of the river Van Riebeeck's Journal explains: *'It is proposed to plough up the land in a strip one rood* [3.7 m] *wide and sow and plant it with bitter almond trees and all sorts of fast-growing brambles and thorn bushes. This belt will be then so densely overgrown that it will be impossible for cattle and sheep to be driven through. Within the compass of this hedge, the whole settlement and all the grain farms, forests etc will be beautifully protected.'*

Although the fortifications and hedge were established, they failed in their purpose and the plundering continued. Parts of the hedge can be seen on this walk.

In 1811, ownership of two areas of Kirstenbosch was granted to British government officials Henry Alexander and Colonel Christopher Bird. After Alexander died in 1818 and Bird returned to England, the land reverted to the government. It then became the property of D G Eksteen, who built a large homestead and slave quarters on the land in 1823. His son-in-law, Hendrik Cloete, became the owner in 1853.

In 1895 Cecil Rhodes (see pg 75) bought the Kirstenbosch property as part of his plan for preserving the eastern slopes of Table Mountain as a national park. Rhodes envisaged a tree-lined road lined extending from his Groote Schuur estate in Rondebosch to Hout Bay. The section of Rhodes' avenue through Kirstenbosch was planted with Moreton Bay figs, camphor trees, Spanish chestnuts and oaks. On Rhodes' death in 1902, Kirstenbosch fell under the control of the state and the land and buildings became derelict.

Fortunately, in 1913 Kirstenbosch was chosen as the site of the South African National Botanical Garden and from this time, development of the Garden was started with great enthusiasm under the direction of Dr H Pearson. At the start there were many setbacks, including the departure of Kirstenbosch's only gardener to fight in World War I, and the death of Pearson in 1916. Despite severe financial constraints, terracing, landscaping and features such as The Dell were built by prisoners. A road link was constructed from Kirstenbosch to Wynberg in 1916, to Claremont in 1920 and to Constantia Nek in 1923.

Today, Kirstenbosch lies in a splendid natural setting of indigenous flowers and trees growing against a spectacular mountain backdrop. It has become a world-renowned centre for education, research, conservation and cultivation of southern African flora. The 528-hectare Garden extends from Rhodes Drive west of Bishopscourt, to Maclear's Beacon on the Eastern Table, and includes Skeleton Gorge and part of the Table Mountain plateau.

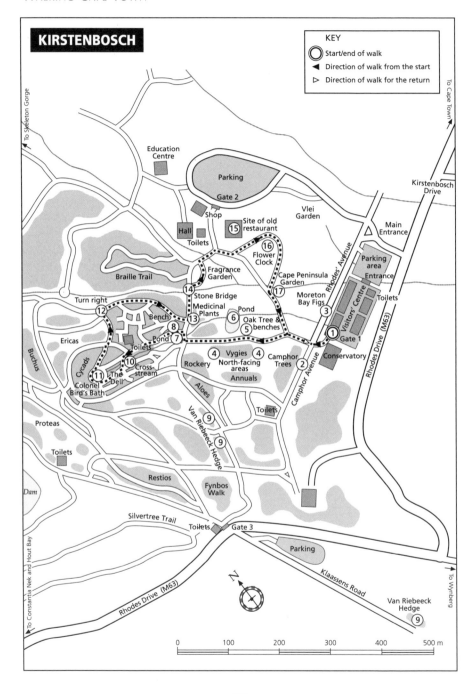

KIRSTENBOSCH

KEY
- ◯ Start/end of walk
- ◀ Direction of walk from the start
- ▷ Direction of walk for the return

Walk through Kirstenbosch

This lovely walk starts at the Visitors' Centre **(1)** and Conservatory, which were completed in 1998. About 15 m from here, the path crosses Cecil Rhodes' avenue of trees. On your left, lines of camphor trees **(2)** form an exquisite vaulted ceiling of branches leading to the south. To the right is an avenue of Moreton Bay figs **(3)** (*Ficus macrophylla*) with their enormous trunks and buttress roots.

About 50 m from Rhodes' avenue the path comes to a fork where, on the left, the large north-facing areas **(4)** planted with West Coast annuals such as Namaqualand daisies are spectacular in spring and summer, and are best viewed on sunny days around midday when the flowers are fully open.

On the right of the path is first a tall clump of wild bananas and then the edge of the path is graced by spectacular crane flowers (*Strelitzia reginae*), named in honour of Queen Charlotte, from the German House of Mecklenburg-Strelitz, who was wife of the British king, George III.

On the other side of the path is a bank of fleshy-leafed sour figs (*Carpobrotus* ssp), once a favoured food of the Khoi, and reputed to have medicinal properties that include treatment for sore throats, allergies, diabetes, thrush and sunburn.

About 100 m from the avenue you will come to a large oak tree and two benches **(5)**. To the left of the path are large beds used for magnificent displays of indigenous annuals. To the right a pond **(6)** is slightly hidden by a dense stand of papyrus (*Cyperus papyrus*), long reeds with tufted fronds at the top, the stems of which are used in South Africa to make traditional hut doors.

About 50 m beyond the oak, on the right, is a puzzle bush or *deurmekaarbos* ('confused bush') (*Ehretia rigida*) with its tangled branches. Its fruit is edible and the powdered roots are used in African medicine to relieve pain by being applied to skin cuts in the abdomen and chest.

At the back of the area, to the left of the path, are thicket plants (e.g. euphorbias) and aloes from the Eastern Cape, most striking when they flower in winter. Closer to the path are vygies (*Mesembryanthemum* ssp), that provide a dazzling display in spring (around October).

Further along on your right is a line of three huge Kosi palms (*Raphia australis*) with leaves up to 10 m long – the largest of any plant in the world. After about 30 years' growth they flower, set fruit and then die. Behind the palms stands a large, broad-leafed wild banana (*Ensete ventricosum*) which is indigenous to the most north-easterly parts of South Africa.

On the left of the path is a stand of assagai strelitzia, and to its immediate right lies a bed of silver-green leafed *Helichrysum patulum*, a medicinal plant traditionally used for ridding bedding of lice. It is popularly known as Hotnotskooigoed ('Hottentot's bedding').

To the right at **(7)** is a small pond. Like all other water features in the Garden, this is fed by springs and streams flowing from Table Mountain. Three water plants flourish here: the beautiful blue Cape water lily (*Nymphaea nouchali*), white waterblommetjie (*Aponogeton distachyos*) which is edible and is traditionally used in stews, and the yellow wateruintjie (*Nymphoides indica*), which is not edible.

Take the path to the right of the pond and on your immediate left stands a magnificent red mahogany tree (*Khaya anthotheca*). About 15 m on, the huge trunk of a wild almond (*Brabejum stellatifolium*) is set back behind a bench **(8)**. This is part of the hedge planted by Van Riebeeck in 1660. (Remains of the hedge **(9)** can also be found at several other places in the Garden leading towards Klaassens Road on Wynberg Hill. Opposite no. 31 Klaassens Road lies a section of the hedge and a National Monument plaque.)

A quinine tree (*Rauvolfia caffra*) stands opposite the bench, but, despite its name, it is ineffective as a treatment against malaria. The latex is used in traditional medicine for infant diarrhoea and other parts of the tree are used to treat skin disorders and abdominal complaints.

About 10 m further along the path, on your left in front of a banana tree, is a bank of a perennial ground cover (*Plectranthus fructicosus*) whose leaves have traditionally been used for ridding rooms of flies.

Although from here the formal path swings to the right, carry straight on across the lawn bearing to the left when you reach the cobbled paths. Cross the stream towards the left at **(10)**. The paths lead into a cool, tranquil area known as The Dell, the oldest part of the Garden and richly planted with tree ferns and other shade-loving plants. Slightly further up you will come to Colonel Bird's

bath **(11)**, an attractive bird-shaped bath constructed of small *klompie* bricks.

On the mountain side of this area you will see numerous strange palm-like plants called cycads. These 'living fossils' were present on earth at a very early stage of plant evolution. It has been found that they evolved to live in an atmospheric carbon dioxide concentration considerably higher than that at present.

From Colonel Bird's bath take the path up the slope to the north (i.e., with your back to the stone railing, go left). Turn to the right when the path reaches a junction. Continue along the bricked path through a section of the Garden specially planted with many of the more than 600 Erica species that form part of the Cape Fynbos (*see* pg 15).

At the end of this path **(12)** turn to the right which takes you in the direction of the old restaurant site **(15)**. On your right is a garden specially planted with geraniums and pelargoniums. If you bruise a leaf you may find it pleasantly scented with a hint of rose or lemon. These sweet-smelling aromatic oils tend to repel insects and are used in perfume manufacture.

On the left, just before a bench, you will pass a wild peach tree (*Kiggelaria africana*) with its distinctive spotted trunk. It is home to the eggs of the rust-red garden acraea butterfly and its blackish spiny caterpillar. The tree can often be distinguished by the caterpillars.

Keeping to the broad path, carry on down the hill, passing another large wild almond tree, recognisable from its star-shaped whorls of leaves.

On the left are specimens of Cape reeds (one of the restios) that are used for thatching. Thatching grass (*Hyparrhenia hirta*), used for traditional hut building, also grows here.

Slightly further down the hill and also on the left is a sweet thorn (*Acacia karroo*), one of the most widespread and useful trees in Africa. The bark is used for tanning, its gum is used in sweet-making and as an adhesive, the wood is used for furniture and fencing, leaves and flowers provide fodder, the roasted pods can be ground to make a coffee, the inner bark

PELARGONIUM AND GERANIUM

The confusion about the difference between 'pelargonium' and 'geranium' has arisen because there have been changes in the botanical classification of our plants from the genus *Geranium* to *Pelargonium*. The cultivated varieties found throughout the world as 'window box geraniums' are now classified in the genus *Pelargonium*, and most derive from the Cape's *Pelargonium cucullatum*. In the Cape there are hundreds of species of pelargonium and just a few geraniums. Geranium flowers are 'radially' symmetrical (like a bicycle wheel) and pelargoniums are 'axially' symmetrical (like an oak leaf). So, to be accurate, you should almost certainly be using the term pelargonium.

provides a usable rope and its considerable amounts of pollen and nectar produce excellent honey. The bark also has medicinal uses for treating cattle.

When the path reaches the broad road, turn to the left at the sundial. This is a fascinating part of the garden where dozens of medicinal plants (13) are

grown. A notice cautions visitors not to try any of the brews! Who would have known that mother-in-law's tongue (*Sansevieria hyacinthoides*) was a cure for intesinal worms, varicose veins, toothache, earache and piles?

Cross the stone-walled bridge (14) and, about 10 m beyond a roofed display area on your right, a small path leads into the Fragrance Garden. Here you can enjoy the scents of scores of aromatic plants with explanatory notes also given in Braille. By bruising a leaf you can discover honey tea, wild garlic, wild mint and many other plants whose fragrances are either intended to attract pollinators or repel insects. Many people find this a particularly rewarding part of their visit to Kirstenbosch.

Continue on the broad path across the stream and then follow the path down the hill to the right of the old restaurant site (15). In the middle of the lawn, beyond the site, is an unusual clock (16) that is sometimes planted with flowers.

Continue down the hill through the Cape Peninsula Garden (17) and back towards the gate near the start. On your left are wild forget-me-nots, perhaps a reminder that Kirstenbosch is the foremost botanical garden on this continent and that it represents areas with the greatest botanical diversity on earth. We are indeed privileged to be able to walk here.

Skeleton Gorge to Table Mountain Plateau

A Forested Ascent up Table Mountain

The origin of the name 'Skeleton Gorge' is obscure, but legend has it that at one time a skeleton of a cow was found near the base of the gorge. It seems to have been known by this name from before the 1860s when mountain climbing became popular at the Cape. Many of Table Mountain's peaks, buttresses and other features were named by climbers.

This walk up Skeleton Gorge to the plateau at the top of Table Mountain is an easy route that runs under a canopy of indigenous trees for most of the way. This was Field-Marshal (General) J C Smuts' favourite route up the mountain. In 1950, the year of his 80th birthday, this most famous South African statesman, philosopher and leader (see pg 20) was honoured when the path from Kirstenbosch Garden up Skeleton Gorge to Maclear's Beacon (the highest point on the mountain, about 1.2 km north-east of Junction Peak) was formally named General Smuts' Track (now known simply as Smuts' Track). As you walk up this path it is easy to visualise how the climb and the beauty of the mountain scene inspired him. To honour Smuts' birthday, a Cape Town Mayoral Committee also raised a fund to endow a fellowship tenable at the University of Cape Town or Kirstenbosch, for the botanical study of South African flora.

In 1923, Smuts wrote with clarity and insight:

'Table Mountain is indeed the greatest monument of South Africa, and incomparably (with the Victoria Falls)the greatest attraction of Southern Africa. What other country can boast such a gatway to its shores? Perhaps Rio de Janeiro is its only rival, and preference is generally given to Table Mountain, rising sheer out of the Southern Ocean, with a pattern of unrivalled beauty of form and setting. To interfere with it is to desecrate what-should be our national temple, our Holy of Holies. We as a nation, valuing our unique heritage, should not allow it to be spoiled and despoiled, and should look upon it as among its most sacred possessions, part not only of the soil, but of the soul of South Africa. For centuries to come, while civilisation lasts on this sub-continent, this national monument should be maintained in all its natura beauty and unique setting; it should be symbolic of our civilisation itself, and it shouldbe our proud tradition to defend it to the limit against all forces of man or nature to disfigure it.'

Walk up Skeleton Gorge to Table Mountain plateau

If you look up towards the mountain from the start **(1)** in Kirstenbosch National Botanical Garden, Nursery Ravine lies to the left of the famous Castle Rock **(5)** landmark above you. Skeleton Gorge is the wooded ravine to the right and the enormous sandstone cliffs of Window Buttress and Window Gorge are visible still further on.

To reach Smuts' Track **(4)** from the start at Kirstenbosch's Gate 2, take the first path to the right (i.e. towards the moun-tain). Walk up the hill for about 100 m until you see a path to the left crossing Skeleton Stream. Follow this to the south side of the stream and then turn right up the hill. The path is signposted 'Smuts' Track' and 'Skeleton Gorge'. Walk up the

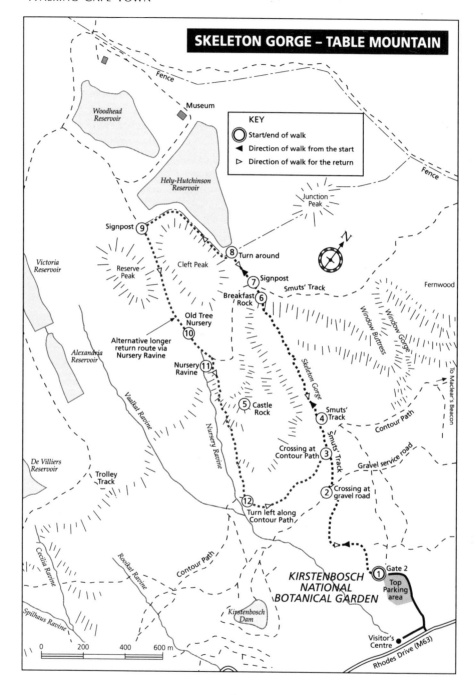

SKELETON GORGE – TABLE MOUNTAIN

KEY

◯ Start/end of walk

◀ Direction of walk from the start

▷ Direction of walk for the return

Woodhead Reservoir

Museum

Hely-Hutchinson Reservoir

Junction Peak

Signpost ⑨

Victoria Reservoir

Reserve Peak

Cleft Peak

⑧ Turn around

⑦ Signpost

Smuts' Track

Fernwood

Breakfast ⑥ Rock

Old Tree Nursery ⑩

Alternative longer return route via Nursery Ravine

Alexandria Reservoir

Nursery ⑪ Ravine

Window Buttress

Window Gorge

Skeleton Gorge

To Maclear's Beacon

⑤ Castle Rock

Smuts' Track ④

Vaalkat Ravine

Nursery Ravine

Crossing at Contour Path ③

Smuts' Track

Contour Path

Gravel service road

De Villiers Reservoir

Trolley Track

② Crossing at gravel road

⑫ Turn left along Contour Path

Cecilia Ravine

Rooikat Ravine

Contour Path

Spilhaus Ravine

Kirstenbosch Dam

KIRSTENBOSCH NATIONAL BOTANICAL GARDEN

① Gate 2
Top Parking area

Visitor's Centre

Rhodes Drive (M63)

0   200   400   600 m

94

side of the stream and then, as the gravel road swings to the left, keep on the walking path that turns to the right into a shady grove of wild almond trees (*Brabejum stellatifolium*). These have a distinctive star-like arrangement of leaves with small gall imperfections on the leaves caused by mites. The nuts are poisonous to humans but are eaten by porcupines. Higher up this path, the much older almond trees that have formed a dense tangle of branches are closer to the effect Jan van Riebeeck hoped to create when he planted his hedge of wild almond trees to keep the Khoi out of the Colony in 1660 (*see* pp 87 and 97).

Looking back over Kirstenbosch towards Wynberg Hill on your right, the north-facing slopes of present-day Bishopscourt are where Van Riebeeck established his farm Bosheuvel in 1658 (*see* pg 87). This whole area and that occupied by Kirstenbosch was once a dense forest. Although the remaining natural forest in Skeleton Gorge is just a minute remnant of the original one, in places on this walk you can get an idea of what it must have looked like before the arrival of the Dutch.

The path crosses the gravel service road (2) and enters the Skeleton Gorge forest which is distinctly different from the scrub you walked through earlier. This is the Afromontane forest-type, typical of mountainous regions of Africa which lie below 1 000 m. There is a high canopy of trees, very little undergrowth and deep roots help resist soil erosion.

Smuts' Track crosses the contour path (3) that winds round the mountain just above the 300-m level and then rises quickly above the boulder-lined stream bed. Here the misty sunlight filters through the tangled branches and there are enchanting views of mossy green cascades. Here and there you will see the tangle of twining monkey ropes hanging between the trees. It is very much as the area appeared when the first settlers arrived.

Eventually, after climbing hundreds of log-lined steps and two ladders (at the 500-m level) and having walked along zig-zagging forest paths, Breakfast Rock (6) is reached about 700 m above sea level. This is a good place to rest and enjoy the spectacular view of the southern suburbs and the Hottentots-Holland Mountains in the distance.

To reach Hely-Hutchinson Reservoir (8) on the Table Mountain plateau, which is the suggested turning point for this walk, continue straight on past the signpost (7). In spring this plateau offers wonderful views of fynbos flowers.

To return, you can either walk back down Skeleton Gorge or, if you want to extend your walk by about an hour, walk down Nursery Ravine. This is a better descent route when it is wet.

ROUTE DOWN NURSERY RAVINE

From (8) carry on along the fence line round the Hely-Hutchinson Reservoir to the signpost at (9) past the old tree nursery area (10) (which gave the ravine its name), and then walk down the path into Nursery Ravine (11). This easy path eventually brings you to the 300-m contour path at (12). Turn to the left along this path and walk for about 400 m until it joins Smuts' Track (3) in Skeleton Gorge. Now retrace your steps to the start.

Liesbeek River Walk

Along the River to the Mill

The walk along the banks of the Liesbeek River takes you through a previously forested area that lies below the hill where Commander Jan van Riebeeck established his farm Bosheuvel in 1658. The river derives its name from two Dutch words, Lies ('duckweed') and beek ('a beck or small river').

The rivers flow into Table Bay near present-day Paarden Eiland. The Diep River reaches the sea at Milnerton, the Black River flows from the south-east. And the tree-lined Liesbeek River runs from the slopes of Table Mountain in the southwest. After winding through the leafy suburbs of Newlands and Rondebosch, it joins the Black River at Observatory, where it is known as the Salt River. Of these three water courses, the Liesbeek is by far the most scenically attractive and unspoiled.

In various early documents it is referred to as the Varsche ('fresh'), Amstel and Soete ('sweet'), but by 1657, when the first farms were granted to 'free burghers', it was generally known by its present name, the Liesbeek.

Today, of the many streams that run from the eastern slopes of Table Mountain to form the Liesbeek, the Newlands Stream and Protea Stream are most easily identified. They flow through Kirstenbosch and converge about 500 m below Rhodes Avenue, near the start of the walk. Just above this confluence there is a wooded area called the Boschenheuvel Arboretum, where the Parks and Gardens Department of the Municipality have planted a large number of indigenous trees and shrubs.

Liesbeek River Walk

From the start at the lawns below Kirstenbosch (1), carefully cross the busy Rhodes Avenue (M63) to the Church of the Good Shepherd (2). The first church building here was constructed in 1864 for villagers who had settled to the north of Kirstenbosch Drive. It was designed by Sophie Gray, the architect wife of Bishop Robert Gray, first Anglican Bishop of Cape Town, who acquired Bosheuvel and renamed it Bishopscourt. The church was rebuilt in 1880 at its present site and a nave was added in 1904. At one time, services alternated between English and Dutch. The church has close links to Kirstenbosch and every October, the Garden's staff holds a service here.

As you pass the church and turn to the right down Kirstenbosch Drive, you will see a wild almond tree (*Brabejum*

stellatifolium) on the corner. This is the species used for Van Riebeeck's hedge (*see* pp 87 and 95) and is distinctive in having leaves with slightly toothed edges, growing in whorls. On the other side of the road are three stone cottages (3) that were built in 1919 for women students and gardeners working at Kirstenbosch.

About 100 m down Kirstenbosch Drive take a turn sharply to the right along Winchester Drive, which will bring you to the Boschenheuvel Arboretum (4). At one time there were playing fields here for the nearby school and Protea village, the small community that lived north of Kirstenbosch Drive.

A footpath takes you along the edge of the Arboretum to the Newlands Stream, which flows from Window Gorge, the mountain ravine above you.

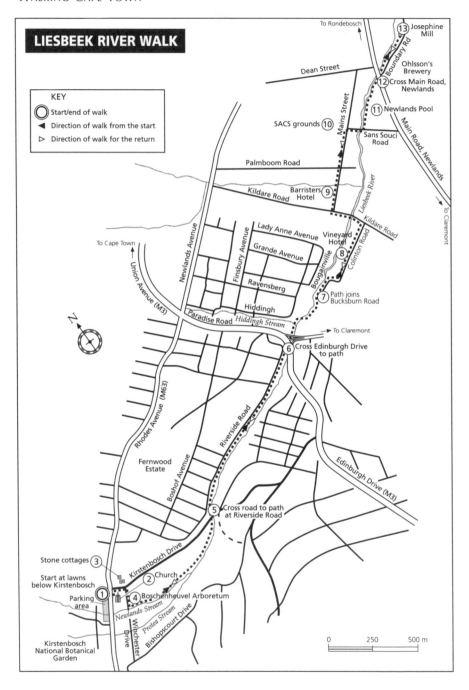

LIESBEEK RIVER WALK

KEY

○ Start/end of walk
◄ Direction of walk from the start
▷ Direction of walk for the return

To Rondebosch

⑬ Josephine Mill

Ohlsson's Brewery

⑫ Cross Main Road, Newlands

Dean Street

Mains Street

⑪ Newlands Pool

SACS grounds ⑩

Sans Souci Road

Main Road, Newlands

To Claremont

Palmboom Road

Liesbeek River

Barristers Hotel ⑨

Kildare Road

Kildare Road

Collinton Road

Lady Anne Avenue

Vineyard Hotel

Newlands Avenue

Finsbury Avenue

Grande Avenue

Bougainville

⑧

To Cape Town

Ravensberg

⑦ Path joins Bucksburn Road

Union Avenue (M3)

Paradise Road

Hiddingh

Hiddingh Stream

Ravensberg

To Claremont

⑥ Cross Edinburgh Drive to path

N

Rhodes Avenue (M63)

Riverside Road

Fernwood Estate

Boshof Avenue

Edinburgh Drive (M3)

⑤ Cross road to path at Riverside Road

Stone cottages ③

Kirstenbosch Drive

Start at lawns below Kirstenbosch

② Church

Parking area ①

④ Boschenheuvel Arboretum

Newlands Stream

Protea Stream

Winchester Drive

Bishopscourt Drive

Kirstenbosch National Botanical Garden

0   250   500 m

For the next 500 m the path winds through fynbos and indigenous trees that are part of the rich heritage of the Cape flora. There are banks of liquorice bush, hotnotskooigoed (see pg 89), blombos, wild rosemary and wild garlic. The trees include real yellowwood, rhus and stinkwood. Much of the river vegetation is alien, but there are some patches of the indigenous palmiet that once stabilised the banks of many Cape rivers.

At the bottom of the Arboretum, cross the road at the bridge (5) and rejoin the path at Riverside Road which runs along the edge of the Liesbeek River below Fernwood Estate. Many beautiful trees, some with identification plates, have been planted along this part of the route, including assegai, liquid amber, waterberry, plane, poplar and Cape beech.

The path eventually comes to the busy intersection (6) between Paradise Road and Edinburgh Drive (M3). Just before the bridge you will see a small brick structure that houses a gauging station used to measure river flows. Incongruously, during floods in 1994, the flow not only exceeded the capacity of the bridge culvert and gauging station, but also flooded the road.

Paradise Road is named after a section of the original forest higher up on the mountain called 'Paradijs'. Paradoxically, the woodcutters named another forest area near Constantia Nek 'Die Hel' (see pg 114).

Cross Edinburgh Drive at the pedestrian crossing and rejoin the path on the mountain side of the river, below the bridge. The Hiddingh Stream joins the Liesbeek River here.

Following the path, you cross the river and walk for about 300 m along the eastern bank. Of the many beautiful trees seen here, some of the most striking are white milkwood and bel ombre, with huge trunks exceeding 4 m in diameter. A short way further on, the path turns to the right to Bucksburn Road (7), where you unfortunately have to leave the river bank because there is no public access here. (For the next 1.5 km the route takes you along suburban roads and paths. Although there is much of historical interest ahead, if you prefer only a leafy walk, this is the place to turn around.)

At the end of Bucksburn Road turn to the left down Colinton Road, past the Vineyard Hotel (8), a place of considerable scenic beauty and historic interest. Lady Anne Barnard, who visited the Cape from 1798 to 1802, lived here and described it in glowing terms. Lady Anne was a writer, artist and poet of distinction. Her famous letters describing her life at the Cape, which were published in 1902, were a best-seller. She and her husband, Andrew Barnard, who was Colonial Secretary at the Cape, also had a country retreat on the mountain at Paradijs.

At the end of Colinton Road turn to the left into Kildare Road. As you cross the bridge you can see the remains of an old bridge handrail in an oak tree. This area has many historical links to Ohlsson's Brewery, sited near here from 1882 until 1900. It then moved to its present site opposite the Josephine Mill. Anders Ohlsson, who came to South Africa from Norway in 1860, imported Irish labourers to work in the brewery and built many of the small houses that crowd the narrow streets in the neighbourhood of Kildare Road. At one time this area was known as 'Irish Town'. As you turn to the right into Main Street, Newlands, you will see Barristers Hotel (9) on your left with its distinctive red lion emblem under the gable. The red lion signifies that Barristers was part of a chain of hotels that Ohlsson built to promote his beer.

As you walk along Main Street you will have views of the South African College School (SACS) grounds (10) on your left. This school is the oldest institution of its kind in South Africa. Founded in 1829 as 'Het Zuid Afrikaansch Atheneum', to provide both school and tertiary (university) education for colonists, it awarded degrees even after the establishment of the University of Cape of Good Hope in 1873. SACS's tertiary education function was passed to the University of Cape Town when it was established in 1918. The school occupied premises above the Company's Gardens in Cape Town until 1955 when it moved to its present location.

Before you turn right into Sans Souci Road, you should be able to see the old Westervoort Mill millstone standing on its edge near a tennis practice wall in the SACS grounds. The mill was operated in about 1801 by the well-known Cloete family (see pg 107).

As you cross the Liesbeek River on Sans Souci Road, on your left you can see the pipe from the Newlands Spring that takes water to Ohlsson's Brewery. It runs under a small corrugated iron 'roof'.

Immediately after crossing the river, take the path to the left that runs next to the river, behind the Newlands municipal

swimming pool (11). If you look around you will notice that there is plenty of broken glass next to the path, and, if you examine a piece carefully, you will see that the glass is very thick and quite unlike modern glass. These pieces are from the glassworks that supplied four breweries in this vicinity in the 19th century.

The path brings you to Main Road, Newlands (12), where you should cross over to the far side at the traffic lights to a white karee tree growing in the pavement. Largely hidden by the foliage is a drinking water tap, which is fed from spring water. If you follow the path under the road bridge on the far side of Boundary Road, you will see the remains of an old stone bridge built around 1800 and designed by the famous military engineer and architect Louis-Michel Thibault (see pg 56). It replaced a wooden structure dating back to the time of Jan van Riebeeck. (Do not explore the area under the bridge alone as several people have been mugged here.) This river crossing was originally called the Westervoort, from which the local name, Westerford, derives.

Continue along Boundary Road until you come to the Josephine Mill (13), at the end of the walk. This is a working mill where flour is still ground between huge millstones. In 1840 a Swedish immigrant, Jacob Letterstedt, built this mill and named it after Princess Josephine of Sweden. Engineering staff and students at the University of Cape Town have carefully restored the waterwheel. The Mill runs a shop and restaurant, and offers a tour with a demonstration of milling.

Return to the start the same way or by car if you have made this arrangement.

Arderne Gardens

Watsonias and Weddings

The Arderne Gardens were once part of the private home of Ralph Arderne, a timber merchant of high repute. He and his son, Henry, persuaded ship captains to bring them exotic plants and trees from all over the world and they lovingly created a vast 5.5-hectare private garden attached to their home, The Hill.

The Arderne Gardens were established over a 69-year period (1845 to 1914) at a time when Cape Town was a crossroads for world shipping plying between Europe, Australia, New Zealand and the East. Among their many botanical accomplishments, Ralph and Henry Arderne collected important specimens from the Cape for the Royal Botanic Gardens at Kew in England, and helped to source exotic plants for the Company's Gardens at the head of Adderley Street (see pg 23). Henry Arderne was also responsible for the cultivation of the white watsonias – appropriately named *Watsonia ardernei* – that now grow along our freeways.

At the turn of the century, the garden was one of the spectacular features of Cape Town and it was visited by many distinguished guests. The famous British evangelist Gypsy Smith joked to Henry Arderne: *'You shall not care to go to Heaven as much as I shall, for you will have to leave this lovely garden'*. Rudyard Kipling, the famous poet and author of many books, including *The Jungle Book*, wrote: *'This place ought to be an imperial possession for the botanists of the Empire – I have broken the 10th Commandment* * *a dozen times and the pieces are scattered all over the lawn – it is a wonderful garden.'* (* 'Thou shalt not covet')

From its start in 1845, one of the garden's most spectacular features was the Norfolk Island pine which arrived by sailing ship and grew to a great height. The Norfolk pines that can today be seen towering above the trees and flats that make up modern-day Claremont are descendants of this tree.

The land was sold in 1914 when Ralph Arderne died and in 1926, when it was being sub-divided for housing, about 3 hectares of the remaining garden was acquired by the City Council who continue to develop it.

A walk through the gardens is a delightful escape from the bustle of the city. Along the winding paths are picturesque scenes of flowers, shrubs and trees from many countries. Although some trees have name plates, more botanical detail is given here for the benefit of enthusiasts. The first route described takes you through most of the southern section of the gardens. The second shorter walk, on the northern side, is focused around the series of ponds that are fed from a perennial spring.

Although beautiful at all times of the year, the gardens are best in spring (September) when they are ablaze with colour: the horizon is fringed by pink and white horse chestnut buds and the paths are lined with banks of brilliant red, pink and white azaleas. The camellias are best in late winter (July–August).

If you visit the gardens over a weekend or on a public holiday you will be doubly rewarded because they are regularly used for wedding photographs by bridal parties of many cultures. A succession of wedding cars and their entourages double-park on the Main Road while bride and bridegroom and immaculately dressed pageboys and flower girls of every size assemble in front of the wrought-iron entrance gates. You will see the splendour of matching silks and satins for the bridal parties and remarkable attention to detail. As they form up on the lawns for their photographs, the picture set against the botanical artistry is enchanting.

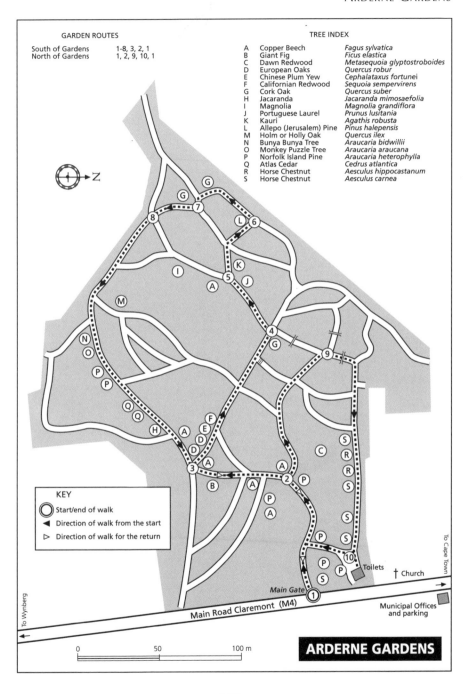

GARDEN ROUTES

South of Gardens   1-8, 3, 2, 1
North of Gardens   1, 2, 9, 10, 1

TREE INDEX

A	Copper Beech	*Fagus sylvatica*
B	Giant Fig	*Ficus elastica*
C	Dawn Redwood	*Metasequoia glyptostroboides*
D	European Oaks	*Quercus robur*
E	Chinese Plum Yew	*Cephalataxus fortunei*
F	Californian Redwood	*Sequoia sempervirens*
G	Cork Oak	*Quercus suber*
H	Jacaranda	*Jacaranda mimosaefolia*
I	Magnolia	*Magnolia grandiflora*
J	Portuguese Laurel	*Prunus lusitania*
K	Kauri	*Agathis robusta*
L	Allepo (Jerusalem) Pine	*Pinus halepensis*
M	Holm or Holly Oak	*Quercus ilex*
N	Bunya Bunya Tree	*Araucaria bidwillii*
O	Monkey Puzzle Tree	*Araucaria araucana*
P	Norfolk Island Pine	*Araucaria heterophylla*
Q	Atlas Cedar	*Cedrus atlantica*
R	Horse Chestnut	*Aesculus hippocastanum*
S	Horse Chestnut	*Aesculus carnea*

KEY

○ Start/end of walk
◄ Direction of walk from the start
▷ Direction of walk for the return

Toilets   † Church

To Cape Town

To Wynberg

Main Road Claremont (M4)

Main Gate

Municipal Offices and parking

0   50   100 m

ARDERNE GARDENS

103

Arderne Gardens
Walk – southern section

Enter the main gate of the Gardens from Claremont Main Road (1), past banks of hydrangeas and spectacular displays of annuals and border plants. The path winds towards a patchwork of rolling lawns, banks of azaleas and camellias, willows, duck ponds and wooden bridges. Towering above are majestic Norfolk pines, an enormous fig tree, copper beeches, an Allepo pine, kauri, palms and clumps of bamboo.

About 70 m from the start (2), you will see a most unusual tree about 25 m to your right. This is the deciduous dawn redwood (C on the map), which grows in a swamp in front of a large dark green tree. This remarkable tree was found in China by Harvard University botanists in about 1947, at a time when it was thought to be extinct and was only known in fossils. It is related to the evergreen Californian sequoia redwoods, and was grown from seed that was brought back from China.

As you continue on the main path, ahead and to the right is a large copper beech from Europe (A) with its distinctive bronze-tinted leaves. About 40 m further on your left, you will come to a giant fig (B) from tropical Asia, with its huge canopy towering above. This is surely one of the biggest trees you will ever see and a wonderful place for children to climb about on its buttress roots which run at surface to form huge ridges and valleys before plunging underground at the edge of the pathway

about 15 m away. The tree is about 140 years old and still growing.

At the next corner (3), about 15 m on, turn to the right and after passing two European oaks (D), a Chinese plum yew (E) and a Californian redwood (F), you come to a bench (4) opposite a wide lawn where there is a very large old cork oak (G) on the right. Looking at the rough surface of this huge tree you may wonder how fine corks can be made from such a gnarled bark. The secret is that, when this tree is cultivated in Spain and other parts of southern Europe, its first layer of rough bark is removed by expert cork strippers. The new growth then produces a fine straight-grained layer which is used for bottle corks.

If you face the lawn from the bench you will see to the right a magnificent bronze-tinted copper beech (A) and a magnolia (I) with large glossy green leaves. From early November to December the magnolia (which comes from Carolina and Texas) has huge white flowers that are exquisitely fragrant.

Turning towards (5), to the right of the path about 40 m on, is Portuguese laurel (J) and high above you, a gigantic round-headed kauri (K) from Queensland, Australia. This is a conifer with very large cones and is related to the Norfolk Island pine. Its wood is used for commercial timber. The path then comes to a 'T' at (6) where on the left there is a gigantic Allepo pine (Jerusalem pine) (L). This tree occurs throughout the

Middle East where its virtues include growing in alkaline limey soils, which are aggressive to most trees, and being incredibly drought resistant.

At this point take the path to the left past two cork oaks, marked **(G)** on the map, and continue straight across the intersection of paths to **(7)** and **(8)**. Further on, where the path forks, keep straight on until, on your left, you come to a green-black holm or holly oak **(M)**. This is an unusual evergreen oak that grows well in windy areas of southern Europe where the climate is similar to that of the Peninsula. Strangely, it is seldom found here. In ancient times it was an important commercial tree – the Romans used it for building their great fighting ships.

Continuing straight along the main path you will see several types of Araucaria tree on the right. The first is a bunya bunya tree **(N)** from Australia, then a monkey puzzle tree **(O)** from South America, followed by two Norfolk Island pines **(P)**. When Captain Cook first discovered these trees on Norfolk Island it was thought that they would be the answer to their problem of finding dead-straight timber for the British navy's ship masts. Unfortunately this was found to be impractical because of the enormous knots formed at branches to the trunk.

Before you reach the corner you will pass two cedars **(Q)** which originate from the Atlas Mountains in North Africa and a jacaranda **(H)** which comes from Argentina (not Pretoria!).

To complete the circuit, carry straight on for about 30 m to **(3)** and turn half-left to rejoin the path at the enormous fig tree **(B)** seen earlier. Carry on along this path for about 120 m and you will have retraced your steps to the start.

You may now wish to explore some of the other paths shown on the map in the northern section of the gardens.

Northern section

The paths near the dawn redwood **(C)** take you to the stream, duck ponds and bridges which children will find delightful. To reach this area, follow the main driveway from the start **(1)** for about 70 m to **(2)** and then take the small path to the right. The copper beech **(A)** will be immediately on your left. Ignore the first turn to the left about 35 m from the beginning of the narrow path, and keep straight on at the next path intersection. You will come to a very large tree marked 'Rimu, Red Pine, New Zealand', surrounded by seats made from sections of upturned tree trunks at **(9)**. To your left, straight ahead and to the right are paths with bridges.

Take the right-hand path where there is a clump of bamboo on your left and, after crossing the bridge, walk straight for about 100 m. You will now be walking down an avenue of two types of beautiful horse chestnuts, marked **(R)** and **(S)**. Taking the next right turn at **(10)** will bring you back to within 25 m of the start at the Main Road.

Useful Information

DISTANCE: 4 km

TIME: About 1.75 hours

PARKING: From Hout Bay Road (M41) at Constantia, take turn-off marked 'Groot Constantia' near High Constantia shopping centre; park at wine-tasting shop next to Bertrams building

START: On lawn outside Bertrams building

ROUTE: Along oak avenue to homestead, round back to cellars, then up hill to pool and vineyards. Up hill to reservoir and then down track to vineyards behind the homestead. Return along oak avenue to start

TERRAIN: Mostly gravel paths

REFRESHMENTS: Restaurants

AMENITIES: Toilets at shop and restaurants

WEATHER: Fairly protected from wind

SUITABLE FOR: Walkers of all ages

Groot Constantia

Valley of the Vines

The farm Constantia was owned by Simon van der Stel, the Commander at the Cape, who established it in 1685. He named it after a little girl – the daughter of the Dutch East India Company Commissioner, Rijckloff van Goens, who authorised the grant of the land.

If you were to have looked down on the Constantia valley 300 years ago, you would have seen a simple country house with small windows set in a leafy scene of thousands of oak trees, vineyards and vegetable fields. Carriages travelling from here to the Castle at Cape Town would have run for about half a kilometre through an oak avenue to an entrance gate on the north-eastern boundary of the farm Constantia.

Simon van der Stel, who is though to have been born at sea, was of mixed Dutch and Indian parentage, and grew up in Mauritius, a small Indian Ocean island to the east of Madagascar. In October 1679 he came to the Cape from the Netherlands with his children and his wife's youngest sister (his estranged wife remained behind).

Van der Stel was remarkably energetic and applied himself to many important tasks. He arranged for farmers to immigrate to the Cape from Europe and assisted them with advice, seeds and rootstock. He was personally involved in exploration for minerals and in 1685, travelling along game paths used by wild animals, he explored parts of Namaqualand in the Northern Cape. In 1687, travelling by horseback, he camped for three weeks along the shore of False Bay while his survey ship took soundings and charted the bay. This venture led to the establishment of the all-weather anchorage for the Company's ships at Simon's Town, which was named after him (see pg 180).

With the objective of making the colony independent of rice imports, Van der Stel established the settlement of Stellenbosch, and in 1681 the wheat crop was so successful that there was enough to export to Sri Lanka. Prior to his arrival at the Cape, Van der Stel had owned two farms in the Netherlands where he had successfully produced wine and brandy. At Constantia he applied this knowledge to the cultivation of vines and even sent wine to the Council of Seventeen in Amsterdam and to Batavia, in the East. The Company officials reported that they preferred the wines of Europe.

At his farm he planted over 8 000 trees, most of which were oaks. In 1699, when Van der Stel retired, he had an immense landholding. His property included the farms Constantia (767 ha) and Witteboomen (58 ha), which he expropriated; Bosheuvel (present-day Bishopscourt, previously owned by Jan van Riebeeck); and Zeekoeyen Valley (which extended from Wynberg to the sea south of Zeekoevlei). When Van der Stel died his farm was divided into Groot Constantia, Bergvliet and Klein Constantia. During the 18th and early 19th centuries this land was further subdivided into six farms, each with a fine homestead (Groot Constantia, Klein Constantia, Nova Constantia, Buitenverwachting, High Constantia and Bergvliet).

After it had changed ownership several times, in 1778 Groot Constantia (193 ha) became the property of Hendrik Cloete. Under Cloete, Constantia wines became world-renowned and he applied himself to developing the estate. He employed the architect Louis Thibault and the sculptor Anton Anreith to build a new wine cellar for him. Hendrik Cloete then commissioned them to enlarge and restyle Van der Stel's simple farm building into the famous, gabled country house that we see today.

In 1885 Groot Constantia was acquired by the Cape Government for use as a demonstration and experimental wine farm, but in 1925 the homestead was practically

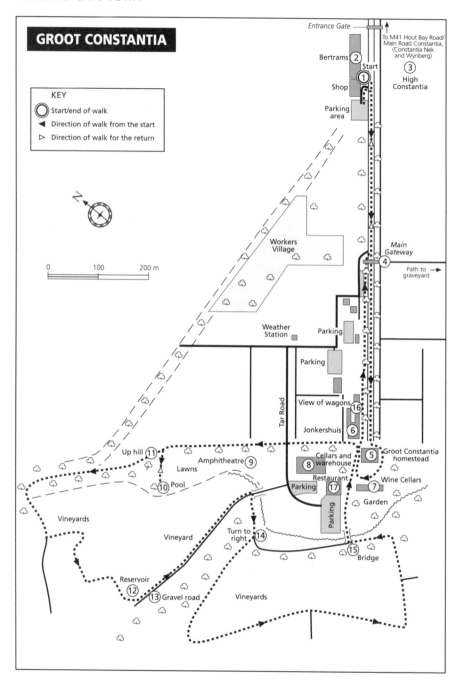

GROOT CONSTANTIA

KEY

⭕ Start/end of walk
◀ Direction of walk from the start
▷ Direction of walk for the return

0   100   200 m

Entrance Gate

To M41 Hout Bay Road/
Main Road Constantia,
(Constantia Nek
and Wynberg)

Bertrams ②
Start ①
Shop
Parking area
③ High Constantia

Workers Village

Main Gateway ④
Path to graveyard

Weather Station
Parking
Parking

Tar Road

View of wagons ⑯
Jonkershuis ⑥
⑤ Groot Constantia homestead

Up hill ⑪
Amphitheatre ⑨
Lawns
⑩ Pool

Cellars and warehouse ⑧
Restaurant
Parking ⑰
Garden
Wine Cellars ⑦

Vineyards

Vineyard
Turn to right ⑭
Parking
Bridge ⑮

Reservoir ⑫
⑬ Gravel road
Vineyards

108

destroyed by fire. It was restored to its appearance of 1791 and parts of the structure were then rebuilt under the direction of the architect, Franklin Kendall, who was an associate of Sir Herbert Baker. In 1936 it was proclaimed a National Monument.

Groot Constantia Walk

The first part of the walk takes you from the enormous building (2) called 'Bertrams' near the entrance of the estate to the restored Groot Constantia homestead.

Bertrams is where Robert Bertram, who acquired the adjacent farm High Constantia (3) in 1902, had his wine cellars. In 1927, after the fire, the Groot Constantia estates were leased to him and the two farms were run together. In 1942, when Bertram died, High Constantia ceased to be farmed. His cellars were expropriated and joined to Groot Constantia to save the area from being subdivided for housing.

About 300 m from the start (1), you reach the main gateway (4) to the homestead where the road narrows and the oak avenue, now only used by pedestrians, begins. If you are interested in graveyards, take a detour to your left, just before the gate, where a path leads for about 300 m to the historical farm graveyard on the far side of the vineyards.

Walking further up the avenue towards the homestead (5), on your far right you will pass the Jonkershuis (6). This and the adjacent stables were part of the Van der Stel farm, but the gable detail is thought to date from 1792. These buildings are now used for a restaurant and other visitor activities.

Although a 'Jonkershuis' is where the *jonkheer* or eldest son of the owner would have lived, this building was probably a *Jongenhuijs* or slave house, and the name has been corrupted.

As you walk further down the avenue, the magnificent Groot Constantia homestead (5) with its well-proportioned windows, stoep and gables lies ahead of you. The gable style is known by many names that incorporate such terms as 'Peninsula', 'Cape', 'Flemish', 'Straight Amsterdam' and 'slendergables'. The style originated in a Flemish architectural patternbook by Jan Vredeman de Vries (1527–1604) and was meticulously implemented by land surveyors who acted as architects in the early days of the Cape. You will notice that there are sash windows (which slide up and down): these replaced Van der Stel's small casement windows (which were pivoted on the side).

When you reach the homestead, turn to the left down a flight of steps and follow the path round to the right which brings you to the front of the wine cellars (7). These are housed in the building that was designed for Hendrik Cloete by the famous French architect Louis Thibault (1750–1815) and the German engineer, Anton Anreith (1754–1822). In the past, a stream ran into the ponds in front of the cellar building where the wine vats were washed. The pediment on the edge of the roof was designed by Anreith and is regarded as one of the finest works of sculpture in South Africa. It shows mythological Ganymede, cup-bearer to Zeus, sitting on an eagle (symbol of Zeus), pouring wine from a jug. On either side are frolicking putti (an Italian art tradition using representations of nude children) with bunches of grapes and panthers (associated with the Greco-Roman god of wine).

Before you walk on, briefly have a look at the underground basement of the homestead behind you. A contemporary description, before the homestead was renovated by Hendrik Cloete, refers to it as two-storeyed and it appears likely that the lowest tiny windows are from the original Van der Stel structure and that the ground level was then much lower than at present.

Carry on round the homestead to the wide path that leads up the hill, past an enormous modern cellar and warehouse facility (8). Now cross a tar road and on your left are wide lawns that form an amphitheatre (9), used for outdoor functions. The vineyards are to your right. Picking the grapes is prohibited and they may have been sprayed.

About 250 m after crossing the tar road, there is a short detour to a large oval-shaped pool (10) which has some curious gables and other elaborate plaster decorations. Inside a niche is a sculptured figure of Triton, son of Neptune, blowing a trumpet. Its significance is not known. In 1985, the teak figure of Triton was replaced with a fibre-glass cast to preserve the original.

Return to the main path and continue up the hill (11). The road curves round the vineyards until you come to a water reservoir (12). This is a good place to stop and enjoy the excellent view of the Constantia valley. When you are ready to walk on, carry on to the gravel road that runs next to the vineyard at (13). Do not walk down the edge of the vineyard because you will find it is difficult to rejoin the gravel road at the bottom. On the way down the hill you will find several colourful protea species have been planted here.

Just before the bridge near the bottom of the hill, take the track to your sharp right (14) and follow the road round so that the walk takes you to a new area of vineyards, south-west of the homestead. When you reach the entrance to the parking area, cross the small bridge (15) and follow on to the west of the homestead. All along there are interesting views of vineyards and picturesque old buildings.

When you reach the 'Jonkershuis' (6) to the west of the long oak avenue, be sure to walk close to these buildings and through a gap (16) you can see the wagons and farming equipment of bygone times.

The walk back to the start is a time to reflect on how these lands were worked at the time of Simon van der Stel. Initially he used the Company's slaves, but by 1688 he personally owned 22 and later bought many more. He freed most of his slaves shortly before he died in 1712. Van der Stel was buried at the Groote Kerk in Adderley Street, Cape Town.

This walk at Groot Constantia can be combined with wine-tasting and visits to the homestead and restaurants.

Constantia Nek to Table Mountain

e Bridle Path to the Plateau

t the time of Jan van Riebeeck, Constantia Nek was called Kloof Pas' (with several variant pellings). It had great strategic importance, because the marauding Khoi often drove cattle stolen from the settlers though this Nek into the Hout Bay Valley. It was also the way that Van Riebeeck's men entered this valley in search of timber.

USEFUL INFORMATION

DISTANCE: About 4 km to Table Mountain plateau (plus a further 2 km to Woodhead Reservoir on extended walk) and equal distances back

TIME: About 3.5 hours to plateau and back (an extra 1.5 hours to go to Woodhead Reservoir and back)

PARKING: Parking area near Constantia Nek traffic circle

START: Under trees near traffic circle

ROUTE: Up bridle path/jeep track from Constantia Nek to Table Mountain plateau; back on same route

TERRAIN: Gravel road

REFRESHMENTS: Restaurant at Constantia Nek near start

AMENITIES: Water tap near De Villiers Reservoir, but carry extra water. Do not drink from any stream, as it may be contaminated

WEATHER: Sheltered from wind

SUITABLE FOR: Walkers of all ages and dogs

The walk along the bridle path that takes you up to the Table Mountain plateau was constructed from Constantia Nek in the 1890s by the Forestry Department to give access to a tree nursery at the top of Nursery Ravine (see pg 95). It is now mainly used as an easy walking path for the public to reach the top of the mountain, for rescue vehicles and as an access for vehicles used by municipal officials working at the dams (there are also several municipal homes on the plateau).

Three major roads join at Constantia Nek, on the ridge between the Constantia and Hout Bay valleys: Rhodes Avenue (M63) leads northwards to Kirstenbosch and Rondebosch, Constantia Road (M41) runs towards Wynberg and on the west is the road to Hout Bay (M63). Although all three routes were in existence as wagon trails in the early 1700s, maps compiled during the 1800s show the only public road on the east of the Nek was from Wynberg. In 1904, Rhodes Avenue was built from Newlands to Constantia Nek under the control of the Claremont Municipality.

In his Journal, Jan van Riebeeck outlined a plan to close Constantia Nek with a stockade to quarter the Khoi in Hout Bay:

'13th August 1657: The Commander accompanied by the skipper of the yacht, Maria, proceeded through Clooffpas to the Hout Bay Valley to explore all the hiding places and passes through which the Hottentots might in any way escape with or without cattle.'

'14 August 1657: This exploration was continued, and it was found that these passes could be closed at no fewer than six different places. These are at the Clooffpas between Steenbergen [present-day Constantiaberg] *and the Bosbergen* [the ridge to the north of Constantia Nek]; *on the knee of the Lion* [present-day Oudekraal]; *further in the kloof between Lion Mountain and the Table Mountain* [present-day Kloof Nek], *and at three other places in the Hout Valley. In all, six places are to be blocked up.'*

But the plan does not seem to have been implemented.

By the time of Commander Simon van der Stel's governorship, in 1679, most of the usable timber had been cut from the slopes above present-day Rondebosch, Newlands and Bishopscourt and the Dutch East India Company's woodcutters moved their operations to the forested area around Constantia Nek. They referred to the new area as 'Die Hel' ('bosun's locker'), possibly on account of the difficulty they had in moving their timber from here to the settlement at the Castle. An earlier encampment above Newlands had been more affectionately named 'Paradijs' ('Paradise') (see pg 99).

In June 1781 the French Pondicherry Regiment arrived at the Cape to assist the Dutch with their fortifications. At this time Britain and France were engaged in the Fourth Sea War and the Netherlands was an ally of the French. Shortly after their arrival, the regiment built an earth redoubt (a small fortification) at Constantia Nek. The remains of Conway Redoubt, named after Colonel Thomas Conway (the Irish regimental commander) are still visible just behind the Constantia Nek Restaurant (to

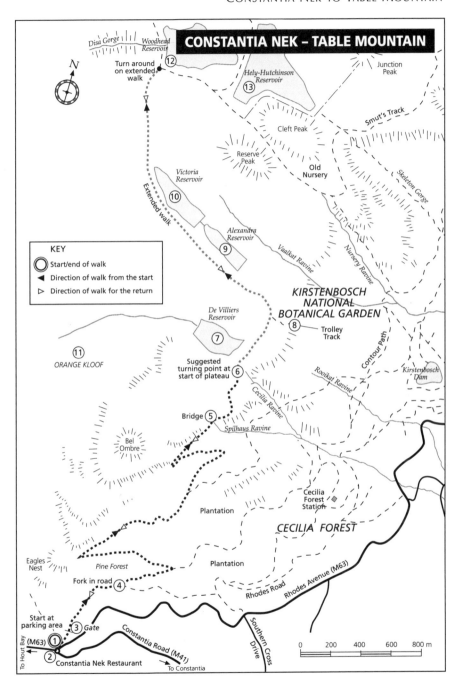

CONSTANTIA NEK – TABLE MOUNTAIN

KEY

Ⓞ Start/end of walk

◀ Direction of walk from the start

▷ Direction of walk for the return

the south of the traffic circle). The troops also established a signal station, with a cannon and flag pole, on the Vlagenberg ('flag hill') immediately to the south.

An arrangement was made with Johannes van Helsdingen, the owner of the Hout Bay farm Kronendal, that, should any ships be sighted in Hout Bay, he would ride up to the signal station. From there the message would be 'telegraphed' to a signal station on Wynberg Hill; then it would be sent to the King's Blockhouse (see pg 79) (above present-day Groote Schuur Hospital); and from there it would go to the Castle. Messages could be coded with cannon fire, flags and bonfires. Military historians estimate that it took about five minutes for a message to be communicated from Constantia Nek to the Castle.

After the British Occupation, produce and refreshments appear to have been sold in the vicinity of Constantia Nek from as early as 1811. The Candle Room of today's Constantia Nek Restaurant was originally built as a tearoom in 1929.

In 1928, when the bridle path was a very rough track, A P Cartwright (later editor of the Rand Daily Mail) made the headlines when he and friends drove and carried a Baby Austin from Constantia Nek up the route of this walk and to Maclear's Beacon (1 085 m). This is the highest point on Table Mountain.

In 1960 this walk was again in the news when it was used in the Cape Argus 'Tip to Top' race between Cape Point and Maclear's Beacon. One competitor was carried along the route on a bed.

Today, although most of the original forest in the vicinity of Constantia Nek has been lost, a small area of 20 hectares of indigenous forest and fynbos, known as 'Die Hel', remains just below the Nek. (It is worth a separate visit and can be accessed from the Cape Town side of the road (M41) leading down to Constantia.)

Walk from Constantia Nek to Table Mountain plateau

From the start (1) at the parking area under the trees, walk northwards for about 200 m up the tarred road to the gate (3) in the forestry fence. The Conway Redoubt is on the far side of the Constantia Nek Restaurant (2), and from the form of the land it is easy to see why the soldiers chose this position to control access over the 'Nek'. Follow the road that leads into the trees for about 500 m and then at the fork (4), turn to the left on the track that leads up into the pine forest. The right fork leads along an avenue (marked 'Rhodes' Road' on the map) that was constructed by Cecil Rhodes (see also pg 75) to link his Groote Schuur Estate to the road to Hout Bay. It runs in the forest above the road that is officially called Rhodes Avenue (M63).

From here you will be walking for about two hours through the pine forest that forms part of the Cecilia plantation, named after Cecil Rhodes. It is a lovely forest scene, with excellent views of the southern suburbs and False Bay.

As the path zigzags higher and higher up the slope you may occasionally spot opportunities for short cuts through the forest. These are not recommended as some are very steep and the best views are from the bridle path. Short cuts are also discouraged as they tend to cause soil erosion. As you follow the bridle path up, you will glimpse a small bridge (5) high above you.

About two hours from the start you will reach the bridge, but do not be tempted to stop here – it is only about ten minutes to the edge of the plateau at the top of the mountain (6) from where there is a wonderful panoramic view of the Peninsula. The effort to get here is well worthwhile and it is a good place to rest and enjoy the tranquillity of the forest. This is the suggested turning point for the walk.

Returning down the bridle path to Constantia Nek takes about an hour and a quarter from here. Avoid any short cuts.

If you want to carry on further there is more to see, although you will now be out of the shade of the trees. Depending on the time of the year, an array of fynbos flowers can be seen, including spectacular red disas (*Disa uniflora*) (February–March in the swampy ground near De Villiers Reservoir), and a wide variety of ericas, which are at their best in winter and spring.

As you walk on towards the north, the path skirts three reservoirs that were built by the Wynberg Municipality at the end of the 19th century. The De Villiers Reservoir (7) is on the left. This

was started in 1907 and was built with the aid of a double-trolley track (8) that ran up the slope of the mountain from Kirstenbosch. As materials were pulled up on one trolley, the other descended (carrying some ballast) ready for the next load. It was initially powered by two horses turning a capstan and was later driven by a steam engine.

As the path rises, you will pass the Alexandra Reservoir (9) on the right, which was finished in 1903, after construction was delayed by the Anglo-Boer War. A few hundred metres on, you will reach the Victoria Reservoir (10), completed in 1896. Water from these three structures is piped down Orange Kloof (11) to a water treatment works near Constantia Nek. Orange Kloof is the first valley to the west, and is only accessible with a special permit obtainable from SA National Parks. It is one of the foremost fynbos sanctuaries in the Cape.

From here the bridle path turns to the right and about 1.5 km further on it skirts the edge of Disa Gorge where there are two large reservoirs built in the 1890s for the Cape Town Municipality – the Woodhead Reservoir (12) and the Hely-Hutchinson Reservoir (13), still important sources for Cape Town's water supply.

When you reach the plateau, also called the 'Back Table', where the reservoirs are, you will find it remarkably flat. The Woodhead Reservoir is some 250 m below the summit of Table Mountain, and the Upper Cableway Station lies about 2 km to the north.

The return from the extended walk to (6) is easy walking on a fairly flat plateau. Restios and ericas line the side of the track.

115

Hout Bay Beach

Of Headlands and Harbours

USEFUL INFORMATION

DISTANCE: 1 km each way

TIME: 45 minutes

START AND PARKING: From Hout Bay Main Road (M6) take the turn-off opposite the Chapman's Peak Hotel towards the beach. Keeping to the left, drive to the parking area at the western end of Hout Bay beach

ROUTE: At the start you can visit the leopard statue on the rocks, then walk in the direction of Hout Bay harbour and back

TERRAIN: Sandy beach

REFRESHMENTS: Shops and restaurants on Main Road before turn to beach parking

AMENITIES: Public toilets and benches near parking area

WEATHER: Exposed to wind, so best in morning and early evening when wind has dropped

SUITABLE FOR: Walkers of all ages, joggers, dogs, kite-flyers; push- and wheelchairs can use 300 m paved walk-way at road behind beach

Hout Bay (meaning 'Wood Bay') was known to British and Dutch fleets at the beginning of the 17th century. The highest peak at the entrance to the bay, Chapman's Peak (593 m), is thought to be the oldest place with an English name in South Africa and was named in 1607 after John Chapman, the mate on a British ship investigating the harbour potential of the bay.

H out Bay beach is fringed on two sides by a backdrop of spectacular mountains and beautiful scenery. The residents, being somewhat separated from the rest of the Peninsula by the mountains, have a strong community spirit and humorously identify their village as 'The Republic of Hout Bay'– tourist shops even sell 'passports'! It is a home for many artists whose craft is sold locally, and is a popular resort for holidaymakers.

In the 17th century the upper slopes of the valley – about 4 km from Hout Bay beach – were thickly wooded with trees that were suitable for ship repair and building construction. This was particularly important because the natural vegetation of the Cape Peninsula provided very little usable timber, and wood was in great demand by the Dutch East India Company and other trading fleets.

Jan van Riebeeck's Journal reports that members of his party found *'a fine large forest of very tall straight growing trees – and a fresh river flowing to the sea, wide and deep enough for rowing boats'*. The Journal mentions an intention to float the timber down the river to the shore. As you will see on the walk, there must have been considerable siltation of this river because it is now very shallow.

Within months of Van Riebeeck's arrival, the timber growing in the Hout Bay valley was being cut and taken by sea to Cape Town: ship masts, fencing, building planks and piling were urgently needed. The structural elements of the first fort that was built by Van Riebeeck's party were constructed entirely from timber. Wood was also used for firing brick and lime kilns.

The lime kilns were fed with shells from beaches in Table Bay and on Robben Island. The lime, produced by heating the shell, was used for building mortar and was mixed with tallow to provide lime-wash paint. Lime mortar cannot be used in wet conditions, however, so for situations such as the lining of canals, a special 'Roman' cement, made with volcanic ash, was brought to the Cape from Europe. (Portland Cement, the building cement that is used today, was only invented in Britain in 1824.)

The Hout Bay River, also known as the Disa River, flows through the centre of the valley to Hout Bay beach. In 1677, the Commander at the Cape, Simon van der Stel, granted the first rights to rent agricultural land on the banks of this river and in 1681 Kronendal and Ruiteplaats were granted as freehold farms. The original Kronendal house has been beautifully restored as a restaurant at 867 Hout Bay Road. It is well worth a visit. From the earliest days the Hout Bay farms have been noted for early spring vegetables, merino sheep and horses.

Hout Bay provides the only natural harbour along the western seaboard of the Cape Peninsula. Although it was considered to be a place of strategic importance and was fortified with guns on both sides of the bay, it was not developed as a port until 1936. This was mainly due to the lack of good road access and the adverse conditions of gusting winds which are due to turbulence caused by the surrounding mountains.

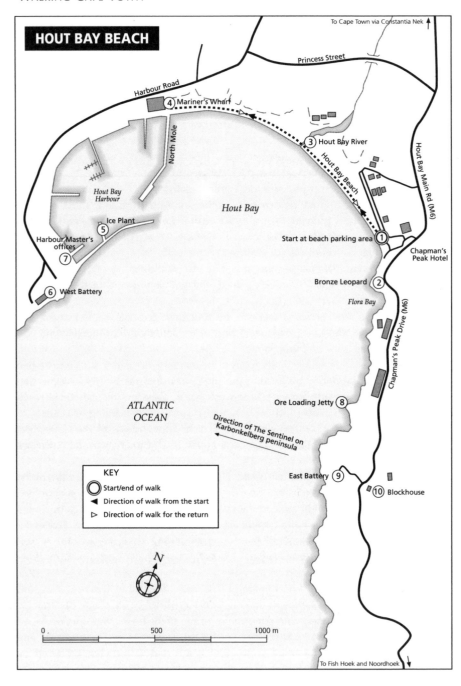

HOUT BAY BEACH

To Cape Town via Constantia Nek

Princess Street

Harbour Road

(4) Mariner's Wharf

North Mole

(3) Hout Bay River

Hout Bay Beach

Hout Bay Main Rd (M6)

Hout Bay Harbour

Hout Bay

Ice Plant

(5)

Start at beach parking area (1)

Harbour Master's offices

(7)

Chapman's Peak Hotel

(6) West Battery

Bronze Leopard (2)

Flora Bay

ATLANTIC OCEAN

Ore Loading Jetty (8)

Chapman's Peak Drive (M6)

Direction of The Sentinel on Karbonkelberg peninsula

KEY

⊙ Start/end of walk

◄ Direction of walk from the start

▷ Direction of walk for the return

East Battery (9)

(10) Blockhouse

N

0   500   1000 m

To Fish Hoek and Noordhoek

Two old batteries, which are not clearly seen from the beach, protect the bay. The West Battery, which is just beyond the fishing harbour to the west of the bay, was constructed in 1781 by the Dutch East India Company with French assistance. Some of it was reconstructed in 1794. The East Battery, high above the rocks on the eastern side of the bay below Chapman's Peak Drive, was built between 1781 and 1784. British forces constructed a blockhouse above the road in 1796.

Hout Bay Beach Walk

The walk along Hout Bay beach can be combined with a swim in summer and is an excellent place to picnic in the evenings or to exercise your dog. Hout Bay is very much a family beach.

Before you set off from the parking area (1), you may like to climb over the rocks to see the bronze leopard (2) mounted on a rock overlooking the beach. This is the work of Hout Bay artist, Ivan Mitford-Barberton, who is also the sculptor of a well-known statue of General Smuts at the top of Adderley Street, Cape Town, near the entrance to the Gardens (*see* pg 25).

As you start your walk along the beach, you may notice a perculiar glinting on the sand. This is due to the presence of millions of thin, fibre-like shells that wash up on the beach. For many years it was erroneously thought that these could be glass-fibre residues from boat building at the harbour.

On your right you will see that the beach sand has been stabilised with brushwood fences to prevent it blowing onto the road and car park. This technique of dune control has proved to be surprisingly effective. It was also used to prevent drift-sands from engulfing the Koeberg Nuclear Power Station near Melkbosstrand during its construction in the late 1970s.

About 500 m from the start, as you ankle-wade across the Hout Bay River (3), visualise the transport of logs and boats here by men of the Dutch East India Company when the river was much deeper. The siltation that has occurred is largely due to removal of stabilising vegetation, and bad farming practice. In the summer months the river practically dries up as there are five dams trapping its headwaters (*see* pg 131). These provide part of Cape Town's water supply.

As you look out across the bay, about 5 km away on your left, you can see Chapman's Peak (593 m), the highest coastal headland to the east. Below this peak, a road has been cut into the rock creating the spectacular Chapman's Peak Drive that was opened in 1922. It was the brainchild of the first Administrator of the Cape Province, Sir Nicholas de Waal, and is one of the Cape's foremost tourist attractions, providing a superlative vantage point for panoramic views of the bay.

As you face the sea, Hout Bay harbour, to your right, is the biggest fishing harbour in this region. The large, conspicuous box-like structure in the middle is a refrigeration plant (5) that provides ice for the fishing boats that operate from here.

The first harbour facilities, built at the beginning of the 20th century in the vicinity of the fishing harbour, consisted of a decking on a sunken vessel, *The Morrow*, to the north of the present slipway at the Harbour Master's Offices (7). A rock lobster cannery operated from here from about 1903, but in 1914 it was destroyed in a huge explosion in which seven men died.

The protected harbour was constructed in several stages. In 1936 a short breakwater was built from the West Battery (6) area to the position of the ice plant and then in 1966 this was extended to its present position and an extra leg, the north mole, was constructed from the shore at the end of the beach.

At the breakwater wall at the end of the beach is a tourist spot called Mariner's Wharf (4) where seafood and curios can be bought. This is the turning point of the walk. If you have time, this is well worth a visit. Inside the harbour there are other tourist activities including boat trips to various parts of the bay.

On your return to the start you will be facing towards the east where Chapman's Peak Drive begins.

If you look at the foothills of the mountains on the Chapman's Peak side (above Flora Bay), you will see that, where roads are cut through these slopes, they tend to form landslides. This has been a problem for road construction and, at the beginning of Chapman's Peak Drive, elaborate anchored retaining walls have been built to stabilise the slopes.

Manganese was once mined on the upper slopes of Chapman's Peak Drive and the remains of an old ore-loading jetty (8) can be seen (easier with binoculars) about 900 m out from the beach on the eastern side of the bay. An overzealous ore loader is said to have sunk a vessel when falling ore punched a hole in the boat's bottom.

After your walk along Hout Bay beach you may like to investigate the East Battery (9), which can be reached by driving for about a kilometre along Chapman's Peak Drive until, on your right, you see a sign 'East Fort'. Take the gravel path down towards the sea and you will suddenly come to the cannons of the fortification facing across to 'The Sentinel' peak (330 m) and Karbonkelberg peninsula on the other side of the bay. Further on along Chapman's Peak Drive even more spectacular views unfold across the bay. The blockhouse (10), constructed by the British, stands above the East Battery on the other side of the road.

The walk along the beach at Hout Bay is fairly short but can be combined with many other activities in the area, such as a visit to nearby craft shops and restaurants in Hout Bay Main Road.

Noordhoek Beach

Waves, Wind and Wrecks

Noordhoek beach is a remote, pristine beach visited mainly by surfers and horse riders from nearby stables, and also by people walking dogs. With many spectacular views and unspoiled natural features, it is one of the last coastal areas in the Peninsula that is virtually undeveloped. At the start of the beach are patches of ancient dune thicket – a rare coastal vegetation-type that was once common in the Cape.

USEFUL INFORMATION

DISTANCE: The beach extends for over 8 km to Kommetjie so any intermediate distance can be chosen. A convenient turning point is at the wreck of the *Kakapo*, 3 km from the start

TIME: A 2.5 hour walk to the wreck and back is ideal

PARKING: Follow signposts marked 'Beach' near the lowest part of Chapman's Peak Drive (M6) near Noordhoek village, to parking area near the sea

START: On the beach

ROUTE: Towards the sea, then southwards to the wreck and back

REFRESHMENTS: Available at Noordhoek shops

AMENITIES: Toilets and water tap at start

WEATHER: Exposed to wind – best in morning and late afternoon

TERRAIN: Sandy beach

SUITABLE FOR: Walkers of all ages, joggers, kite-flyers, dogs and horses

The first settlement in Noordhoek was in 1743 when Baron Gustaaf van Imhoff granted the farms, De Goede Hoop and Imhoff's Gift, to a widow, Christina Diemer. Imhoff, who acted as Commissioner reporting to the Dutch East India Company during his short stay at the Cape (21 January to 28 February 1743), was travelling from the Netherlands to Batavia to take up office as Governor-General of the Dutch East Indies.

Because of poor access, until the 1920s this area was virtually inaccessible to the public. From Fish Hoek and Kommetjie there were only sand tracks, and to the north the route from Hout Bay, some 6 km away, was blocked by a mountain ridge with cliffs dropping almost vertically to the sea. The steepness of these cliffs can be judged from the fact that the highest point, Chapman's Peak (593 m), which is nearly two-thirds the height of Table Mountain (1085 m), is only 450 m away from the coast.

In 1922 the spectacular Chapman's Peak Drive, linking Noordhoek to Hout Bay, was opened after seven years of construction. It was a remarkable achievement involving some 10 km of road cut into the steep mountainside. More than 2 km of this road was constructed by blasting into the solid rock. The project was master-minded by Sir Frederick de Waal, first Administrator of the Cape after the formation of the Union of South Africa in 1910. (De Waal Drive, the road linking Cape Town to the southern suburbs, was named after him.) Although Noordhoek has now become part of a popular scenic drive around the Peninsula, it remained a remote farming area and it took about 50 years before there was significant residential development here.

In 1923 an imposing mansion, Noordhoek House, was built high up on the hillside above Chapman's Peak Drive for Sir Drummond and Lady Chaplin. The house was designed by Sir Herbert Baker's firm of architects. Prior to his retirement, wealthy mining magnate Chaplin had been Administrator (Governor) of then Rhodesia.

Since about 1950, several farming areas in the valley have been subdivided for housing and the roads to the area have been greatly improved. Parts of Noordhoek, particularly on the hillside near the start of the walk, have become attractive residential areas. As in many other parts of the Peninsula this development has raised issues of conflict between the wishes of some to preserve the coastal vegetation and others for whom this has no value. Close to the beach an attempt has been made to integrate a large time-share development and conference centre (Monkey Valley Beach Nature Resort), into an area of ancient white milkwoods.

Slightly inland of the walk, and for much of the length of the beach, are imperma-nent lagoons that are filled by waves at high tide. These tend to dry up in summer. Further inland is a wetland Nature Area with extensive reedbeds and several perma-nent vleis, including Papkuilsvlei and the Wildevoëlvlei, which in winter links to the sea about 700 m beyond the wreck of the Kakapo.

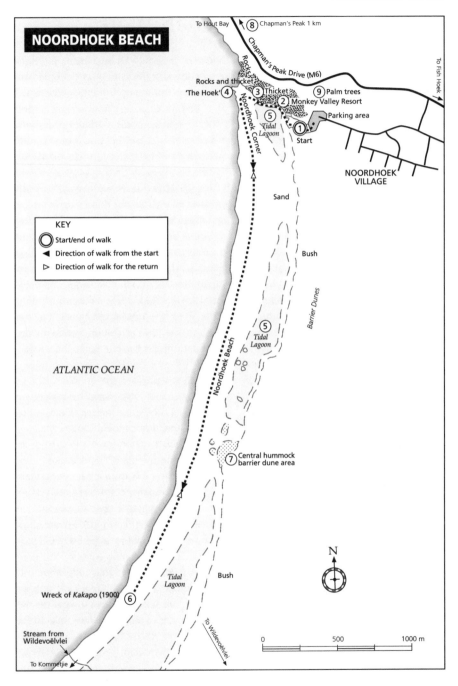

NOORDHOEK BEACH

To Hout Bay
⑧ Chapman's Peak 1 km
Chapman's Peak Drive (M6)
To Fish Hoek

Rocks
Rocks and thicket
'The Hoek' ④
③ Thicket
⑨ Palm trees
② Monkey Valley Resort
Noordhoek Corner
⑤
Tidal Lagoon
Parking area
① Start
NOORDHOEK VILLAGE

Sand

Bush

KEY
Ⓞ Start/end of walk
◀ Direction of walk from the start
▷ Direction of walk for the return

Barrier Dunes

⑤ Tidal Lagoon

Noordhoek Beach

ATLANTIC OCEAN

⑦ Central hummock barrier dune area

Bush

N

Wreck of *Kakapo* (1900) ⑥
Tidal Lagoon

To Wildevoëlvlei

Stream from Wildevoëlvlei

0   500   1000 m

To Kommetjie

Noordhoek Beach Walk

This peaceful walk is a balm to the soul. Mid-week the beach is virtually deserted so do not go alone; many more walk here over weekends and on public holidays.

At the start of the walk **(1)**, take the sandy path that winds towards the sea. Before you head towards Kommetjie village in the south, take a detour slightly to the north-west where you can overlook the sea. This famed surfing spot is known as 'The Hoek' **(4)**, and, if the conditions are favourable, it is an excellent spot to view surfers riding the waves.

As you walk towards the sea you will see that on the mountainside there is a dense band of dark-green trees **(3)** below Chapman's Peak Drive. Many of these are white milkwoods (*Sideroxylon inerme*) and are distinctive in having dark green, waxy, oblong rounded leaves and a light green midrib. They form a very dense canopy with cavernous areas underneath. Some of these trees are very old – certainly hundreds of years and possibly much older. The wood of this tree was greatly sought-after by the early settlers as it is heavy, hard and durable even in damp conditions. An infusion of the bark is reputed to dispel nightmares. The species, which is found in coastal regions from the Western Cape to Mozambique, is now legally protected in South Africa.

If you climb a short way up the slope you will find a network of paths and 'caves' running under the white milkwood canopy. It is easy to visualise these distinctive trees giving shelter to prehistoric man, and stone implements are occasionally found here. In more recent times this area was occupied by Khoi and Strandloper hunter-gatherers.

Before you reach the sea, look up one of the narrow paths leading up the hillside and you will notice several access tracks have been cut through the dense indigenous bush to the Monkey Valley Resort **(2)** and housing areas. This bush is part of the ancient dune thicket which is naturally shaped and pruned by the wind. Botanists are concerned about protecting this area and avoid cutting into it. The reason is obvious if you compare the bush on the two sides of a path: on the windward side you will see that the thicket is dense and intact. On the other side, where the protection of the shaped thicket has been lost, the vegetation is sparse and is struggles to survive.

When you reach the sea you will find that, because the wind continuously blows sand off the beach, it is very loose above the tideline and makes walking quite difficult. It is much easier to walk on the wet sand, especially at low tide.

Turning now towards the south, walk in the direction of Kommetjie. A large number of different species of bird are attracted by the tidal lagoons **(5)** and nearby vleis. You should see groups of the pale grey-backed Hartlaub's gulls and the more solitary large kelp gulls (black-backed with white-margined wings and a large yellow bill with an orange spot). In the nearshore waves you may see black cormorants diving for fish. In winter the large southern giant petrels course above the waves beyond the surf. These are grey-brown seabirds, about 90 cm long, with a large bill. In summer, in the shallow water of the lagoons, you are very likely to see flocks of thousands of curlew sandpipers which are small, olive-grey waders with a distinctive downturned bill. There are also the common sandpipers, which are small, grey-brown waders with short grey-green legs and thin, pointed, straight bills. Their tails constantly bob up and down as they walk. Another summer migrant is the sanderling which is a small, pale grey wader with white underparts and dark shoulder patches. These birds run together along the beach and catch mussels as the waves retreat.

This shore is exposed to the wind and the huge rollers from the Atlantic and there is generally plenty of flotsom after a storm. Unusual finds on this beach have included glass buoys, used by foreign fishermen to float their long tuna fishing lines, and 'sea beans', the large shiny brown seeds that have floated here from tropical estuaries.

About 3 km from the start you will come to the wreck of the *Kakapo* **(6)**, where parts of the film, *Ryan's Daughter*, were filmed. The *Kakapo*, which is named after a New Zealand flightless parrot, was accidentally beached here on 25 May 1900 in a north-westerly gale. It was on its delivery voyage from England to the owners in New Zealand. This wreck, and several others that had occurred previously along the beach, are thought to have been caused by the officer on the bridge confusing the rounding of the Karbonkelberg (at the left of the entrance to Hout Bay) with their intended rounding of Cape Point. After attempts to pull the *Kakapo* off the sand failed, the salvage was abandoned and the steel plates of the hull were reportedly later removed by the SA Railways.

In the distance, beyond Kommetjie, you can see the lighthouse at Slangkop which was built in 1914 to improve navigation along this section of coast. The light has a range of 29 km and is one of the most powerful in Africa.

On the way back to the start, look out for several features which are of particular interest. About 500 m landwards of the shoreline is a barrier dune **(7)** that was formed at a time, about 5 000 years ago, when the sea was some 3 m above its present level. The geological period is known as the Flandrian transgression of the Holocene.

Chapman's Peak is the high peak **(8)** immediately in front of you and Sir Drummond Chaplin's mansion is about 2 km to the east (on your right).

Above the parking area on the hillside near the start stands a line of twelve palm trees **(9)** that were identified in old British Admiralty sailing directions as landmarks to be seen from the sea.

This pleasant, relaxing walk is particularly attractive in the early morning when there is likely to be little wind.

Zandvlei

Grassy Banks and Shimmering Water

At the time of the Dutch settlement at the Cape in 1652, Zandvlei was a marshy area fed by rivers draining the Constantia valley and nearby low-lying sand dune areas of the Cape Flats. In winter the water level rose until the sandbar was breached at the sea and then, during summer when there was much less rain, the mouth silted up. The vlei was named by Jan van Riebeeck in the 1650s.

Zandvlei is a small estuarine lake, about 2.5 km long, lying just east of Lakeside and Muizenberg. In 1973 amenities for the public were improved by dredging the vlei, stabilising the banks and landscaping the parkland, and it was joined by canals to a waterside residential development, Marina da Gama, in the east.

In Jan van Riebeeck's time the area was wild and there are reports of an abundance of game including leopard, lion, hippo and even rhino. In 1672 a commissioner of the Dutch East India Company reported *'one of the Company's herdsmen residing in the recently erected kraal behind Steenberg (just north of Zandvlei) informed us that a lion had eaten two or three sheep there, but had been entertained with a musket in such manner that shortly afterwards he succumbed'*. A cattle post was started by the Company on the shore at Lakeside in the following year.

At this time the only safe anchorage for ships at the Cape was at Simon's Town, where the bay was well protected from storm winds and waves. Because of this, the road to the anchorage from Cape Town became an important link and in 1744 a fortified staging post was established at Muizenberg (*see* pg 148).

Zandvlei remained a relatively inaccessible marshland until 1882 when an embankment was built across the vlei to enable the suburban railway to connect to Muizenberg and residents of the more northerly suburbs could travel there by train.

In June 1884 the first rowing regatta was held at Zandvlei with 70 boats. Three months later another regatta was cancelled because the water level was too low.

Lakeside Boating Association (later the Imperial Yacht Club) was founded in 1907 and pavilions were constructed at Lakeside to the west of the railway and, after that, near today's yacht club. Boating was difficult because of the shallow depth and water weed. Old photos show masts being stepped (lowered and re-erected) so that the boats could pass under the railway line. The vlei has been partially dredged several times and the water depth at present varies from about 1 m to 2 m. It is shallowest in the south.

Of the many types of waterweed that exist in the vlei, the bullrushes, pondweed and reed swamps are the most evident. The pondweed, which floats close to the surface and grows in water up to about 1.5 m in depth, is the most problematic and is systematically harvested by a weed cutter. After cutting, the weed is lifted out to prevent it from rotting in the water.

Zandvlei Walk

Before walking towards Muizenberg, you will notice Marina da Gama on the far side of the vlei. This was the first housing development to be constructed in South Africa in which the engineering, architectural and landscape design were integrated and strict design controls were applied. The land form, alignment of canals and architectural design of the buildings

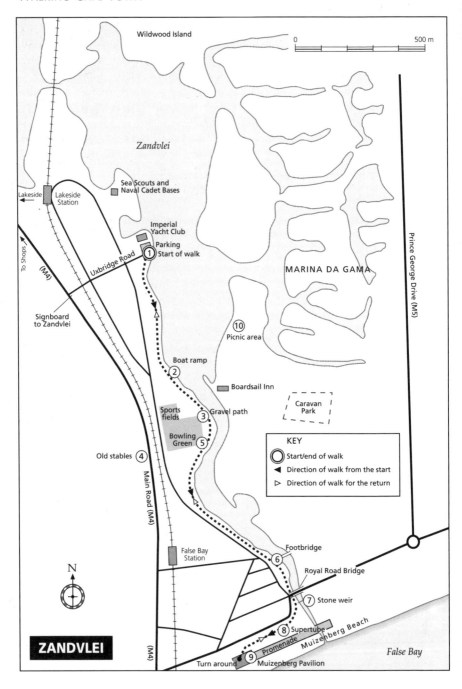

S ADEY/SIL; PREVIOUS PAGE E THIEL/SIL

A PROUST

PREVIOUS PAGE: Greenmarket Square (*see* pg 21), a lively, bustling flea market in the heart of the city.

TOP: Completed in 1679, the beautifully preserved Castle of Good Hope (*see* pg 29) now houses an art galllery and museum.

ABOVE: Much of the Bo-Kaap (*see* pg 34), the traditional home of the Cape Malays, has been restored to retain its original character.

RIGHT: Once a parade ground, the Grand Parade (*see* pg 29) now hosts a colourful market unique to Cape Town.

S ADEY/SIL

S ADEY/SIL; PREVIOUS PAGES M SKINNER/SIL

A PROUST

PREVIOUS PAGES: In the 1600s the Dutch gave Lion's Head (*see* pg 41) its name, which relates to is sphinx-like appearance when viewed from the Castle.

OPPOSITE TOP: Rhodes Memorial (*see* pg 75) is a tribute to Cecil John Rhodes, a man who had a great influence on Africa in the 1800s.

LEFT: A walk in Newlands Forest (*see* pg 81) provides a peaceful escape from the bustle of the city.

BELOW: The Victoria and Alfred Waterfront (*see* pg 47) successfully combines numerous tourist attractions, shops and restaurants in the context of a working harbour.

S ADEY/SIL

OPPOSITE: The unrivalled beauty of Kirstenbosch National Botanical Garden (*see* pg 86) in spring.
ABOVE: Groot Constantia (*see* pg 106), an important part of the Cape's cultural heritage.

ABOVE: Muizenberg beach (*see* pg 147) along the False Bay coastline stretches for over 20 km to the east. It is one of Cape Town's most popular beaches, with its warm waters, safe bathing and good waves for surfers.

TOP: The view across Hout Bay beach (*see* pg 116) towards the harbour and the Sentinel.
ABOVE: Unspoiled Noordhoek beach (*see* pg 121), popular haunt of horse riders, walkers,
surfers and kite-flyers.

L VON HÖRSTEN/SIL

OPPOSITE TOP: Sailing, swimming, sunbathing – Fish Hoek beach (*see* pg 169) has it all.

LEFT: Historic Simon's Town (*see* pg 179) retains much of its 19th-century character and still has many links with its Dutch East India Company and Royal Naval past.

BELOW: Boyes Drive (*see* pg 159), the mountain road overlooking False Bay, offers spectacular views of Kalk Bay harbour (*see* pg 164), where the timeless ways of local fisherfolk continue.

S ADEY/SIL

PREVIOUS PAGES, TOP AND ABOVE: Cape Point and the surrounding Cape of Good Hope Nature Reserve encompass a virtually unspoiled rocky headland and a unique ecological sanctuary. This lovely view from Kanonkop (top) forms part of the walk on page 185.

were based on the outcome of wind measurements and laboratory wind-tunnel tests in California. Measurements after construction confirm that the design reduced the wind speed in the Marina da Gama area by about 50% of what it was previously. Looking due east you can see the distinctive white walls with their black roofs pitched to deflect the wind.

Wildwood Island, at the extreme north, is a reeded conservation area that includes a bird sanctuary. It is unfortunately not open to the public.

From the start (1) you will find no difficulty in following the route of the walk – keep to the edge of the vlei all the way. Non-walkers in your party may choose to picnic near the start, where there is good wind protection near the swings, climbing frames and ablution facilities. Fires are, however, not allowed at this point, but there are braai areas about 500 m further south.

As you walk you are likely to see many different types of bird, including moorhen, coot, sandpiper (these migrate from breeding grounds in Siberia), black duck, yellow-billed duck and many types of seabird (the most common are the white-headed gulls which thrive on scavenging the refuse dumps about 8 km to the east), sacred ibis (they were revered in ancient Egypt) and blacksmith plover. When the water level is low, as in summer, flamingo and pelican can also occasionally be seen at the north of the vlei. Over 130 bird species have been recorded at Zandvlei.

The vlei is well populated by fish and you may see them jump out of the water.

The fish, which include carp (introduced in 1896) and tilapia, are tolerant to wide swings in salinity. This is relevant because at times there is an inflow of seawater into the vlei, whereas in winter, when the rivers flow strongly, there is freshwater. At the southern end of the vlei, where it is most salty, there are haarder and springer which live on material in the weed beds, and predatory fish such as white steenbras, white stumpnose, elf and leervis. Biologically, Zandvlei is considered to be the only estuary of significance in False Bay and it is important as a nursery for fish which move in and out of the bay when the mouth is open in winter. (Permits for fishing in certain areas of Zandvlei are obtainable in Cape Town from the Chief Directorate: Sea Fisheries.)

About 500 m from the start is a concrete ramp (2), used for launching boats into the vlei. (Another more wind-protected ramp lies to the west of the Imperial Yacht Club.) When you come across braai areas, you must follow the gravel path (3) that leads between the vlei and the sports fields. In the distance, on the far side of the Main Road looking towards the mountain, you can see unusual long buildings (4) with arches. These used to be the stables for horses drawing the municipal refuse carts. A regional refuse dump used to be in the area now occupied by Marina da Gama.

The manatoka trees (*Myoporum insulare*) along the banks, although bent and shaped by the south-easter, are remarkably resistant to the salt spray. Most of the picnic and braai areas are protected by these fleshy leafed trees, which originate from Australia, and their seeds are spread by birds. They are also grown as a hedge in other windy areas of the Peninsula such as Milnerton, Muizenberg and Fish Hoek.

The path takes you past the municipal bowling green **(5)** where you may also see wild pelargoniums (geraniums) growing in the grass. Interestingly, the bright red geraniums which are grown in window boxes in Holland, Spain and other parts of western Europe originally came from the Cape (*see also* pg 91).

ZANDVLEI LAWNS

The lawns around Zandvlei always look surprisingly green, even in the dry late summer. This has been achieved by cultivating four different types of grass, each of which grows in its area of preference. The light green kikuyu grass, which covers most areas, is from East Africa. In areas too dry for kikuyu there is a naturally occurring fine 'kweek gras' with a distinctive seed head split into four spikelets. This is tolerant to salt and dry summer conditions with practically no need for watering. There is also the dark leafed indigenous buffalo grass, its coarse leaves on runners which grow close to the ground and forming a hard mat. On the water's edge, another local grass (*Paspalum vaginatum*) grows even into the salty vlei water. Lawns planted on sand are easily damaged by traffic so they have been underlain by a thin layer of ferricrete gravel, which helps to resist the abrasion of walkers, traffic and sporting activity. You may see some orange-coloured patches of the ferricrete in the grass.

Ahead, opposite a small embayment on the bank, you will see four Norfolk Island pines which grow well in quite salty conditions. These trees are indigenous to remote islands in the Pacific and also a few places in South America, such as Chile.

As you walk further south you will pass a footbridge **(6)** leading to the eastern side of the vlei. Then, just past the Royal Road Bridge on your left, you will see the stone-packed weir **(7)** that is used to control the water level of the vlei, when the mouth is open to the sea.

The Royal Road Bridge is a good place to turn round but, if you want a cup of tea or a cool drink, continue southwards for about 100 m towards the blue Supertube **(8)** at the beachfront and then turn to the right past the children's amusement park and on towards the large red-roofed Muizenberg Pavilion **(9)** and the nearby shops.

The picnic area at **(10)** has excellent views of the mountains and vlei. As there is quite a lot to do at Zandvlei you may want to come back later to try your hand at board or dinghy sailing, bowling or rowing. Dragon boat racing is also organised here by the Canoe Club.

146

Muizenberg Beach

Along the Tideline

In 1743, a cattle post and fortified staging post for horse-drawn traffic was established by the Dutch East India Company under the command of Sergeant Wynand Muys, near present-day Muizenberg railway station. The post became known as Muysenburg (meaning 'Muys's stronghold'), which became corrupted to its present name, Muizenberg.

USEFUL INFORMATION

DISTANCE: 2 km each way

TIME: About 1 hour each way

START AND PARKING: Parking area near Muizenberg Pavilion

ROUTE: On raised promenade and then along beach

TERRAIN: After short paved section, along flat sandy beach

PUBLIC TRANSPORT: Train to Muizenberg, then 5-minute walk to beach pavilion

REFRESHMENTS: Available at start

AMENITIES: Benches and public toilets at start, children's playground with swings, supertube and boat rides near start

WEATHER: Exposed to south-easter wind

SUITABLE FOR: All ages, joggers, kite-flyers, surfing, swimming. Dogs allowed on leads 1 May–30 October; from 1 November–30 April no dogs from 9 am to 6 pm

Muizenberg's strategic relevance was due to the fact that carts, wagons and other vehicular traffic bound for the Dutch East India Company's winter harbour at Simon's Town had to travel through the narrow gap between the mountains at Muizenberg .

The original garrison building (Oude Pos) of Sergeant Wynand Muys of the Dutch East Indian Company has been restored and can be seen on the mountain side of the Main Road, 200 m south of the railway station.

In 1756 further fortifications were built by the Company at Muizenberg Pass, slightly to the south, at the narrowest point between the mountain and the sea. One of its functions was to prevent farmers from sending provisions to ships at Simon's Town, because at the time there was a scarcity of food in the settlement. They also wished to force the farmers to pay duties on their produce to the Company.

On the night of 16 October 1788 the French frigate, *Penelope*, was grounded on Muizenberg beach while trying to reach safe refuge at Simon's Town. Although most of the 430 men aboard were saved, the vessel was broken up by the waves.

A few years later, on 1 July 1795, a large British fleet arrived at Simon's Town to seize the Cape of Good Hope from the Dutch East India Company. An advance force of 450 soldiers were sent ashore. The Dutch set up batteries of cannon at Muizenberg and Kalk Bay and prepared to defend with 670 men together with slaves, Khoi and others. The English then sent a small boat to take soundings near the Muizenberg beach to plan for a landing. On 7 August 1795, while four large British ships sailed up and down offshore of the Muizenberg coast, troops were advancing overland from Simon's Town. After a cannonade was fired by the ships at the Kalk Bay redoubt, these forces withdrew. Then British ships engaged with eleven Dutch guns at Muizenberg. The Dutch withdrew to a position about 3 km inland (now called Retreat) and the Cape came under British rule. This was the First British Occupation of the Cape.

In the same year, British troops built a battery and other defensive works at 'The Fort'.

By 1900, with the development of the diamond and gold fields at Kimberley and the Witwatersrand, Muizenberg had developed into a most prestigious seaside resort. Many of the most wealthy mining and industrial magnates had seaside homes here.

Although the town of Muizenberg has not retained its earlier splendour, its beach is one of the most beautiful parts of the Cape.

Muizenberg Beach Walk

The walk starts at Muizenberg Pavilion (1) from where the beach extends more or less continuously for over 20 km towards the east. The walk is particularly popular over weekends. Because it becomes remote in places, the recommended turning point is about 2 km or one hour's slow walk from the start.

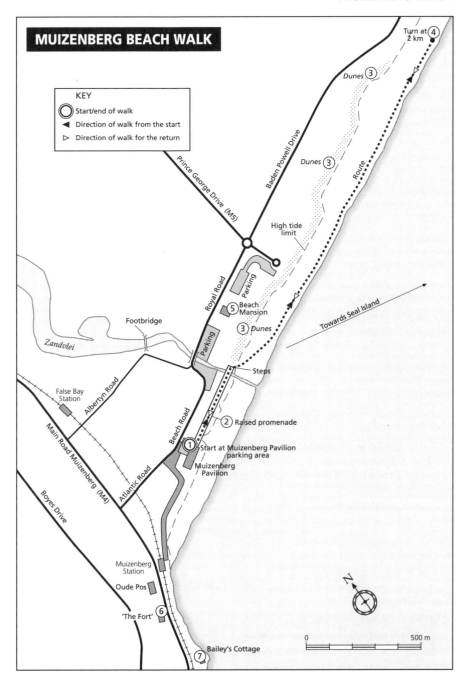

MUIZENBERG BEACH WALK

KEY

◯ Start/end of walk
◄ Direction of walk from the start
▷ Direction of walk for the return

Turn at (4) 2 km

Dunes (3)

Prince George Drive (M5)

Baden Powell Drive

Dunes (3)

Route

High tide limit

Royal Road

Parking

(5) Beach Mansion

Footbridge

Parking

(3) Dunes

Towards Seal Island

Zandvlei

Steps

False Bay Station

Albertyn Road

Beach Road

(2) Raised promenade

Main Road Muizenberg (M4)

Atlantic Road

(1) Start at Muizenberg Pavilion parking area

Muizenberg Pavilion

Boyes Drive

Muizenberg Station

Oude Pos

'The Fort' (6)

Bailey's Cottage

(7)

N

0   500 m

From the parking area at the pavilion, begin by walking along the raised promenade **(2)**, heading towards the east (i.e. away from the mountain). From this vantage you can see a panorama of mountains that surround False Bay. The Hottentots Holland Mountains are to the east, with Cape Hangklip in the far distance. To the west, the mountains of the Cape Peninsula end at Cape Point. Seal Island is about 10 km to the south-east, in the direction shown on the map. On a clear day you can sometimes see the white flecks of waves breaking on the island's rocky shore.

The promenade crosses a small river which is the outlet from Zandvlei (*see* pg 146) to the sea. Except during mid-winter, when the flow from the vlei is strong enough to scour the mouth open at all stages of the tide, this channel is generally blocked by sand. When the first rains come at the beginning of winter (about the end of April), the water level rises in the vlei, but because the mouth is blocked there is often a danger of flooding the residential parts of the vlei (i.e. Marina da Gama). To solve the problem a bulldozer is used to push the sand plug away and to cut a lead to the sea. The plan is to let the outflowing water scour the rest of the sand plug. If this is not done at low tide, the mouth

WHY ARE THE FALSE BAY BEACHES SO FLAT ?

The reason why the beach is so flat at Muizenberg is quite complex, but the basic mechanism can be easily understood from the following: when waves travelling in deep water reach shallows which have a depth of about half their wave length (which occurs in False Bay), they tend to change their direction slightly through an effect known as refraction. The further the waves travel across a changing gradient of 'shallowing' water depths, the more the direction of the incoming waves change.

In False Bay the underwater contours are such that waves entering the bay from deep water are sufficiently strongly refracted so as to come to the shore on the beaches at Simon's Town, Glencairn, Fish Hoek and Muizenberg, with their crests more or less parallel to the shoreline, as can be seen if you look down on the bay from Boyes Drive.

This implies that, regardless of the initial direction of the deep water waves, they break on the shore in a manner that hardly moves the sand. It gives us wonderfully stable beaches which are in marked contrast to the situation at Milnerton where, as a result of the construction of the harbour at Cape Town, the direction of the waves has changed, the movement of sand has increased, the slope of the beach has become steeper and the beach line has been generally eroded.

can silt up before the sand plug has washed away fully and the whole job of clearing the mouth has to be repeated.

At the end of the promenade, walk down the steps to the beach and stroll along the tide line that is just damp enough for comfortable walking; very dry sand is tiring to walk across. You will notice that Muizenberg's beach is remarkably flat (see box pg 150).

The beach always holds surprises for visitors. For example, towards the end of March and until early winter you may find a spectacularly beautiful nautilus shell which has been blown in by the south-east wind. To be sure of getting a perfect specimen, you will need to get to the beach at first light before the gulls and other collectors get there. (For safety reasons do not go alone at this time.) At other times you may find the tide line is littered with bright blue shells which are washed in with bluebottles (be careful not to stand on their blue threads or you will be stung).

Although all shell collecting is seasonal and you cannot be sure of finding anything other than mussel shells, you can often find coloured fans, about the size of your thumb nail, or tiny 'corkscrew shells' which in Victorian times were sewn onto the edge of lace milk covers (a hole was made with a thick needle). The best place to look for shells that have just washed up is on the tide line but sometimes there are also shells in the shallow cusp depressions that are characteristic of this type of beach.

A fun activity for the kids is to make bugles out of kelp. Dry kelp fronds can always be found where there is loose sand, and these can be cut across the bulb to form a trumpet and then cut across the thin end to form a mouthpiece. A surprisingly satisfactory bugle noise can be produced by an expert. The fun comes to an end when the bugler's lips become too sore to blow. Remember that bugles, like trumpets, require a 'beep' with the lips and do not depend on mere blowing.

As you walk along the beach, you will notice that there are lines of dunes above the limit of the high tide. The important purpose of these dunes (marked (3) on the map) is explained on page 152.

The recommended turning point for this walk (4) is based on the issue of safety. For the first 2 km or so, there are generally plenty of other people about. Rather turn back if you find yourself alone here – particularly mid-week when there are few other walkers. It is generally very popular over weekends.

On the return journey you will be facing towards the mountain. To your right at (5) is an imposing gabled beach mansion called Vergenoeg, built in 1914 for Alpheus Williams, the General Manager of de Beers. This was designed by the famous architect Sir Herbert Baker. Baker was responsible for the revival of the vogue for old Cape Dutch architecture in southern Africa. Ahead, slightly to the left of the railway station on the mountain side, you can see what was once the palatial home of Count Labia. It was built in 1929 on the site of the British 'Fort' (6) of 1795, as the home of the Italian Legation. It is now the Natale Labia Museum. On the seashore rocks to the left of The Fort is the beach cottage of Sir Abe Bailey (7) (see pp 26 and 157), another early 20th-century mining magnate.

While you are walking back to the start, look at the profile of the surrounding mountains. You will see some interesting forms that relate to times when the sea level was very much higher than at present. At about 6 m above sea level, notice that there is a clearly defined flat area on the edge of all the mountain slopes. This is the remains of a prehistoric beach which was formed when the sea level was some 6 m higher than at present. The suburban railway line from False Bay to Simon's Town has been built on this terrace.

At 18 m above the present sea level is another prehistoric 'raised beach'. This is at the same level as the floor of the Fish Hoek valley, the ancient wave-cut terraces at Millers Point and, on the other side of the Peninsula, the Green Point Common and at Oudekraal (near Bakoven). At many places rounded 'beach' boulders can be found at this level on mountain slopes. Similar 'raised beaches' are found throughout the southern hemisphere and relate to growth and shrinkage of the northern hemisphere ice-sheets during the glacial or Pleistocene period of the last million years. Many of the prehistoric caves in the southern Cape relate to times when the sea was at a higher or lower level than at present (*see* pg 14).

When you've returned to the start, you may find interest in the small shops in the many old commercial areas of Muizenberg that sell a wide variety of curios, shells and interesting memorabilia.

WHAT ARE THE COASTAL DUNES FOR ?

You may have noticed that at many places on the coast (for example at Muizenberg, Fish Hoek, Hout Bay and Milnerton), great trouble has been taken to stabilise the first line of dunes on the shore and there are fences, irrigation systems and board walks to try to ensure that the dunes remain vegetated and protected. The reason for this work is that, under certain storm conditions, the sea may erode the first line of dunes. Unless these dunes are there, intact, and can supply the necessary bulk to withstand erosion by the stormy sea, the whole coastline will be permanently eroded and the high-tide line will move inland. (At Milnerton the high-tide line has been eroded by more than 70 m.)

You may then ask 'Why does one not protect these foredunes with a solid wall, so that they cannot be eroded?' The interesting answer is that, as soon as you build this type of solid protection against the sea, you increase the amount of turbulence which leads to a catastrophic increase in the problem. Unfortunately, many South African beaches and much of the coastline have already been unnecessarily and irrevocably lost in this way.

Along the Coast from Muizenberg to St James

Shells and Rock Pools

This delightful walk winds along the rocks past an ever-changing scene of seascapes, rock pools and small shelly beaches. It is one of the most beautiful walks in the Peninsula, particularly in the early morning, when there is generally very little wind.

USEFUL INFORMATION

DISTANCE: 1.5 km each way

TIME: About 1.5 hours

PARKING: From Atlantic Road, Muizenberg, turn towards sea at Beach Road, past shops, then turn sharp right. At the traffic circle keep straight on to the car park at Muizenberg Station

PUBLIC TRANSPORT: Train to Muizenberg Station

START: On lawn on seaward side of Muizenberg Station

ROUTE: Along paved pathway at water's edge to St James Station and back

TERRAIN: Paved

REFRESHMENTS: Shops at Beach Road, Muizenberg, and at St James Main Road

AMENITIES: Benches on path; toilets at Muizenberg Station and on St James beach

WEATHER: In shadow by late afternoon. Exposed to south-easter wind

SUITABLE FOR: Walkers of all ages, push- and wheelchairs

This coastal pathway was constructed from about 1985 as a result of an initiative and launching donation by a St James resident, Mr Mendel Kaplan. With sufficient funding it may eventually be extended by about 3 km to link to Fish Hoek beach.

Although this walk is chosen primarily for its outstanding natural beauty on the seaward side, it is also of considerable historical interest as it is only about 20 m from the Main Road, where there are 14 buildings that have been declared National Monuments. (A guide to these buildings is given in a booklet, *Historical Walk – Muizenberg to St James* published by the Civic Gallery of the Cape Town City Council.) Close to the walk there are also three museums: the Police Museum, Natale Labia Museum (an extension of the SA National Gallery) and Rhodes' Cottage Museum (which contains Cecil Rhodes memorabilia) (*see also* pg 75).

As you walk along this shoreline path, the scores of rock pools that you pass will tempt you to stop and marvel at the incredible beauty of marine life. The species variety is astonishing but is difficult to discern without some guidance how each interacts with the environment.

The principal factor here is a situation of a constantly changing water level. Marine biologists have identified three broad zones, which relate to how long the animals are submerged in the sea. In each quarter of the lunar day (6 hours, 12.5 minutes), the sea level changes from a condition of high to low tide. At the highest level, on rocks which are hardly ever submerged by the sea, there are tiny black snails known as the Knysna littorina. Further down, where the rocks are bared by the low tides, you will see thousands of barnacles. Most of these are the volcano (grey cones) and white barnacles, but among these are many other shellfish including granulate limpets (oval with tiny white granules texturing fine radiating ribs) and common winkles or topshells (about 15 mm diameter with mottled 'tabby' colouring) which feed on microscopic seaweeds.

About half way down the barnacle zone, at low tide, you will see that there is a band of seaweed. At this level the amount of animal life increases greatly. Here you can see pink-lipped topshells (rounded, dark purple-black up to about the size of a ping-pong ball) and long-spined limpets. At the lowest tide, which is almost halwas submerged, you can see a band of pear limpets (shaped like a pear) clinging to the rocks. Below the lowest tide are tufts of weed, as well as crabs, starfish, anemones and sponges in colours that defy description.

If you wait quietly and look carefully into the rock pools, you should also see the small fish which live in depth zones. In the shallowest pools, you are most likely to see the common goby, which is fairly dull coloured. In the deeper pools various species of klip-fish are common. Many of them have stripes and speckles which provide excellent camouflage among the rocks.

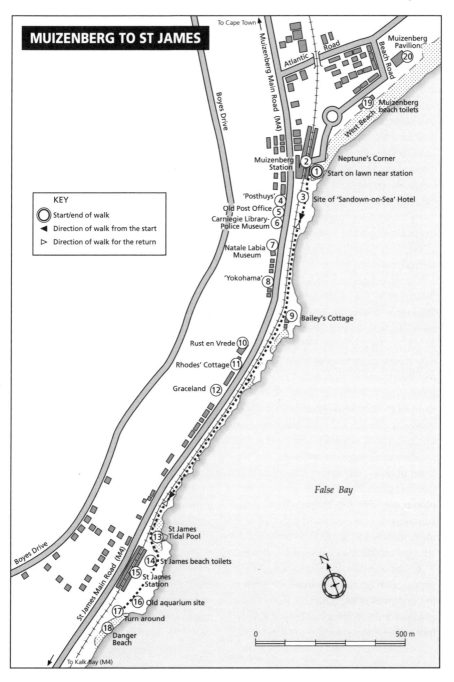

MUIZENBERG TO ST JAMES

To Cape Town

Muizenberg Pavilion

20

Atlantic Road

Muizenberg Main Road (M4)

Boyes Drive

Beach Road

19 Muizenberg beach toilets

West Beach

Muizenberg Station

2

1 Start on lawn near station

Neptune's Corner

KEY

⊙ Start/end of walk

◀ Direction of walk from the start

▷ Direction of walk for the return

'Posthuys' 4

Old Post Office 5

Carniegie Library- 6
Police Museum

3 Site of 'Sandown-on-Sea' Hotel

Natale Labia 7
Museum

'Yokohama' 8

9 Bailey's Cottage

Rust en Vrede 10

Rhodes' Cottage 11

Graceland 12

False Bay

St James 13
Tidal Pool

14 St James beach toilets

Boyes Drive

15 St James Station

16 Old aquarium site

St James Main Road (M4)

17 Turn around

18 Danger Beach

N

0   500 m

To Kalk Bay (M4)

Walk from Muizenberg to St James

From the lawn at the start **(1)**, the path winds towards the sea, skirting the remains of the Sandown-on-Sea Hotel **(3)** that once overlooked the beginning of spectacular Muizenberg beach. This hotel, whose bathrooms were plumbed with seawater, was so close to the sea that the spray from large breakers reached the windows. In 1789 the Dutch East India Company had used this site for a gunpowder magazine. In the early 1970s the hotel was converted to offices for the planning of Marina da Gama (*see* pg 127).

On the mountain side of the Main Road, to the left of Muizenberg Station **(2)**, is the 'Posthuys' **(4)** which was built for a Dutch East India Company garrison in about 1740. The garrison was tasked with intercepting farmers trading directly with ships in Simon's Bay at a time when the Dutch East India Company tried to tax all sales of wine and produce. Old maps show that there was a building here in 1673, the year before the completion of the Castle of Good Hope (*see* pg 31). From about 1790, during the period of the European Napoleonic wars, it was used by the Dutch as an observation post guarding against invasion, and was part of their defence in 1795 when British troops invaded the Cape and defeated them at the Battle of Muizenberg (1795) (*see* pg 148). The Posthuys, a single-storied thatched building with white walls and boarded windows, has been carefully restored to its original form by the Anglo-American Corporation. It is by far the oldest building on the False Bay coast.

South of the Posthuys is a gabled building **(5)** built in 1911 which, as Muizenberg's Post Office, was the first South African post office to receive airmail. On 27 December 1911, as a promotional venture intended to sell the idea of airmail postage, a South African aviator, Evelyn Driver, flew specially prepared postcards from Kenilworth Race Course to Muizenberg (flying time 7.5 minutes). The postmaster then cancelled the stamps for collectors. Earlier, in September 1911, Driver had been one of four pilots who inaugurated an airmail service between London and the royal residence at Windsor. Despite Driver's enthusiasm, the first official South African airmail service only started in 1929.

The next building to the left of the old Post Office is where a tollhouse stood from 1815 to 1884 **(6)**. The tollhouse had previously been located about 3 km to the south, on the seaward side of the Kalk Bay-Clovelly Main Road, where the house nearest Clovelly Station (*see* pg 168) now stands. In 1884 the tollhouse was moved again, to a building close to Zandvlei (*see* pg 127). Tolls, which were used to pay for road construction, were abolished in 1901. The finance for roads was then obtained by rates on property.

In 1909 the Carnegie Library was built on the site of the tollhouse. You can identify this building by its small cupola, or dome, on the roof. It was one of many libraries that the American steel millionaire Andrew Carnegie funded throughout the English-speaking world.

Muizenberg received a grant of £5 250, and Stellenbosch University has another Carnegie-endowed library. Until 1934, in a building behind the Carnegie Library, there was a detachment of the Cape Mounted Police. The library and Posthuys now house the Police Museum.

If you walk further along the coastal path you can see, on the southern side of the library, a large double-storey building (7) with an imposing entrance of stonework and columns. This is 'The Fort', once the premises of the Italian Legation and palatial home of Count and Countess Natale Labia. It was built in 1929 on the site of fortifications dating from the time of the First British Occupation of the Cape in 1795 (see pg 11). The Fort was donated to the SA National Gallery and is now known as the Natale Labia Museum. It is used as a cultural centre and houses an outstanding collection of art treasures.

Five houses after the museum is a long single-storied cottage (8) with a whitewashed walled-staircase in the middle. This home, named 'Yokohama', is distinctive in that it is made of papier-mâché. It was shipped here in sections from Japan in about 1900.

About 500 m from the start of the walk, the rocks widen on the seaward side of the coastal path and you will come to a small cottage (9) on your left, behind a fence. This is Bailey's Cottage, built for the guests of Sir Abe Bailey (see inset and pp 26 and 151). It now belongs to the state and has been used as a holiday home by members of the parliamentary cabinet. Bailey lived at Rust en Vrede (10), the large steep-gabled and red-tiled building that you can see on the other side of the Main Road, south of the cottage (9). This famous building, designed by Sir Herbert Baker, is considered by many to be one of this famous architect's most outstanding designs. The site was originally purchased by Cecil Rhodes (see pg 75) who commissioned Baker as follows: *'so that from the house and stoep the public road would be hidden, and there would be seen through white columns the fullest sweep of the blue sea and rhythm of white surf, and the two far-off mountain promontories which shelter*

SIR ABE BAILEY

Sir Abe Bailey (1864-1940) was a wealthy mining magnate and at various times a member of both the Cape and Transvaal parliaments. At the age of 20 he became extremely wealthy as a result of the gold rush at Barberton in 1884. After the discovery of gold on the Witwatersrand he moved to Johannesburg where he became a prominent figure in mining and on the Johannesburg Stock Exchange. He was a close friend of Cecil Rhodes and succeeded him as Member of Parliament for Barkly West (the district of Kimberley) from 1902 to 1905. He spent most of his later life in England where he was well known as a racehorse owner. Much of his wealth he left in trust to improving the relations between white races in South Africa.

the entrance to False Bay.' After the foundations were laid, the site was purchased by Bailey, who had it completed to its original design.

About 100 m on stands the small thatched cottage **(11)** where Rhodes died in 1902. On the south wall you can see where Rhodes had a small window installed to improve the ventilation. The cottage now houses a museum relating to Rhodes' life and is much as it was at the time of his death. His Cape cart, which is parked in the garage to the south, was a standard high-speed conveyance in South Africa in the days before the arrival of the railway and motor car. It has two very large wheels and was drawn by two horses.

Further along the walk at **(12)** is a Spanish-styled double-storied mansion with a green glazed-tile roof. This was built at the beginning of World War I for John Garlick who, in 1891, started the famous store 'Garlicks' in Adderley Street, Cape Town. Its original name 'Watergate' relates to a perennial spring that fed a horse drinking trough on the edge of the Main Road. In the 1980s it was renamed 'Graceland' after Elvis Presley's home in Memphis, Tennessee.

The path gently meanders along the coast and eventually comes to the St James tidal pool **(13)**, a delightful place for children. It was built in 1911 in response to the need for safe bathing and is backed by colourful bathing boxes which are rented to locals.

Examine the sand where the southern pool wall joins the beach – it is brownish-black here. If you study it carefully you will see that it is composed of a most surprising material – this is an ancient peat dating from a time when the sea was very much below the present level, and this part of the shore was covered in reeds and grass. Between 18 000 and 20 000 years ago the sea was about 130 m below its present level and the whole of the area now occupied by False Bay was dry land.

Beyond the bathing boxes and toilets **(14)**, on the sandy area above the rocks in front of St James Station **(15)**, is another interesting artefact – a mast from a sailing vessel that foundered on the coast more than 100 years ago. You can still see the hardwood and cast iron insets that were part of the rigging.

About 100 m further to the south is the site of the old St James aquarium and laboratory **(16)** which, from 1902 to 1936, was the centre of study in marine biological research at the Cape. The work was initiated by Dr John Gilchrist, a Scottish biologist, who is regarded as the father of South African marine biology. After his death in 1926 the research laboratories were moved to the beachfront at Sea Point (*see* pg 62), which were recently upgraded. St James aquarium was demolished in 1954 after it had stood vacant for many years.

The turning point for the walk is about 50 m ahead **(17)** at the beginning of Danger Beach **(18)** which is so named because bathing conditions are much less safe here than at the very flat beaches of nearby Muizenberg and Fish Hoek. On your return to the start take time to see what shells you can discover on the edges of the little beaches. You should find periwinkles, small fans, limpets and scores of others.

Boyes Drive

Bird's Eye View over False Bay

Boyes Drive is named after a resident magistrate at Simon's Town, C J Boyes who, in about 1917, motivated for its construction. Prior to it being built the area of Boyes Drive was a steep mountain slope with streams cascading down ravines towards the sea.

USEFUL INFORMATION

DISTANCE: Up to 2.5 km each way

TIME: About 2 hours for the whole distance

PARKING: Access Boyes Drive from Main Road (M4) at False Bay or Lakeside. Park your car on seaward side of Boyes Drive just south of the dip in the road, above Muizenberg. Here is a small green signboard on the mountain side of the road marked 'Peck's Valley'

START: On Boyes Drive above Camp Road

ROUTE: Along Boyes Drive from Muizenberg to Kalk Bay and back

TERRAIN: Paved

REFRESHMENTS: Take your own. Do not drink from mountain streams as water may be contaminated

AMENITIES: Benches en route

WEATHER: Fairly sheltered from wind. Best in the morning – shady in afternoon

SUITABLE FOR: Walkers of all ages, push- and wheelchairs

This walk is along the mountain road that overlooks Muizenberg, St James, Kalk Bay and the panorama of False Bay. As you look down on the crests of the breakers, particularly at the start, the view is quite spectacular.

C J Boyes, after whom the drive was named, was also largely responsible for persuading Parliament to finance construction of the Kalk Bay harbour in 1913. The estimated cost of the breakwater, quay, slipway and reclamation was £55 766. Boyes later became a judge in the Cape Supreme Court.

The construction of Boyes Drive was started by ex-servicemen returning from Europe at the end of World War I. Later, from 1920 to 1927, teams of convicts worked on the road and its many masonry walls under the supervision of armed guards. The site of the prison compound was at 'Petrava', a large house on the route of the walk.

Along the Main Road there were holiday houses belonging to wealthy mining magnates, industrialists and many of the most prominent people in the country. The road from Muizenberg to St James at that time was a 'millionaires' mile' and Kalk Bay was largely a village of fishermen. Long flights of steps linked the Main Road to the higher properties; these were extended to Boyes Drive when this road was constructed.

During the whale-watching months (from about the end of September to early November), Boyes Drive is an excellent vantage point to see the southern right whales in False Bay. Sometimes more than 50 have been seen at one time.

Boyes Drive Walk

At the start of the walk (1), on the sea side, you will see a line of steps marked 'Camp Road'. This relates to a British military convalescent camp that stood where you see the bowling greens below you, during the Anglo-Boer War (1899-1902). The camp did much to establish Muizenberg as the premier holiday resort in the country.

The name board 'Peck's Valley' (2) on the other side of the road refers to a famous inn called 'Farmer Peck's' that was built in Muizenberg Main Road in 1828 and traded there for 84 years. The sign-board outside the inn included the quaint verse and spelling: *'Lekkerkos as much as you please, Excelent beds Without any*

fleas'. In 1912 the inn was upgraded and renamed 'The Grand Hotel'.

About 50 m ahead you will suddenly see the spectacular panorama of False Bay. The white sands of Muizenberg beach below you stretch for about 40 km to Gordon's Bay where the mountains of the Hottentots Holland form a grey-blue curtain on the bay's eastern limits. At the end, the mountain ridge drops and runs on to the headland at Cape Hangklip. On the right, Cape Point, the furthest point on the western side of the bay, is just visible 28 km away. Seal Island is 11 km away in the direction of Gordon's Bay.

Muizenberg Station (3), with its distinctive, elegant Edwardian clock tower, is

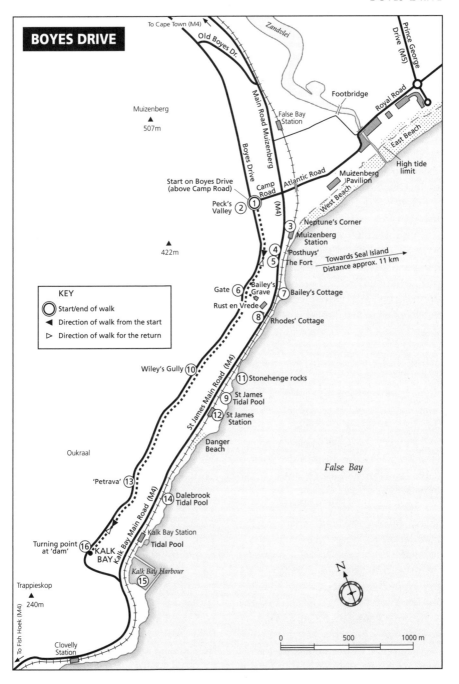

immediately below you. This building is an outstanding example of construction with brick and dressed stone, built in 1913 by stonemasons John and William Delbridge, who came to South Africa from Cornwall to assist in the construction of the Woodhead Reservoir on Table Mountain (see pg 115). William Delbridge lived in the stone-faced building immediately below you. John was the last Mayor of the Kalk Bay-Muizenberg Municipality before this area became incorporated in the City of Cape Town in 1913.

As you walk further up the hill you will have a clear view of four historic buildings just above the Main Road. (The walk on page 156 gives additional background on these buildings.) From left to right is the thatched-roofed 'Posthuys' (4), dating from about 1740 and one of the oldest buildings in South Africa; then there is a gabled-roofed building that was the first post office in South Africa to receive airmail; followed by the Carnegie Library with the small dome on top. Finally, on the right, is the light-red tiled roof with two chimneys of Count Labia's mansion, 'The Fort' (5). This is now the Natale Labia Museum, and houses works of art from the SA National Gallery.

Hidden by the bush, on the mountain slopes below you and further to the right, are several places where the Dutch East India Company's forces constructed 'breastworks' (low-level walls giving cover) for the defence of the Cape. In January 1795 the Dutch leader, William Prince of Orange, had fled to England when the French occupied the Netherlands and the Cape was threatened by the invasion from both French and English forces. On 14 July 1795 English troops landed at Simon's Bay and defeated the Company's forces at the Battle of Muizenberg (see pg 148).

As you walk further up the slight hill, on your left about 400 m from the start is a stone wall with a chained wrought iron gate (6). This leads down to the grave of Sir Abe Bailey, mining magnate (see pp 26, 151 and 157), whose high-gabled mansion, Rust en Vrede, can be seen just above the Main Road. His seaside guest cottage (7) is the thatched building on the coastal promontory below you. The next building to the south of Rust en Vrede is the thatched cottage where Cecil Rhodes died in 1902 (8) (see pp 75 and 158). This is now a museum relating to Rhodes' life. The Natale Labia Museum and Rhodes Museum and are accessed from the Main Road and are well worth a visit.

On your right you will pass a valley cut by a small stream where a sign-posted path leads up the mountain to the Silvermine Nature Reserve, an excellent area for more energetic hiking.

Shortly after reaching the crest of the hill there are good views of the St James coast with its tidal swimming pool (9) and colourful bathing boxes. You will pass a number of large dark green cedar trees, probably descendants of those planted at Kalk Bay's Holy Trinity Church (near Dalebrook tidal pool), which dates from 1873. At (10) the road crosses a deep ravine, known as Wiley's Gully, where it is supported by a high masonry retaining wall. Facing the sea, on the left of the gully, are terraces where in about 1900 fruit farming was attempted by a member of the well-known Wiley family.

On the mountain side of the road, at Wiley's Gully, a small path leads up the mountain to hiking paths. The valley above the road is known as St James Ravine.

If you look straight down towards the sea, left of St James' tidal pool **(9)** and the bathing boxes, you will see several large rocks about 40 m offshore of a promontory. These rocks and the large red-roofed house on the landward side (where there are distinctive palm trees) are known as 'Stonehenge' **(11)**. During World War II, General Smuts, South Africa's Prime Minister, arranged for the Greek Royal Family to live in exile in this house.

About 80 m beyond the bend at Wiley's Gully, on the slopes immediately below the road, you can just see the round base of a summer house, and, below it, a house once owned by the son of Charles Rudd (there is a single palm standing in the front of this garden). Charles Rudd was one of Cecil Rhodes' partners. In 1910, the year of the Union of South Africa's provinces, General Smuts and many other notables are said to have visited this home and were seen to be having tea on the lawn at the palm tree. Rudd had a private railway siding built in front of his house, to the left of the gabled St James Station **(12)** that you see below you.

The walk passes the signboards 'St James Road' and 'Jacob's Ladder' at the head of flights of steps from the Main Road. At the time Boyes Drive was built, it was decided that Jacob's Ladder should have 365 steps. This necessitated that the convicts should extend the steps beyond the road for a way up the mountain.

Its name refers to the biblical story of Jacob's dream of a stairway to heaven.

As you walk down the hill you pass some beautiful flowering gum trees and then the large house 'Petrava' **(13)**, where the convict camp stood. About 80 m away, up on the mountain, you may notice an extraordinary pipe standing 'in the middle of nowhere'. It is actually a flue from a pump station about half a kilometre away (near the Main Road), built in 1906 as a result of a court order brought by a Kalk Bay resident who objected to the pump station's smell.

As you look down towards the sea, Dalebrook tidal pool **(14)** is below you. Nearby, on the mountain side of the Main Road, is a thatched-roofed cottage, once the home of Sir John Molteno. He was the first Premier of the Cape Colony under 'responsible government' (1872).

To the right you can see the Kalk Bay harbour **(15)**, a colourful scene of fisherfolk, boats and restaurants (*see* page 167).

A short way further along Boyes Drive you will notice a small wall at the base of a waterfall on the mountain side. Before the construction of Boyes Drive there was a large dam here which supplied water to the Kalk Bay washhouses and to steam trains. Kalk Bay was 'the end of the line' from 1883 until 1890, when it was extended to Simon's Town. The site of the dam **(16)** is a convenient turning point for the walk.

Returning to the start you will enjoy an entirely different view looking towards the north. The vistas are outstanding. It is not surprising that Boyes Drive is the vantage point from which many postcards and tourist photographs are taken.

Kalk Bay Harbour and Clovelly

A Taste of the Old Cape

Kalk Bay was named by the Commander at the Cape, Simon van der Stel, during his exploration of False Bay in 1687. The name 'Kalk' ('lime' in Dutch) refers to the plentiful supply of black mussel shells on the beach that were converted to building lime by heating them in kilns that were situated on today's parking terrace above the harbour.

Kalk Bay harbour is a colourful part of ethnic Cape Town where the local fishing community gather when the boats come in – generally about lunch time, when it is also a good time to sample the excellent fish and chips sold at the cafeteria. This picturesque harbour also attracts artists, photographers and sightseers.

When Simon van der Stel became Commander of the Cape, one of his principal interests was to find an alternative to the anchorage in Table Bay, where the ships were vulnerable to winter storms. Simon's Bay was identified as offering suitable shelter (*see* pg 180). In 1743 a sea ferry was established between Kalk Bay and Simon's Town to avoid the difficulties in crossing the rivers and driftsands of the Fish Hoek and Glencairn valleys. The small rocky promontory, to the south of present-day Kalk Bay harbour, provided limited protection for small boats.

In 1803 a grant of land was made for a whale fishery at Kalk Bay. This became a highly profitable industry until about 1816 when there was a depletion in the population of whales and due to rival whaling activities based at Fish Hoek and Gordon's Bay.

In 1841 five plots were sold at Kalk Bay for the erection of 'marine villas' and the area quickly developed into a fashionable seaside resort for Capetonians. When a hotel was opened in 1851, the *Cape Monitor* described Kalk Bay as *'this salubrious and fashionable watering place – the Brighton of the Cape'*. By 1853, the village had become so popular that a daily horse-drawn coach service was operating from Wynberg to Kalk Bay.

By the mid-1850s fishing activities had greatly increased at Kalk Bay as a result of settlement by fishermen from the Philippine Islands, north of Australia, who had jumped ship at Simon's Town. They encouraged their countrymen to join them and a community of more than 100 Filipino families developed near the harbour. A Roman Catholic church was built close to today's St James railway station in 1858, largely in response to the needs of this community.

When the suburban railway line was extended from Wynberg to Kalk Bay in 1883, Kalk Bay became such a popular seaside destination that many of the well-to-do owners no longer saw it as an exclusive place and moved to other areas.

In 1911 a tidal pool and wooden bathing pavilion were constructed on the seaward side of the railway station. The popularity of Kalk Bay as a holiday destination at this time can be gauged from the fact that the tearoom could accommodate '700 people a day' and already there were several hotels in the area.

The breakwater, which was built from 1913 to 1919, was constructed using a technique called 'slice work', requiring a great deal of precision. The method is no longer used because there are now other more economical systems. Huge 10-tonne elaborately shaped concrete blocks were cast in Cape Town and sent to Kalk Bay by rail. At that time a railway spur ran to the Kalk Bay breakwater where there were two large steam cranes that lifted the blocks off the railway wagons. Each block was accurately positioned and keyed, like a jigsaw puzzle, to form part of the wall.

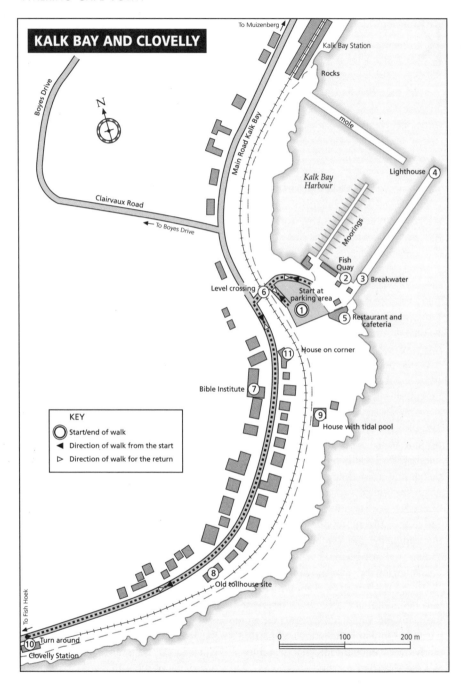

KALK BAY AND CLOVELLY

To Muizenberg

Kalk Bay Station

Rocks

Boyes Drive

mole

Main Road Kalk Bay

Lighthouse ④

Kalk Bay
Harbour

Clairvaux Road

← To Boyes Drive

Moorings

Fish
Quay

Level crossing ⑥

② ③ Breakwater

Start at
parking area
①

⑤ Restaurant and
cafeteria

House on corner

⑪

⑨ House with tidal pool

Bible Institute ⑦

KEY

⬭ Start/end of walk

◄ Direction of walk from the start

▷ Direction of walk for the return

⑧ Old tollhouse site

To Fish Hoek

0   100   200 m

⑩ Turn around
Clovelly Station

During World War I, guns and submarine nets were railed to Kalk Bay harbour, lifted by the construction cranes onto lighters (barges) and then towed to Simon's Town. This was because there was no link between the suburban railway line and the Simon's Town naval dockyard.

The Kalk Bay harbour mole, extending from near the railway station towards the breakwater, was built between 1930 and 1945. This greatly improved the mooring conditions by restricting the amount of wave energy entering the harbour.

Kalk Bay Harbour Walk

From the parking area (1) walk down to the corner of the harbour quay at (2) where the breakwater (3) starts. If you have arrived at about midday, boats are likely to be coming in from Rocky Bank and other fishing grounds off Cape Point, where they have been fishing with handlines. At this corner there are concrete fish-cleaning tables where, as the fish are off-loaded and sold, a group of women gut and fillet them to order – an incredible display of knife-work – but certainly not for the fainthearted. Wallowing in the murky water nearby is often a huge seal that has arrived for lunch. With little encouragement it demonstrates an ability to climb up the great concrete steps on its flippers to take bits of fish that onlookers throw to it. You can buy a variety of fresh fish here at extraordinarily low prices – yellowtail, snoek, red roman and many others, depending on the season and weather.

Along the breakwater, a crowd of patient enthusiasts fish at all hours of the day and night, depending on the weather. On warm evenings and particularly over weekends this place doubles as a 'beer garden' for the locals.

If the sea is calm, walk to the small lighthouse (4) at the end of the breakwater. Around midday, you could see fishing boats, each with a crew of about 10 weather-etched men, strung across the bay to the horizon. The fleet usually goes out at about 4 o'clock in the morning.

If the sea is rough and there is high wind the boats approach the harbour entrance with extreme caution because at this moment they are exposed to potential 'broaching' – a dangerous situation in which the vessels are broadside to the waves. There are times when wind and waves close this harbour and locals remember tragedies when boats have not cleared the entrance and have been swept onto the rocks near the railway station. Periodically, storm waves occurring at high tide come right over the breakwater, hit the boats moored inside the harbour and damage inner harbour structures. Do not venture onto the breakwater if there are high winds or waves.

Retracing your steps to the fish-tables you are now probably ready to sample the fish and chips sold at the harbour cafeteria (5). If the weather is fine sit on one of the benches in the sun while gulls swoop overhead and hover as close as they dare. If you thought that gulls were nice to each other you will soon discover otherwise for they squawk, peck and demonstrate a full range of bad manners. From the end of winter to the beginning of summer you may also be lucky to see whales about 500 m away in the ocean.

Walk to Clovelly Station

When you are ready for the walk to Clovelly Station **(10)**, retrace your steps to the car park **(1)**, cross the railway line at the level crossing **(6)** on foot and then, at the Main Road, turn left. This part of the walk can be as long as you like. The road takes you to Clovelly Station, about 1 km away, or, if you wish to walk further, Fish Hoek is some 3 km further on. Once you are round the corner past Kalk Bay the road is high above the sea and the views are excellent. There may be whales in Fish Hoek bay, most likely southern right whales, which are distinctive in having no dorsal (back) fin or throat grooves. They are migratory and in early summer they move about 2 000 km south towards Antarctica to feed. They were named 'right' because whalers found them easy to hunt and they float after being harpooned. Fortunately, these whales have been protected since 1935.

Clovelly Station is so close to the water's edge that there are notices forbidding fishing from the platform! Since the bridge over the line became corroded and had to be demolished, the train only stops here when it is northbound.

On your return journey, look out for Victorian houses with 'carpenter's lace' woodwork, dating from times when Kalk Bay was a prestigious seaside resort. On the sea side of the road, the first house you come to from the Clovelly side, is the site of the tollhouse **(8)**, where until 1815 travellers proceeding to Simon's Town had to pay for the use of the road.

Closer to the harbour, on the mountain side, is the Bible Institute **(7)**, where students come for residential Bible study courses from many parts of southern Africa. The last house before the harbour, on the sea side, is a ship-shaped home **(11)** which has been continuously under renovation for over 40 years. Behind this, on the sea side of the railway line at **(9)**, is one of the few buildings on the coast that have water frontage and a private tidal pool. It pre-dates the Seashore Act that now makes such ownership impossible.

Returning to the harbour you will see that the parking terrace is at more or less the same level as the railway. It is the remains of a beach surface when the sea was at a much higher level. Stone implements, found in the vicinity of the parking area, date from the Middle to Late Stone Age. Near the railway line the remains of kitchen-middens from the dinners of hunter-gatherers that pre-date colonisation of the Cape have been found.

Fish Hoek Beach and the 'Catwalk'

The Jewel of False Bay

Fish Hoek is a popular residential suburb with a strong community identity. Its beach walks are part of its social fabric where many locals meet their friends. The town has unique features that include numerous clubs, a ban on bottle stores, more than 20 churches, and one of the safest of bathing beaches in the Peninsula. A significant number of retired people and families with children live here.

The area which is now Fish Hoek was relevant from the very beginning of the Dutch settlement at the Cape. Jan van Riebeeck's Journal recorded on 5 August 1659 that a corporal *'came upon an encampment of three reed huts, where there were 18 able-bodied men in addition to approximately the same number of women and children. He heard them beating out assegais, and would have taken them by surprise, had their dogs not begun to bark – they leapt out from the back of their huts in great astonishment, completely naked and without even skins to clothe their bodies.'* At that time Fish Hoek was reportedly an 18-hour journey from Table Bay, where visiting sailing ships moored in open water between Robben Island and the shore.

In 1687, because the Table Bay moorings for ships were dangerously exposed to northerly winds and many ships had been wrecked (*see* pg 47), Commander Simon van der Stel investigated alternative moorings in False Bay. He confirmed the suitability of the anchorage at Ysselsteijn's Bay, which became known as Simon's Bay (*see* pg 180).

In that same year, in response to a petition, Van der Stel granted the free burghers and settlers the right to free fishing in False Bay, and the area of Visch Hoek (literally 'Fish Corner') soon became prominent for fishing and whaling. A report dated 1740 mentions that two donkeys were kept at Fish Hoek to convey a regular supply of fish to the Castle for the Governor's table.

With ships mooring in Simon's Bay the road that passed through Fish Hoek from Table Bay became an important route for supplies. At that time it crossed through the back of the Kalk Bay Mountain to avoid the quicksands on the Silvermine River near the beach.

The whole beach area that lies to the east of the suburban railway line was originally a large dune-field. The Silvermine River, which is now constrained to crossing the beach near Clovelly to the north, used to meander between the dunes and at times broke out as far south as the car park near the starting point for the walks.

Beach Walk towards Clovelly

From the start from the popular beach restaurant (1), walk northwards along the paved pathway in the direction of Clovelly. On your left, after a line of colourful bathing boxes (3) which are rented out by the Municipality, is the Surf Lifesaving Clubhouse and an observation tower. The walkway ends at a miniature lighthouse (4), after which you walk on the sandy beach for about 800 m before reaching the Silvermine River (5). The boardwalks and small fences on your left have been built to protect the dunes from being damaged by pedestrians. Selected dune grasses and other salt-tolerant vegetation has been planted to stabilise the dunes so that they can provide a reserve of sand when winter storms erode the beach.

This beach has become so popular that it has become necessary to designate different areas for swimming, boat

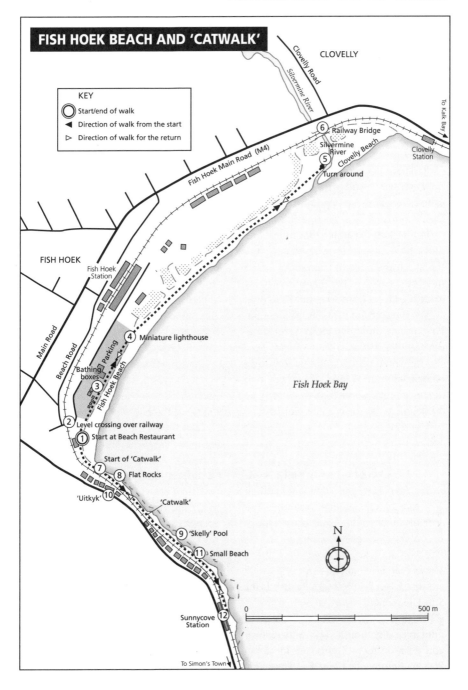

FISH HOEK BEACH AND 'CATWALK'

CLOVELLY

Clovelly Road

Silvermine River

To Kalk Bay

KEY

◯ Start/end of walk

◀ Direction of walk from the start

▷ Direction of walk for the return

⑥ Railway Bridge
Silvermine River
⑤ Turn around

Clovelly Beach

Clovelly Station

Fish Hoek Main Road (M4)

FISH HOEK

Fish Hoek Station

Main Road

Beach Road

Parking

④ Miniature lighthouse

Fish Hoek Beach

Bathing boxes

③

② Level crossing over railway

① Start at Beach Restaurant

Start of 'Catwalk'

⑦ ⑧ Flat Rocks

'Uitkyk' ⑩

'Catwalk'

⑨ 'Skelly' Pool

⑪ Small Beach

Fish Hoek Bay

N

0   500 m

Sunnycove Station ⑫

To Simon's Town

171

launching and board sailing. Swimming is not recommended in the Silvermine River or in the two stormwater streams that cross the beach in the winter as the water may be contaminated. Although quicksand conditions used to be a problem at the railway bridge **(6)** crossing the Silvermine River, and there is still a warning, it does not appear to have occurred here for many years.

At all times of the year you are likely to find cuttlefish, sponges, shark's eggs and kelp fronds washed up on the tideline on Fish Hoek beach. There are few shells here other than white sand mussels and black mussels from rocks on the sides of the bay. At the Silvermine River you may be lucky to find small brightly coloured or white fan shells, particularly high up on the dry, loose sand area, where they are blown by the wind. After strong winter storms, piles of kelp and redbait are often strewn along the length of the beach. This material is cleared by the Municipality before it begins to rot.

The Silvermine River is the turning point of this walk. On your way back, you can see some of the historical features of this area. At the Simon's Town end of the beach, and slightly to your left behind the railway line, are two low buildings with gables. These are 'Uitkyk East' and 'Uitkyk West' **(10)**, which were once part of the whaling stations that operated from here around 1687. Originally there were three cottages, built of mud and stone, which formed part of a lookout post. They were converted to two homes in 1918 by the Mossop family who owned the Tannery on the Liesbeek River in Rondebosch. Their building operations at Uitkyk were delayed by the devastating Spanish influenza epidemic that swept across the world in that year. Worldwide, more than 30 million people died.

The original farm homestead of Fish Hoek, and other buildings which date from about 1710, stood to the west of Uitkyk and immediately behind the railway subway at the end of the beach. The homestead was damaged in a fire in the early 1950s and was later demolished. The old Homestead Hotel, now a women's residence for the SA Navy 'swans', is near the railway level crossing **(2)** at the entrance to the beach.

As you pass the bathing boxes **(3)**, you are in the area where Col. Fletcher Smith Baden-Powell, brother of the founder of the Boy Scouts Movement, experimented with man-carrying kites in 1900. He was in charge of the British Army's Balloon Section during the Anglo-Boer War.

Walk Along 'Catwalk'

Start your stroll along the 'Catwalk' (officially 'The Jager Walk' after an early Mayor of Fish Hoek) at the beach restaurant **(1)** and head towards the mountain. About 150 m from the start at **(8)** you come to some low flat rocks at the water's edge, where whales were once flensed. There were large pots for boiling whale oil at the 'Uitkyk' buildings **(10)** on the other side of the railway line.

When whaling started in Fish Hoek Bay in the 1700s about 40 southern right whales were harpooned in a typical season. British Naval records of 1825 mention that there were whaling stations at Fish Hoek, Kalk Bay and Gordon's Bay, but that the whalers could barely cover costs with fewer than four whales killed at each station in a year. At one time, there were virtually no whales in False Bay. Today it is heartening that, with an international whaling ban, the whales have returned and on many days, from about August to November, more than 50 can again be seen in the bay.

As you stroll along the Catwalk you will see several structures from much earlier times. About 75 m beyond the flensing rocks there are the remains of a stairway leading into the sea in front of a curious open shed now used as a changing room. At several places on the route there are the remains of cast iron winching rings set into the rocks.

Many of the rock pools along this walk have descriptive local names. There is 'Canoe Harbour' (just in front of the next railway subway) and then, as the path winds further over the rocks, you will pass the 'Skelly' pool **(9)** (after a rock resembling a skeleton). Beyond 'Skelly' you will come to a very small beach (about the size of a blanket) at **(11)** where at low tide you can find tiny shells. The path then rises up past huge granite boulders to the level of the railway line at Sunnycove Station **(12)**,

which is the turning point. As you return along the Catwalk examine the granite rocks at the water's edge. These are of a coarse granite with particularly large milky white feldspar crystals and are of the same formation that occurs at Sea Point and other parts of the Peninsula. When these rocks were formed about 540 million years ago the granite was molten and it was brought towards the surface under great pressure. Another distinctive geological feature of the area is a 'fault' or vertical break in the underground rocks that runs through the whole length of the Fish Hoek valley.

As you walk back to the start, visualise the scene in about 1918 when the first plots in Fish Hoek were sub-divided as a township. At this time, the beach and foreshore were covered in dunes and a broad swath of sand connected the beach to the hills behind. (A small white patch of sand is still visible on the high ground in the middle of the valley.) In 1918 there were fewer than a dozen houses in the village. If you are interested in the history of this area, take a look at the very old photographs displayed at the restaurant near the start.

Fish Hoek is now one of the most attractive suburbs in the Peninsula. The friendliness of its residents, the tranquillity of the beach scene and its safe bathing, and the manner in which the town has developed with a strong community spirit are all evident as you enjoy these two beach walks. Fish Hoek is a place where you are still likely to be greeted by passersby.

Peers Cave

Walk in the Footsteps of Prehistoric Man

A visit to Peers Cave is a fascinating outing. Here an incredible time warp links the use of the cave by prehistoric man to the present, and archeologists are confident that it has been occupied for at least 100 000 years. Little is known of what its original inhabitants looked like but, from artefacts found here, it is clear that they used stone implements and lived largely on what they could find along the seashore.

This is not an easy walk and should only be attempted by fit adults and children. In several places you will need plenty of energy to get up the steep, sandy paths and to scramble over the rocks. But you will, nevertheless, find this a very satisfying expedition and be rewarded by the wonderful view across the Fish Hoek valley.

In 1928 Fish Hoek residents Victor Peers and his son, Bertie, investigated this cave and, in addition to a finding a large number of stone implements, they unearthed a skull which has been dated to between 10 000 and 12 000 years old. At that time parts of Europe were still covered by the glaciers of the last Ice Age. The skull, which has some San (Bushman) characteristics, relates to a people who were ancestral to the hunters and gatherers who were living at the Cape when Jan van Riebeeck arrived.

At a higher level, in the soil filling of the cave floor, two, more recent skeletons have been found, with features which suggest they are from a Khoisan-type of people. These bones are now in the South African Museum, but for reasons of sensitivity skeletons are no longer displayed.

About 60 m to the west of Peers Cave, towards Kommetjie, there is another rock shelter known as Tunnel Cave from where you can look out towards the Silvermine valley to the north. A large number of stone implements were found here during an archaeological dig in 1942.

Prehistoric stone flakes and scrapers, for flensing skins, are still found around Peers Cave and hand-axes have been found at the foot of nearby Peers Hill. These rock shelters clearly provided a remarkably safe home for their Stone-Age occupants who were able to collect shellfish from the nearby coastal rocks and to catch fish in tidal fish traps built of rocks placed across suitable gullies. One of these was in the rocks near the start of Kommetjie beach. The cave's occupants also ate plants and caught small antelope and tortoises.

The stone tools found near Peers Cave are made of hard and durable rocks such as silcrete, quartzite and quartz, which do not occur in the vicinity. They have been brought from places where the rock is much harder, such as from the Tygerberg, near Bellville. It is clear that implements were made near Peers Cave because 'cores' (which are the remains of the lumps of raw material after the implements have been flaked off) and loose flakes are found in this area.

Peers Cave Walk

Be sure that you are prepared for this walk. Wear closed shoes as you will be walking across the dunes and up a sandy path. Take hats and water in summer, choose a day when there is no chance of strong wind (you do not want to be sand-blasted) and allow enough time to enjoy the walk. If you have small children with you, ensure that they stay with your party

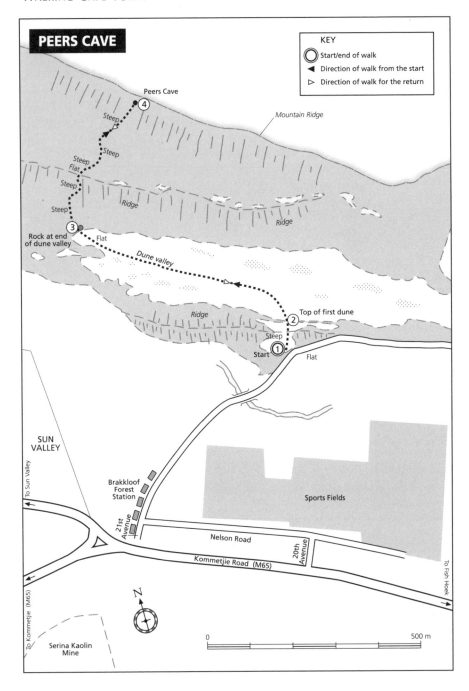

PEERS CAVE

KEY
- ⭕ Start/end of walk
- ◄ Direction of walk from the start
- ▷ Direction of walk for the return

Peers Cave

④

Steep

Mountain Ridge

Steep

Steep
Flat

Steep

Steep

Ridge

Steep

③
Rock at end
of dune valley

Flat

Dune valley

Ridge

Top of first dune

②

Steep

Start ①

Flat

SUN
VALLEY

To Sun Valley

Brakkloof
Forest
Station

21st Avenue

Sports Fields

Nelson Road

20th Avenue

Kommetjie Road (M65)

To Kommetjie (M65)

To Fish Hoek

N

Serina Kaolin
Mine

0   500 m

as it is easy to get lost on the winding path up the mountain.

From the start **(1)**, walk up the steep dune **(2)** ahead of you and look out across the valley in the sand dunes. You will be able to see the dark mouth of the cave near the top of the mountain, about a kilometre away, almost due north at **(4)**. Above the cave on the mountain ridge there is a distinctive survey beacon with a metal vane.

Before you cross the valley to the cave, take note of your starting position in relation to landmarks on the other side of the valley. This will simplify your return later. A useful marker is the white sandy path on the mountain immediately in front of you.

For the next stage of the walk, cross the sand dune valley to a large rock **(3)** on the other side, about 500 m away. From the first dune you are too far away to see it clearly, so just head towards the bush on your far left (west) at the end of the valley, as shown on the map.

As you cross the valley floor to the 'marker' rock you will be walking on a hard layer of dark brown soil. This colour is due to the presence of manganese which occurs as a mineral deposit in the surrounding mountains. It has been mined on the slopes above Chapman's Peak Drive, near Hout Bay (*see* pg 120).

When you reach the rock at **(3)** you will find a painted notice 'Peers Cave' and an arrow showing the route to the left. From here take the steep sandy path up to the cave. You will cross a second dune area on the slopes which is used by local children for sand tobogganing.

Although there are many routes up to the cave it is easiest to take the main path which is clear all the way. Avoid short-cuts as some of these are very steep and your action may lead to soil erosion. Along the path follow the arrows that will eventually bring you to the mouth of the cave, high above the valley. On the way up there are many places where you can stop, take a breather and enjoy the view.

The cave is large enough to accommodate several dozen people. In 1652, when Van Riebeeck's party arrived at the Cape, it was still occupied by Khoi hunter-gatherers. At that time elephant, lion, many types of antelope, hippo, leopard and baboon roamed the Peninsula and this cave would have provided an ideal protection from the animals and the north-west wind and rain. Van Riebeeck's Journal indicates that there was intense rivalry between different local groups of Khoi, so the cave's commanding position would have been important.

On the floor of the cave you will notice shells that are remains of dinners of previous occupants, and the ground is black from the fires of these people, decomposed organic material and manganese soil. Do not remove or deface anything – this is part of our unique heritage and is protected by the National Monuments Act.

From here there are clear views towards the coast at Fish Hoek on the extreme left (east) of the valley, towards Kommetjie (near the present-day lighthouse on the right) and to Noordhoek on the extreme right.

Long before its investigation by Victor Peers and his son this cave was known as 'Skildergat' ('Painters Cavern') because there were rock paintings here. If you look carefully high up on the wall at the entrance, you can distinguish a series of human hands painted in yellow and reddish-yellow ochre. There are also several mysterious lines and comb-shaped signs that have been painted in light red.

As you look out towards the south it is easy to visualise prehistoric times when this cave was occupied by primitive man. A changing world climate has periodically resulted in large changes in sea level and there have been times when the sea filled the valley and part of the Peninsula to the south of Fish Hoek was an island. At other times, when the sea level dropped, the shore would have been far seawards of its present position.

* 5 000 years ago the sea level was about 3 m above the present level
* 20 000 years ago it was about 130 m below the present level
* 125 000 years ago the sea was about 12 m above the present level and much of the Fish Hoek valley was flooded

On your way back to the start, notice the changes in the vegetation. As you walk down the hill, you will move through fynbos on the higher slopes to an area of dense bush where the sand dunes start. This bush is composed mainly of acacias, or wattles, which were introduced to the Cape Peninsula from Australia in about 1835, to combat soil erosion. This alien vegetation has become a serious problem as it easily invades and supplants the fynbos. One of the most common wattles here is rooikrans (*Acacia cyclops*) which has seeds with a small red surround and golden ball-shaped flowers. The two other common wattles in the Cape Peninsula are Port Jackson, with lemon ball-shaped flowers; and the long leafed wattle (*Acacia longifolia*), which is characterised by brown galls on the stems that have formed in response to attack by wasp larvae. These have been recently introduced as a biological control.

If you are interested in Stone Age implements you should visit the display at the SA Museum near the Dutch East India Company Gardens in Cape Town (*see* pp 4 and 27). Some are shaped like small leaves with markings where stone flakes were knocked off. The oldest implements are the largest, some about the size of your fist.

After your walk, if you are interested in examining the fish trap in the rocks at Kommetjie, continue west along the Kommetjie Road (M65) to the village of Kommetjie. Seawards of Beach Road (near the post office) is the large rock pool where prehistoric man caught fish in a dam that was filled by the high tide. This is a good place to relax and reflect on man's occupation of this area for many thousands of years.

Simon's Town

Historical Harbour Town

Simon's Bay, which is seawards of this walk, was initially named Ysselsteijn Bay, after a Dutch vessel with that name had found storm refuge there in 1671. Sixteen years later it was renamed 'Simon's Bay' after the Commander at the Cape, Simon van der Stel, had identified its potential as a natural harbour.

In 1741, after suffering repeated shipwreck and damage to vessels moored in Table Bay during winter storms, the Dutch East India Company resolved that their trading fleets must use Simon's Bay as their winter anchorage between 15 May and 15 August. Two year's later, guidelines for the construction of a naval station and hospital at Simon's Bay were then provided when Baron van Imhoff, Governor-General of the Dutch East Indies, visited the Cape.

On 1 July 1795 a British naval squadron anchored in Simon's Bay. The British disembarked troops on the beach and on 7 August, moved along the coast to Muizenberg, where there were minor skirmishes. The Dutch surrendered and the British troops took over control of the Cape in what is known as the First British Occupation (*see* pg 148).

The British occupied the Cape for several years, but under the Treaty of Amiens they were obliged to hand the colony back to the Dutch forces, which were under control of the revolutionary Batavian Republic in the Netherlands.

In 1806 British forces re-invaded the Cape at the Battle of Blouberg (*see* pg 72). (They avoided Simon's Town as the Dutch had fortified its approaches.) In 1813, after seven years of unsatisfactory use of Table Bay, the British decided to establish a base for the Royal Navy at Simon's Town. The move brought great prosperity to the town and many buildings were constructed which still remain today.

In 1815 Napoleon was defeated at the Battle of Waterloo and was exiled on the Island of St Helena in the mid-Atlantic. Simon's Town was a convenient supply base and local merchants benefited greatly.

During much of the 19th century, Simon's Town was also the base for Royal Naval vessels intercepting slave trading on the African coasts. Between 1806 and 1816, 27 French and Portuguese ships were intercepted around the Cape and their cargoes of over 2 000 slaves were forfeited to the Crown. (Britain had abolished the slave trade in its Empire in 1807, but it was only in 1834 that the slaves were freed at the Cape.)

From 1899, during the Anglo-Boer War, Simon's Town and Cape Town became the chief ports of entry for the British forces and supplies. In 1902, the last year of the war, construction of Simon's Town East Dockyard (also known as the Selbourne Dock) commenced. It was opened in 1910 and was an important repair and replenishment facility for Royal Navy vessels in World War I.

During World War II Simon's Town was a closed security area. The dockyard repaired ships damaged in protecting the 'Cape Route' and thousands of troops visited the Peninsula.

In April 1957 Simon's Town Dockyard was handed back to the South African Navy by the British Royal Navy. Since this time the dockyard has been substantially modified to accommodate submarines and to undertake the refitting of modern naval vessels. Despite the changes the town retains much of its 19th century character and it still has many links with its Dutch East India Company and Royal Naval past.

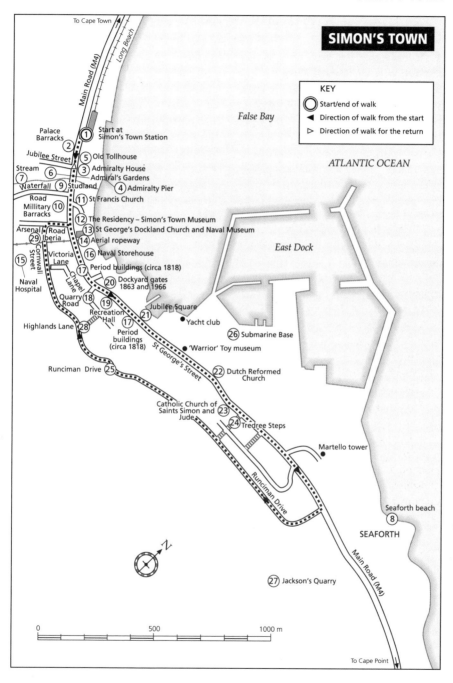

SIMON'S TOWN

KEY
- ◯ Start/end of walk
- ◀ Direction of walk from the start
- ▷ Direction of walk for the return

To Cape Town

Main Road (M4)

Long Beach

False Bay

ATLANTIC OCEAN

Palace Barracks
① Start at Simon's Town Station
②
Jubilee Street
⑤ Old Tollhouse
Stream
⑦
⑥
③ Admiralty House
Waterfall ⑨ Studland
② Admiral's Gardens
④ Admiralty Pier
Road Millitary Barracks ⑩
⑪ St Francis Church
⑫ The Residency – Simon's Town Museum
Arsenal Road ⑬ St George's Dockland Church and Naval Museum
⑭ Aerial ropeway
② Iberia
⑯ Naval Storehouse
Victoria Lane
⑰ Period buildings (circa 1818)
Cornwall Street
⑮
Chapel Lane
② Dockyard gates 1863 and 1966
Naval Hospital
Quarry Road ⑱ ⑲
Recreation Hall ⑰
② Jubilee Square
Highlands Lane ②
Period buildings (circa 1818)
● Yacht club

East Dock

② Submarine Base
Runciman Drive ②
St George's Street
● 'Warrior' Toy museum
② Dutch Reformed Church
Catholic Church of Saints Simon and Jude ②
② Tredree Steps

Runciman Drive

● Martello tower

Seaforth beach
⑧
SEAFORTH

② Jackson's Quarry

N

0   500   1000 m

To Cape Point

Simon's Town Walk

From the start at Simon's Town Station (1), walk southwards along the sea side of the main road (St George's Street). On the opposite side of the road notice the building with the large semi-circular gable called the Palace Barracks (2), owned by John Osmond from 1813 to 1847. During the First British Occupation of the Cape, he was in charge of ship repair at Simon's Town. When the British left in 1803, he set up his own repair yard and acquired enormous areas of land, subsequently bought from him in 1813 by the Royal Navy after they returned to the Cape in the Second Occupation. As a result of his wealth Osmond became known locally as 'King John' and his house was called 'The Palace'. This property has served many military functions and was used as a hospital during the Anglo-Boer War (1899–1902).

On your left, behind the stone wall, lies Admiralty House (3) which dates from the time of the Dutch East India Company. After the arrival of the Royal Navy in 1813 it became the home of the Commander-in-Chief of the naval base.

On the seaward side of Admiralty House is Admiralty Pier (4) from where the Commander-in-Chief started on his inspections of the fleet in the roadstead. The pier was constructed of stone and timber beams in 1871 and replaced an earlier structur, built in 1828.

Until 1904 there was a tollhouse (5) near the gates of Admiralty House. Tolls, which were used for road upkeep, became impractical to implement when motor cars were introduced.

Looking up towards the mountain you will notice a steep cliff behind the Admiral's Gardens (6). In winter a water-fall – part of the perennial stream (7) flowing from the Klaver Plateau – can be seen here. This stream has played an important part in the development of the town as, besides fresh produce, fresh water was one of the essential require-ments of visiting ships. The Dutch East India Company had vegetable gardens above Seaforth beach (8), to the south of the dockyard and at Oatlands, near present-day Froggy Pond.

On your right, just before you pass Waterfall Road, are three old buildings which have been declared National Monuments. The building with the rec-tangular gable and pergola (on the south side of the stream) is Studland (9), built as a winehouse to attract the sailors away from the main landing jetty that had developed into an area of drunken layabouts. Behind the old semi-detached houses (called 'Yarra-Yarra') on the corner is an old brewery, linked to Studland and dating from before 1845.

The military barracks (10) are on the other side of Waterfall Road. These were built on the site of the Dutch East India Company's hospital which stood here from 1765 to 1815.

Further along St George's Street is a long curved brick wall on your left, which forms a boundary to the naval dockyard. On the seaward side of the wall are many buildings relating to the very early history of the town, which now form part of the West Dockyard.

St Francis Church **(11)** is first on your left. This is the oldest Anglican church in South Africa and dates from 1837. It was named to compliment Lady Frances Cole (sic) who was an early church fundraiser. The first church to be built in Simon's Town was the Wesleyan (Methodist) Chapel, off Quarry Road **(18)** further along the walk.

The next building on your left is the Residency **(12)**, now home to the Simon's Town Museum. It is one of the oldest structures in the town and was built in 1772. A contemporary writer described it as 'another large and handsome house for the accommodation of the Governor when he chooses to retire thither for his pleasure'. The main living area was on the middle floor, which now houses the museum. Slaves lived in the basement and the attic was for stores. This building has been used for many purposes including offices, a customs house, gaol (until 1942) and a school. The Magistrate's Court was located here until 1979.

The Anglican St George's Dockland Church **(13)**, with its prominent clock tower, is two buildings further on. The church has been housed in an old sail loft since 1825, after two earlier places of worship had collapsed. The Naval Museum is at the back of this building.

Close to the clock tower is the first of a line of pylons leading up the mountain. These are the remains of an aerial ropeway **(14)** that operated here from 1904 to about 1932. It was built to carry people and supplies to the Naval Hospital **(15),** just above Runciman Drive, and to a naval sanatorium and a shooting range at the top of the hill. The journey from the dockyard to the top of the ropeway took about 15 minutes.

The next building on your left is the enormous Naval Storehouse **(16)** that was built by the Dutch East India Company and later modified by the Royal Navy. Construction started in 1743 and took 25 years to complete. It is some 135 m long – well over the length of a rugby field – and is still used as a store and as the SA Navy's Diving Centre. This building was once the hub of the town's naval activity.

On the opposite side of St George's Street is a Shell Garage where once there were stables. The next building is the Lord Nelson Inn. You will notice that there are rows of period buildings **(17)**, circa 1818, where the building names, window styles and architecture are reminiscent of an old English sea port. The British Hotel was the scene of a spectacular banquet hosted by Cecil Rhodes (*see* pg 75) to mark the arrival of the railway from Cape Town to Simon's Town in December 1890.

Further to the south you will pass Quarry Road **(18)**, once called Chapel Hill Road because it led to the Wesleyan Chapel. The Recreation Hall **(19)**, at the corner, used to be the assembling point for animals that were to be taken aboard calling vessels. In 1808 this land was used as a cooperage making wooden casks and barrels for packing salted beef, pork, pickled vegetables and liquids. It was then used as a recreational facility from 1834 to about 1957, and was once called the 'Africa Station Club'. Since 1986 it has been used as a reference library and offices.

On your left you pass two sets of imposing dockyard gates **(20)** which are elegantly monogrammed in wrought iron – VR 1863 and RSA 1966.

The walk now passes Jubilee Square **(21)**, originally called Market Square and the hub of everyday activity of early Simon's Town. Today it is a tourist spot with restaurants and curio shops. A statue of Just Nuisance, the celebrated Great Dane that caught the interest of visiting troops during World War II, is the focal point of the square. The jubilee that is commemorated is the 25th Anniversary of King George V in 1935, when local school children planted the line of 11 palm trees along St George's Street.

Continuing past the square, you will find the Dutch Reformed Church **(22)** on the left, where the music for South Africa's old National Anthem, *Die Stem van Suid-Afrika*, was written by the minister, Rev M L de Villiers.

Carry on past the old East Yard Gate and bell tower until you come to the Catholic Church of Saints Simon and Jude **(23)** on the right, dating from 1885. A church record from 1887 commented: *'much drunkenness and immorality as usual in a seaport town. Besides the civilian congregation there has been a number of soldiers and sailors attending church here. The number has varied from 6 to 58!'* In the dockyard wall on your left you can see an old cast iron postbox emblazoned with the monarch's monogram, ER VII.

Just before the Caltex garage, cross the road and climb the Tredree Steps **(24)** leading up to Runciman Drive **(25)**. From here you will have an excellent view of the harbour and bay. The large modern building **(26)** in the dock area below you is the Submarine Base. Above you, to the south, is the enormous cut of Jackson's Quarry **(27)** above Seaforth beach **(8)**, which provided stone for the Selbourne Docks, built for the Royal Navy in the early 1900s. An inclined railway took stone from here down to the harbour.

Runciman Drive was named after William Runciman, Mayor of Simon's Town for five terms from 1888 to 1925. Near Highlands Lane **(28)** further along the drive is the site of his once imposing home which overlooked the town.

As you walk down the hill, you will see on your left the gateway to the old Royal Naval Hospital **(15)** that was served by the aerial ropeway **(14)**. This is now used as the headquarters of the SA Naval Band. On the sea side of the road is 'Blofield', which was the nurses' quarters. Further on is the stone-faced rectory of St Francis Church.

Further down the hill, a magnificent view of the Klaver Stream waterfall can be seen in winter. Several Victorian houses are in the area, the last one on the left being Iberia **(29)** (built in 1916 and now a National Monument). It is on the site of one of the first two properties that were sold to the public in Simon's Town. At the bottom of the hill, turn right into Arsenal Road and follow it down to St George's Street where, after turning left along the road, you return to the start.

If you want to explore the historical side of Simon's Town further, two excellent places to visit after the walk are the Simon's Town Museum **(12)** and the Naval Museum **(13)**.

184

Cape of Good Hope Nature Reserve

Coastal Paths and Pools

Cape Point and the surrounding Cape of Good Hope Nature Reserve is a virtually unspoiled rocky headland and a unique ecological sanctuary. Inside the boundaries of the 7 750-hectare reserve an unbelievable diversity of indigenous plants and animals occurs. In this small area, more than 1 000 plant, 250 bird and 50 mammal species are found.

USEFUL INFORMATION

DISTANCE: About 3.5 km each way

TIME: About 2.5 hours

PARKING: From Cape of Good Hope Nature Reserve entrance gate on M4 follow signboards to Buffels Bay

START: Picnic area at Buffels Bay

ROUTE: Along coastal path from Buffels Bay to Venus Pool and back

TERRAIN: Grass, beach, gravel and tar

REFRESHMENTS: Fresh water at picnic sites

AMENITIES: Toilets at ablution blocks along route

WEATHER: Exposed to wind

SUITABLE FOR: Walkers of all ages

SAFETY: Isolated, so do not go alone. If you encounter baboons, ignore them and definitely do not show or offer them food

N early a million people visit Cape Point each year, thinking that this is either the most southerly point in Africa or the meeting point of the Atlantic and Indian oceans. It is neither. Cape Agulhas, 52.7 km further south, is the most southerly point of Africa and also where the two oceans officially converge.

But the Cape of Good Hope, which lies at the end of the Cape Peninsula, is an area of considerable historic interest. It is was one of the most significant landmarks on the voyages of discovery that eventually led to finding the sea route from Europe to India (*see* Historical Background pg 8).

After more than a thousand years of belief that sailors would fall off the edge of the earth if they proceeded too far south, eventually at the end of the 15th century Portuguese explorers rounded the Cape of Good Hope.

Their rate of progress in exploration over a twelve-year period is astonishing. In 1486 the explorer, Diego Cão, sailed south from Portugal and reached a point just north of the present-day Namibian town of Swakopmund. Two years later, Bartholomeu Diaz rounded the Cape of Good Hope and after sailing to Kwaaihoek, near the Bushman's River in the Eastern Cape, was forced by his crew to turn back. He and his party are then thought to have spent about a month in the Cape Peninsula. Finally, in 1498, Vasco da Gama rounded the Cape and eventually reached India on a voyage lasting almost a year.

Vasco da Gama's journal of November 1497 describes their arrival at St Helena Bay, about 150 km north of Cape Town:

'On Tuesday we came to tack towards the land, and had sight of low land, which had a great bay. The Commander-in-Chief sent Pero de Alenquer in a boat to sound and see if good anchorage could be found. He found it to be good, with a clean bottom, and sheltered from all winds except the north-west; it lies east and west. To the bay they gave the name Santa Helena. In this land the men are swarthy. They eat only sea-wolves (seals) and whales and the flesh of gazelles and the roots of plants. They go about covered in skins; their weapons are staffs of wild olive trees tipped with fire-treated horns. They have many dogs like those of Portugal and they bark the same way as they do.'

After sailing south they reached the Cape Peninsula, but they struggled to round Cape Point for four days because of adverse winds.

'On Saturday in the afternoon, we had sight of the said Cape of Good Hope. This same day we stood out on a tack to sea and that night we turned on a landward tack. On Sunday, the 19th day of November, in the morning, we were once again level with the Cape but we were not able to round it, because the wind was south-south-east. That Wednesday at midday we passed the said Cape and sailed along the coast with the wind astern.'

186

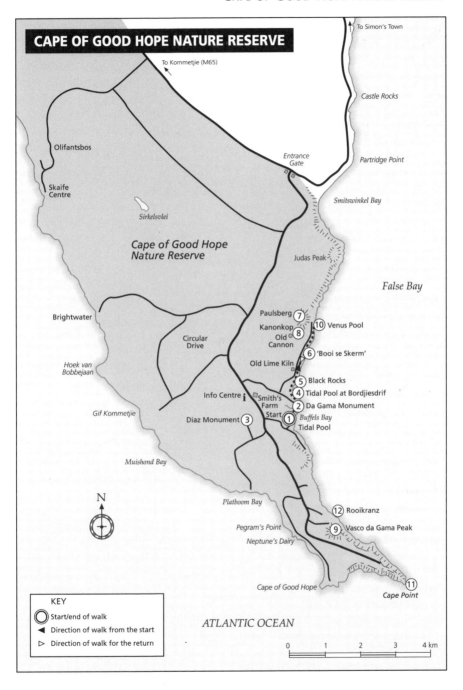

CAPE OF GOOD HOPE NATURE RESERVE

To Simon's Town

To Kommetjie (M65)

Castle Rocks

Olifantsbos

Entrance Gate

Partridge Point

Skaife Centre

Smitswinkel Bay

Sirkelsvlei

Cape of Good Hope Nature Reserve

Judas Peak

False Bay

Brightwater

Paulsberg ⑦
Kanonkop ⑧ ⑩ Venus Pool
Old Cannon

Circular Drive

⑥ 'Booi se Skerm'

Hoek van Bobbejaan

Old Lime Kiln

⑤ Black Rocks
④ Tidal Pool at Bordjiesdrif
② Da Gama Monument

Info Centre
Smith's Farm
Start

Gif Kommetjie

① Buffels Bay Tidal Pool

Diaz Monument ③

Muishond Bay

N

Platboom Bay

⑫ Rooikranz

Pegram's Point

⑨ Vasco da Gama Peak

Neptune's Dairy

Cape of Good Hope

Cape Point ⑪

KEY

◯ Start/end of walk
◄ Direction of walk from the start
▷ Direction of walk for the return

ATLANTIC OCEAN

0   1   2   3   4 km

Cape of Good Hope Walk

At the start at Buffels Bay (1), you will find a carefully planned recreation area with landscaped lawns, parking, ablution facilities and braai areas. It is an excellent place for a picnic. Although very popular in the summer holidays it is practically deserted for the rest of the year.

Walk northwards for about 100 m to a lovely sandy beach and, if there has been a recent storm, you are likely to see an abundance of coloured seashells on the sand – fans, limpets and small 'Venus ear' shells. Near the end of the beach is the Buffels River which, in winter, you will have to wade across. On the far side of the beach a sandy path takes you towards a small headland where there are brick buildings behind a wire fence. This was part of a naval installation built in the 1970s for characterising the underwater sounds emitted by naval vessels. Offshore there are acoustic sensors on the seabed.

Keep to the mountain side of the buildings and walk on towards the next bay, Bordjiesdrif, where there is another popular summer recreation area. Slightly higher up the slope you can see the monument (2) commemorating the voyage of Vasco da Gama, the Portuguese explorer who sailed past here on his epic voyage from Portugal to India in 1497. A similar monument to Diaz (1488) lies on the inland plateau (3).

Walk on past the tidal pool (4) and you will come to a boulder-lined shore that is covered in soft grass above the tide line. About 300 m further on you will notice that on the shore are huge boulders of dark brown ferricrete. This is a rock-type that is formed by a fluctuating water table depositing iron salts in ancient sand layers. The place is known as Black Rocks (5) on account of the ferricrete.

As you walk further along the path, look up towards the hillside where you can see many small caves. Archaeologists have found evidence of prehistoric man here. These cliffs are composed of a band of calcrete that was formed by deposits of calcium carbonate cementing ancient deposits of shell and sand.

Some of the holes in these cliffs are where the calcrete was mined in about 1860 by John Mackellar, who was the landowner at the time. Because there were no remaining midden deposits of large shells here, and the available fine shell grit could not be easily burned, Mackellar mixed the calcrete with coal which he brought from Simon's Town, a process that he had seen in Britain. Despite this innovation he went bankrupt and the farm, which became known as Smith's Farm, was transferred to a new owner. Mackellar's previous ownership is still shown on maps by the alternative name for Buffels Bay, Mackellar's Bay.

In 1938, Smith's Farm was bought by the Cape Divisional Council to form part of a nature reserve. As a result of further purchases and donations, the Cape of Good Hope Nature Reserve now covers 77.5 square kilometres.

Continuing along the grassy path, you will come to a short section that becomes soggy in winter and you may need to detour across the rocks. Ahead, on the left is a stone structure, about 6 m high, which is one of Mackellar's lime kilns, that has recently been restored. At the kiln you can join the tarred road which leads to a small parking area called 'Booi se Skerm' (6) ('boy's hiding place') where you will find ablution facilities and a freshwater tap. Booi se Skerm is thought to have been named after an event when a member of the Khoi took refuge in one of these shallow caves.

LIME KILNS

The remains of several lime kilns, built to provide building (slaked) lime, are seen along this walk. Until the introduction of Portland Cement, which was patented in England in 1824, lime was the basis of mortar, plaster and whitewash for all building work. The process of preparing the lime involved heating seashells until they had been converted to quicklime (calcium oxide) and then adding fresh water which hydrated it to calcium hydroxide, which is the slaked lime used for building.

Keep walking to the north along a narrow tarred path that leads towards the towering Kanonkop with the highest peak, Paulsberg (7), immediately ahead. This is a spectacular sight where the land rises to a height of 369 m in a sheer cliff straight from the sea.

In 1957, an old cannon was found on Kanonkop (8). This was one of a series of cannons that were used for signalling the arrival of Dutch ships in the 18th century, and details were provided for the reconstruction of the gun carriage by the Netherlands government.

Another nearby historic lookout is on Vasco da Gama Peak (9), the mountain behind Cape Point, where the first radar station on the African continent was built during World War II to monitor enemy shipping. At that time radar was a military secret.

Along this section of coast a series of shallow pools runs behind the rocky wave barrier. After about 500 m the path reaches the deepest of these, the crescent-shaped Venus Pool (10), which is the turning point for the walk. The rocky scenery is quite spectacular here and is a good place to stop and relax.

On the way back you will be looking towards Cape Point (11) where the 19-million-candlepower light casts its beam 37 km offshore. This is the most powerful lighthouse in Africa and was installed in 1936 to replace a half-million-candlepower light that had operated previously.

The high cliffs on the curve of the bay about 4 km away, in front of you, are known as Rooikrantz (12). This has been one of the most famous fishing spots in South Africa for over a century, and, despite over-fishing, it is still regarded as a good place to spin for yellowtail. Above the cliffs you can see buildings that were constructed for the secret radar establishment during World War II.

On a clear day, if you look east across False Bay, you can see the Hermanus mountains in the gap between Cape Hangklip and the Hottentots Holland Mountain ridge on the far side of the bay.

Index

Page numbers in **bold** refer to photographs.

Adderley, Sir Charles 12, 17
Admiral's Gardens 182
Admiralty House 181, 182
Admiralty Pier 181
Alexander, Henry 87
Alfred Basin 48
Alfred Dock 10
Alfred, Prince 48
Anglo-Boer War 20, 26, 31, 48, 50, 115, 160, 182
Anreith, Anton 20, 31, 32, 107, 109, 110
Arderne Gardens 101–105
Arderne, Henry 102
Arderne, Ralph 102
Athens 48, 54, 56
Auwal Mosque 35, 37, 39

Baden-Powell, Colonel Fletcher Smith 172
Bailey, Sir Abe 26, 151, 157, 162
Bailey's Cottage 149, 155, 157, 161
Baines, Thomas 27
Baker, Sir Herbert 19, 20, 23, 25, 26, 151, 157
Barnard, Lady Anne 99
Barristers Hotel 98, 100
Bertram, Robert 109
Bible Institute 166, 168
Bird, Colonel Christopher 87
Bishopscourt 9, 97
Black River 97
Black Rocks 187, 188
Blinkwater Ravine 64
Blockhouse Aqueduct 64, 65
Blouberg, Battle of 10, 71, 180
Bloubergstrand 71
Boers, Willem 32
Bo-Kaap 34–39, **130**
Bo-Kaap Museum 36, 39
Booi se Skerm 187, 189
Bordjiesdrif tidal pool 187, 188
Boschenheuvel Arboretum 97, 98
Bosheuvel 81, 95, 107
Boyes Drive 159–163

Boyes, C J 160
Breakwater Lodge 57
British, First Occupation 9, 23, 26, 35, 57, 79, 148, 157, 180
British, Second Occupation 10, 19, 35, 72
Brock, Sir Thomas 33

Caledon Square 29, 30, 32
Camps Bay 41, 44, 64
Cape Argus 21, 62
Cape Floral Kingdom 13
Cape of Good Hope 6, 186
Cape of Good Hope Nature Reserve **144**, 185–189
Cape Peninsula, geology of 11–12, 62, 71, 173
Cape Point **142–143**, 187
    lighthouse 189
Cape Times 21
Carnegie Library 156, 162
Castle of Good Hope 1, 9, 17, 18, 29, 30, 31, 55, **130**
Catholic Church of Saints Simon and Jude 181, 184
'Catwalk' 171, 173
Cecilia Forest 113
Chaplin, Sir Drummond 122, 125
Chapman's Peak 119, 122, 125
    Drive 118, 120, 122, 123, 177
    Hotel 118
Chiappini, Antonio 36
Church of the Good Shepherd 97
Church Square 30
City Hall 18, 30, 31, 131
Cloete, Hendrik 107, 109
Clovelly Station 156, 161, 166, 168, 171
Company's Gardens 9, 20, 23
Constantia Nek 111–115
Constantia Nek Restaurant 113
Conway, Colonel Thomas 112
Currey, John Blades 77
Custom's House 30

Da Gama Monument 187
Da Gama, Vasco 6, 186, 188
Da Saldanha, Antonio 7
Dalebrook tidal pool 161, 163

Danger Beach 155, 158, 161
Darling, Sir Charles 31
De Beers Mining Company 75
De Goede Hoop Lodge 30, 32
De la Queillerie, Maria 8
De Nieuwe Haerlem 7
De Tuynhuis 24, 26, 30
De Villiers Graaff, Sir David 69
De Villiers, Reverend M L 184
De Waal Drive 76
De Waal, Sir Frederick 122
De Waal, Sir Nicholas 119
De Wet, Hendrik 21
Delbridge, William 162
Delville Wood Memorial Garden 24, 26
Diaz Monument 187
Diaz, Bartolomeu de Novaes 7, 55, 186
Diep River 69, 72, 97
Diepsloot 64, 66
Disa Gorge 65
District Six Museum 30, 31
Drake, Sir Francis 7
Drill Hall 30
Driver, Evelyn 156
Drommedaris 8
Duncan Dock 10, 48
Duncan, Sir Patrick 48
dune erosion 71, 152, 170
Dutch East India Company 8, 9, 32, 41, 53, 65, 148, 156
Dutch Reformed Church 17, 19, 32, 181, 184

early settlement 8, 9, 23, 87
Effendi, Abu Bakr 39
Eternal Flame 30
Evangelical Lutheran Church 18, 21
explorers 6–10, 186

False Bay 11, 12, 160, 161
    beaches 150
Fehr, William 32
First National Bank 18, 19
Fish Hoek beach 169–173, **140**
flower sellers **spine**, 19, 33
Fort Wynyard 54, 56, 57
Fountain Ravine 66
Freeman, Charles 26, 33
fynbos 13, 42, 44, 45, 78, 84, 115, 178

Garlick, John 158
General Post Office 29
geraniums 91
Gilchrist, Dr John 158
Goede Hoope 8, 41
Golden Acre 18, 19, 30
Government Avenue 18, 20, 23, 24, 25, 27
Graaff, David 61
Graaff's Pool 60, 61
Grand Parade 17, 18, 19, 28, 29, 30, **131**
Granger Bay 56
Granger, Captain Robert 56
Granite Aqueduct 65
Gray, Bishop Robert 20, 25, 97
Gray, Sophie 97
Great Synagogue and Jewish Museum 24, 26
Greaves, Henry 26
Green Point 53, 59, 60
lighthouse 53, 54, 55, 60
Stadium 54
Greenmarket Square 18, 21, **129**
Grey, Sir George 25, 27, 47, 48
Groot Constantia 9, 106–110, **137**
Groote Kerk 17, 18, 30, 110
Groote Schuur 77, 85, 87
Groote Schuur Hospital 77
Guillaume, François 33
Guru, Tuan 35, 39

Harpley, Sidney 26
Heerengracht 17
Hiddingh Hall Campus 24, 26
Hofmeyer, Jan Hendrik 33
Holy Trinity Church 162
Hottentots 7, 81
Houses of Parliament 24, 25, 30, 32
Hout Bay beach 112, 116–120, **139**, 152

Imhoff's Gift 122
Islam 35, 39

Jack, David 50
Jackson's Quarry 181, 184
Jacob's Ladder 163
Jager Walk 172
Jameson, Dr Leander 75
Janssens, General 72
Janszen, Leendert 7

Jonkershuis 109
Josephine Mill 98, 100
Jubilee Square 181, 184

Kakapo 122, 123, 125
Kalk Bay 161
harbour **140–141**, 165, 166
station 166
tidal pool 161, 165
Kanonkop **144**, 187, 189
Kaplan, Mendel 154
Karbonkelberg 125
Kasteelspoort 65, 67
Kendall, E K 23
Khoi 7, 8, 10, 23, 55, 89, 95, 112, 124, 177, 189
King's Blockhouse 76, 79, 114
Kipling, Rudyard 77
Kirstenbosch National Botanical Garden **front cover**, 86–91, 94, 98, 113, **136**
Kloof Buttress 66
Kohler, William 25
Kommetjie 124, 175, 176
Koopmans-de Wet House 18, 21
Koopmans-de Wet, Maria 21
Kronendal 117

Lakeside 127
Leendert's Bosch 81
Letterstedt, Jacob 100
Liesbeek River 85, 87, 96–100
lime kilns 117, 189
Lion's Head 8, 12, 14, 41–45, **132-133**

Mackellar, John 188
Maclear's Beacon 13, 69, 87, 114
Magistrates Courts 30, 32
Malays 35, 36
cuisine 39
head coverings 38
Mandela, Nelson 29, 55, 59
Marais, Pieter 61
Marina da Gama 50, 127, 128, 150
Mariner's Wharf 118, 120
Martello Tower 181
Masey, Francis 20, 25
Mayor's Garden 30, 33
Metropolitan Golf Course 54, 56, 59
Michaelis, Sir Max 21

Military Barracks 181
Millers Point 152
Milnerton 69, 152
beach 68–73
Lagoon 69, 73
lighthouse 69, 70, 73
Milton Pool 60
Mitford-Baberton, Ivan 20, 25, 119
Molteno, Sir John 45, 163
Monkey Valley Resort 122, 123, 124
Montagu, Sir John 55
Mouille Point 47, 53, 54, 56
Mount Nelson Hotel 24, 26
Muizenberg 9, 128
beach **138**, 147–152
Pavilion 146, 149, 155, 161
Post Office 156
station 155, 160, 161
Muizenberg, Battle of 67, 148, 156, 162
Murray, Reverend Andrew 19
Muslim leaders 39
Muys, Sergeant Wynand 148

Natale Labia Museum 151, 154, 155, 157, 162
Naval Hospital 181
Neptune 29
Newlands Forest 81–85, **135**
Newlands Pool 98
Newlands Stream 82, 85
noon gun 42
Noordhoek 12, 123
beach 121–125, **139**
Nursery Ravine 93, 95, 112

Ohlsson, Anders 90
Ohlsson's Breweries 85, 90, 98
Old Slave Lodge 18, 19, 20, 24, 25
Old Supreme Court Building 30
old tollhouse 166, 181
Old Town House 18, 21
Oliphant 8
Orange, William Prince of 29, 162
Osmond, John 182

Palace Barracks 181, 182
Palm Tree Mosque 35
Paulsberg 187, 189
Pearson, Dr H 87
Peers Cave 6, 174–178

Peers, Bertie 175
Peers, Victor 175
Pegram, Thomas 27
pelargonium 91, 146
Penelope 148
Penny, Joshua 66
Petrava 160, 161, 163
Pilgrim's Mosque 37, 38, 39
Pipe Track 63–67
Planetarium 24, 27
Platteklip Gorge 13
Police Museum 155, 157
Posthuys 155, 156, 161, 162

Queen Victoria 31
Queen Victoria Statue 30

Reijger 8, 41
reservoirs 17
  Alexandra 113, 115
  De Villiers 113, 115
  Hely-Hutchinson 65, 95,
  113, 115
  Kloof Nek 65
  Mocke 65
  Molteno 45, 65
  Victoria 113, 115
  Woodhead 65, 115, 162
  Wagenaar's 16, 19
Rhodes' Avenue 98, 113, 114
Rhodes' Drive 94
Rhodes Memorial 74–79,
  83, **134**
Rhodes, Cecil John 25, 27, 75,
  87, 114, 157, 158, 162
Rhodes' Cottage 154, 155, 161
Rietvlei 70, 72
Robben Island 8, 50, 55, 56, 69
Robinson Graving Dock 48,
  49, 50
Rocklands Beach 60, 61
Rohland, Jacob 32
Rooikrantz 187, 189
Rudd, Charles 163
Runciman Drive 181, 183
Runciman, William 184
Rust en Vrede 155, 157,
  161, 162
Rust en Vreugd 30, 32

Salt River 87, 97
San (Bushmen) 23
Saunders Rocks 59, 60
Schutte, Herman 31, 32
Sea Point **back cover**, 45, 60, 61
Seaforth Beach 181, 182, 184

Seal Island 150
Shafi Mosque 37, 38
Signal Hill 8, 35, 41, 53, 56
Silvermine Nature Reserve 162
Silvermine River 170, 171, 172
Simon's Bay 165
Simon's Town 9, 11, 47, 107,
  127, **141**, 148, 167, 179–184
  Museum 181, 183, 184
  Naval Museum 181
Skeleton Gorge 87, 92–95
Slangkop lighthouse 125
Slangolie Ravine 65, 67
Smitswinkel Bay 11, 187
Smut's Track 20, 93, 95
Smuts, Jan Christian 20, 25,
  93, 163
Solomon, Saul 62
Somerset Hospital 54, 57
Somerset, Lord Charles 26, 57
South African Library 24,
  25, 47
South African Maritime
  Museum 49
South African Museum 6, 24,
  27, 178
South African National
  Gallery 24, 26
South African Navy 180
Spilhaus Ravine 113
St Francis Church 181, 182
St George's Cathedral 18, 20,
  24, 25
St George's Dockland Church
  181, 183
St George's Mall 18, 21
St James 77, 154
  Ravine 163
  station 155, 161, 163
  tidal pool 155, 158, 161, 163
St Mary's Cathedral 30, 32
Stal Plein 30, 32
Standard Bank 18, 19
Strelitzia 89
Sturrock Graving Dock 48
Submarine Base 181, 184
Sun Valley 12, 176
Swan, J M 78

Table Bay 7, 8, 41, 47
Table Mountain **2–3**, 11, 12,
  20, 134–135
Tafelberg Kerk 30, 32
Tafelberg Road 43, 64
Thibault, Louis Michel 31, 32,
  56, 100, 107, 109

Three Anchor Bay 53, 54,
  59, 60
Tommy's Aqueduct 64, 66
Trafalgar Place 18, 19
Tulbagh, Governor Ryk 21, 33
Twelve Apostles 44, 64, 67
Two Oceans Aquarium 49

Uitkyk 171, 172
University of Cape Town 76,
  77, 93

Van der Stel, Simon 9, 23 25,
  107, 112, 117, 165, 170
Van der Stel, Willem Adriaan
  9, 33
Van Imhoff, Baron Gustaaf
  122, 180
Van Riebeeck, Jan 8, 17, 23,
  29, 41, 47, 67, 81, 84, 87,
  112, 117, 127, 170, 177
Van Riebeeck's hedge 9, 84,
  87, 90, 95, 97
Vasco da Gama Peak 187
Venus Pool 187, 189
Vergenoeg 151
Victoria and Alfred Waterfront
  46-51, 54, **134-135**
Victoria Basin 50
Vineyard Hotel 98, 99

Wagenaar, Zacharias 9, 19,
  29, 55
Wagenaar's Reservoir 16, 19
Walvis 8
Watts, G R 78
Welgelegen 77
Wiley's Gully 162
William Fehr Collection 32
Williams, Alpheus 151
Winton 70, 73
Woodbridge Island 69, 70, 73
Woolsack 77
World War I 42, 57, 65, 69, 167
World War II 42, 48, 55, 57,
  69, 160, 163, 180, 189

Yokohama 155, 157
Yonge, Governor Sir George 23
Ysselsteijn's Bay 170
Ysterplaat 69

Zandvlei 126-128,
  145-146, 150
Zonnekus Mansion 70, 73
Zuid Afrikaan 33